PENG[illegible]

THE PENGUIN B[illegible]

Mudar Patherya was born in [illegible] *Sportsworld* magazine in Calcutta, where he specializes in cricket writing. He is interested in the stock market and reviews stocks and shares for *The Telegraph*, Calcutta.

Barry O' Brien was born in 1963 and also works with *Sportsworld*. A keen sportsman himself, his other interests include drama, public speaking and conducting quiz contests.

Very specially for Syedna Mohammed
Burhanuddin Saheb, Syedi Mazoon
Saheb, our parents (Neil and Joyce, Tyeb
and Zarina) and our family at
Sportsworld.

Contents

Acknowledgements

The authors wish to express their gratitude and indebtedness to the following people; without their help and encouragement this book could not have been put together:
E.W. Swanton, David Frith, Leo Wijesinghe, MJ Akbar, Dickie Bird, Dennis Waight, Amrit Mathur, Bishen Bedi, Geoff Boycott, Duleep Mendis, Roy Dias, Ranjan Madugalle, Ravi Shastri, Viv Richards, K. Srikkanth, Richard Streeton, Dicky Rutnagur, Debashis Bandopadhyay, Raju Mukherjee, Dr. Surapriya Mukherjee, Gautam Bhattacharya, David McMahon, Asif Iqbal, Raj Singh Dungarpur, Lekha Dhar, Shabana Azmi, Rohit Brijnath, Imran Khan, Dilip Vengsarkar, Swaroop Kishan, Mohinder Amarnath, Sir William Golding, Dipen Sanghvi, Kavita Kapoor, Yasmin Matcheswalla, Sagarika Basu, Mansur Ali Khan Pataudi and all at *Sportsworld.*

Foreword

Any game that can take 27 hours and more to play and still remain inconclusive must need plenty of "characters" in order to survive. That Test cricket has managed to survive despite many meaningless games (that dull attitudes and duller wickets have produced over a hundred years) and with luck will continue to be played in the future is a suitable tribute to these characters who, through their skill and personality, have enriched the game and taken it beyond the bounds of a straightforward contest. The game has known its moments of tragedy, but thankfully these have been few and far between, and very rarely fatal. While the tragic moments in cricket history cannot be ignored, there has been enough drama without the tragedy to afford endless delight to those following the exploits of various characters who've taken their rightful place in cricketing folklore. Some like Nash, whom Sobers clouted for six consecutive sixes in one over, may perhaps have preferred to stay outside a book of records. They are victims rather than perpetrators of a vicious assault; some have achieved fame because they happened to be a part of a greater design, but there are many who can justifiably claim and hope to get a mention on the strength of their individual merits alone in a book of this nature.

It has been said that there have been more "intelligent" words written about cricket than any other game. While the following collection of interesting facts gathered by Mudar Patherya and Barry O' Brien can hardly claim to be a work of literary genius, the book can sit quite comfortably alongside weightier works. The authors have gone to considerable trouble and have produced a book which will engage both the casual and the avid follower of cricket, no matter to which age group he or she may belong.

New Delhi,
July 1988

M.A.K.Pataudi

Introduction

Forty-hour-long journeys by train in India are not unusual. As a result , the vast majority of rail travellers have to, perforce, find ways of keeping themselves occupied. Card games are commonplace and strangers soon find themselves drawn into familial arguments and pastimes. Sometimes conversations veer toward the whimsical. On a train we were on recently, the conversation drifted to cricket and soon a group of us were trading questions such as 'Who are the five greatest cricketers of all time' and 'Who would captain a joint India-Pakistan side?' Everyone seemed to have something to contribute. The journey ended and we went our respective ways. But the idea wouldn't go away and soon the two of us were making and collecting lists as we could find them. Initially we had no idea they would be material for a book but then it struck us that if so many people found such trivia engrossing then perhaps it should be widely available between covers.

We stepped up our efforts. The number of lists we had grew. They varied from the serious (Donald Bradman's five greatest matches) to the enjoyable (Ten immortal Cardus lines); from things cricket (Seven arguments in defence of Bodyline) to topics distantly related (The five women Ravi Shastri would love to spend an evening with).

Soon we had well over a hundred lists. Two hundred, five...a thousand. It was then that the problem really began. Which ones would select themselves. What appealed to one of us was rejected by the other. A lot of compromises were eventually made and the book gradually took shape. We believe that the items here should interest anyone with an interest in the game (and even some of those without). Our intention has been to produce a book you do not have to read at one sitting. Leaf through it, laugh about it and use it to challenge your friends in conversations about cricket.

Some advice, though, for those who take the book too seriously; we didn't!

Calcutta,
July 1988

Mudar Patherya
Barry O' Brien

Achievements and Honours

EIGHT SPORTSMEN WHO PLAYED CRICKET FOR ONE COUNTRY AND *RUGBY* FOR ANOTHER

1. M. P. Donnelly (cricket for New Zealand, rugby for England)
2. M. K. L. Gee (cricket for South Africa, rugby for Scotland)
3. R. H. M. Hands (cricket for South Africa, rugby for England)
4. W. H. Milton (cricket for South Africa, rugby for England)
5. R. O. Schwarz (cricket for South Africa, rugby for England)
6. C. B. van Ryneveld (cricket for South Africa, rugby for England)
7. F. Mitchell (cricket for England and South Africa, rugby for England)
8. S. M. J. Woods (cricket for Australia and England, rugby for England)

MIKE BREARLEY'S THREE ACHIEVEMENTS AS A *STUDENT*

1. Secured a First Class Honours Degree in Classics
2. Secured a Doctor of Philosophy Degree
3. Got an upper second in Moral Science at Cambridge

...AND AS A *TEACHER*

1. Taught philosophy at the University of California
2. Taught at a clinic for disturbed adolescents

WHEN *LEN HUTTON* BROKE DON BRADMAN'S RECORD OF 334...

Len Hutton of England established a Test 'high' when he scored 364 at The Oval vs. Australia in 1938

1. ...the square leg umpire 'Fanny' Walden said : 'Thank God, that's over'
2. ...Hutton's mother broke into tears while doing the family washing with the radio by her side
3. ...Maurice Leyland ordered two bottles of champagne ('One for me and one for thee')
4. ...the Pudsey parish church rang a peal of 364
5. ...Hutton received 500 congratulatory messages at tea!

– *Fifty Years in Cricket* by Sir Len Hutton

TWENTY-SIX CRICKETERS WHO HAVE FIGURED AT *MADAME TUSSAUD'S*

1. W.G. Grace
2. Arthur Shrewsbury
3. A. E. Stoddart
4. Joe Darling
5. Jack Hobbs
6. Herbert Sutcliffe
7. Bob Wyatt
8. Douglas Jardine
9. W. Hammond
10. Bill Woodfull
11. Don Bradman
12. Alec Bedser
13. Len Hutton
14. Peter May
15. Bill Edrich
16. Norman Yardley
17. Denis Compton
18. Jim Laker
19. Ted Dexter
20. M. J. K. Smith
21. Colin Cowdrey
22. Sir Gary Sobers
23. Tony Greig
24. Geoff Boycott
25. Vivian Richards
26. Ian Botham

FOURTEEN CRICKETERS WHO PLAYED *RUGBY* FOR THEIR COUNTRY TOO

1. J. H. Anderson (South Africa)
2. T. A. Harris (South Africa)
3. A. N. Hornby (England)
4. P. S. T. Jones (South Africa)
5. G. MacGregor (cricket for England, rugby for Scotland)
6. A. W. Powell (South Africa)
7. A. R. Richards (South Africa)
8. A. E. Stoddart (England)
9. J. H. Sinclair (South Africa)
10. M.J.K. Smith (England)
11. R. H. Spooner (England)
12. E. W. T. Tindill (New Zealand)
13. M. J. Turnbull (cricket for England, rugby for Wales)
14. G. F. Vernon (cricket for England)

TEN CRICKETERS *TALENTED* IN OTHER FIELDS

1. Qasim Omar (Pakistan) ... can speak five languages fluently – Punjabi, Urdu, English, French and Swahili.
2. Bevan Congdon (New Zealand) ... was a member of a jazz band – 'played the trumpet as well as Spike Milligan'.
3. Jock Edwards (New Zealand) ... his card tricks were of a professional standard.
4. Don Bradman (Australia) ... was once a scratch golf player.

5. Bob Crisp (South Africa) ... climbed Mount Kilimanjaro twice.
6. David Acfield who plays county cricket for Essex...was a member of the British Olympic fencing team at Mexico City and Munich; was the British champion from 1969 to 1972 and won a gold medal for the team event at the 1970 Commonwealth Games.
7. Percy Chapman (England) ... once ate 210 oysters in Brisbane on the 1928-29 tour of Australia.
8. John Snow (England) ... wrote two volumes of poetry.
9. Lance Gibbs (West Indies) ... his ability at predicting winners at the race course was second only to his proficiency as an off spinner – sometimes better!
10. Terence Harris (South Africa) ... played rugby for his country; rode a horse at the age of 3, shot wonderfully by the time he was 5, drove a truck at the age of 7, played tennis when 9, started rugby when he was 12, won his province's junior tennis championship at the age of 12 and was also competent at soccer, squash and golf.

TEN MEMORABLE *PERFORMANCES* WHILE IN PHYSICAL PAIN

1. Eddie Paynter, suffering from tonsilitis, left his hospital bed to play a historic four-hour innings of 83 for England against Australia at Brisbane in 1932-33. In the second innings, he struck the winning hit – a six – to enable England to regain the Ashes.
2. Len Hutton retired after being hit on the hand by H. H. Johnson in the match between England and West Indies in 1950 at Old Trafford. Hutton came back and batted virtually with one hand to score 39 and 45.
3. Australian batsman Bill Woodfull was twice hit by bouncers during the Adelaide Test of 1932-33. He carried his bat through the second innings, secoring 73 out of a total of 193.
4. Sunil Gavaskar scored 124 and 220 at Port of Spain, Trinidad, 1970-71, in spite of a severe toothache right through the game. He refused tablets on the grounds that they would make him drowsy.
5. Dennis Lillee, greatly restricted by a vertebral injury, bowled unchanged throughout the 138 minutes of play on the last day of the Sydney Test versus Pakistan in 1972-73. With Walker at

the other end, Pakistan, needing 159 to win, was bowled out for 106.

6. Trevor Bailey retired in England's second innings against South Africa in 1956-57 at Durban. He suffered a fracture in his right hand. He resumed batting with a plaster and stayed for 55 minutes with Cowdrey. The match was saved in the process.
7. Ramakant Desai continued batting even after his jaw had been fractured by a delivery from Motz during the Wellington Test between India and New Zealand in 1967-68. Bedi and he added 57 to give India a vital first innings lead. India went on to win her first Test outside the Sub-continent.
8. Rick McCosker, his jaw wired after being struck by Bob Willis, went on to add important runs with Rod Marsh during the Centenary Test, 1977. Australia eventually won the game.
9. Everton Weekes scored 90 versus England at Lord's in 1951 with a broken finger.
10. Viv Richards batted in pain when the effects of a pain-killing injection wore off while batting for West Indies against Australia at Melbourne in 1979-80. Richards, who was suffering from a back injury, scored an unforgettable 153, not out.

Advice

THREE GOLDEN RULES FOR GETTING *AUTOGRAPHS* BY W. BROOKS

1. Approach a player only at the start or finish of a day's play; NEVER at mealbreaks
2. Don't push or jostle the player
3. Always remember to say 'Please' and 'Thank you'

– *Wisden Cricket Monthly*

FIVE WAYS OF IMPROVING THE *CONFIDENCE LEVEL* OF A CRICKETER

By Dr Arthur Jackson, a noted hypnotherapist based in Australia

1. Breathing deeply in the middle
2. Conjuring up different deliveries in the mind and playing them accordingly

3. Imagining facing a particular bowler and playing him at your best
4. Physically ticking off different muscles
5. Mentally summoning up an image of a place that has had happy associations

World Series Cricket

FIVE *ESSENTIALS* TO BE A SUCCESSFUL CRICKETER...BY MIKE BREARLEY

1. Selfish enough to do well for yourself
2. Unselfish enough to be acceptable to the rest of the team.
3. Should be phlegmatic
4. Courageous
5. And should have self-control, particularly when a fast bowler is bowling straight at your head

THE FIVE BASICS OF *WICKET KEEPING* ACCORDING TO WASIM BARI

1. Having a good view of the ball
2. Being evenly balanced, ready to move either way
3. Most importantly, concentration, watching the ball all the time
4. Whenever possible, getting your body behind the ball
5. And remember, do not 'snatch'

***SECRETS* OF THE SWEEP ACCORDING TO ALAN KNOTT**

A cricket writer recalled Knott, a fine player of spin bowling, attempting sweeps off 15 successive deliveries on the tour of India in 1976-77; he didn't miss a single one !

1. Watch the ball 2. Get low 3. Don't try to hit the ball too hard

***DIETARY* RECOMMENDATIONS FOR CRICKETERS BY DENNIS WAIGHT**

(The contributor was Australia's physiotherapist during Packer's 'circus' days. He has also taken charge of several Australian rugby sides, and is currently attached to Somerset's cricket team and the West Indies).

1. Stay off soft drinks 2. Keep your sugar intake down to the very minimum 3. Cut down on your salt intake 4. Eat a lot of fruits

But watch it, an excess of citrus fruits could cause gout 5. Dairy products are recommended i.e. milk, Scottish cheese and yoghurt 6. Green, leafy vegetables 7. Don't forget the proteins – fish and meat 8. The fibrous intake of course, for the roughage – wholemeal bread, cornflakes and wheat 9. You can have beer provided you don't over indulge. Some doctors feel that a couple of pints does more good than none at all !

RICHARD HADLEE'S RECIPE FOR SUCCESS

'The motivation card that has become my Bible,' says Hadlee of the following list. He always carries it around in his kit bag.

1. Fear is negative. Desire is positive
2. Your mind is your brain. It is better than a computer
3. Attitude is a frame of mind
4. Simulation...putting yourself back in a situation in which you last enjoyed success
5. Visualizing what you want to see happen. It works if you believe it strongly enough
6. Belief is another crucial factor. Once confidence is there, success nearly always comes
7. Think of the rewards of success – winning
8. Self esteem – know your own worth/ability/value
9. Goals, aims, and targets are an essential part of my philosophy
10. 'Wanting to achieve' is the next stage in the formula
11. 'Control' refers to the way you have to convert all your dreaming and visualizing into physical action
12. Enjoyment is the next part of the equation
13. Never get tired, just pleasantly weary
14. Winning is being happy with your performance, even if someone does it better

– *At the Double* by Richard Hadlee

FIVE SUGGESTIONS BY GREG CHAPPELL TO *DISCIPLINE* YOUR CRICKET

1. Write down a list of things you don't like about your game, be they mental or physical faults. Then list the things with which you would like to replace these faults, and forget about the things you wish to get rid of
2. Set aside 10 or 15 minutes a day, either first thing in the morning or last thing at night, somewhere by yourself and start

to programme these success ideas into your mind

3. Try to find a secluded spot where you can relax completely and imagine yourself doing the things you want to do successfully. If you like to improve your footwork, spend your 15 minutes for 4 days, mentally using the footwork you want to use. You will find the physical job of achieving the change far simpler
4. Be positive in what you do and say each day – in all walks of life. This will flow over into your cricket
5. If you approach each net session with the feeling that it is one of the tough periods, and are determined not to get out in the first three quarters of your stint, you will more easily get through these in the middle

– *World Series Cricket*

FIVE TIPS FROM GEOFF LAWSON ON HOW TO GET YOUR *EYE* IN

The Australian fast bowler is a qualified optometrist!

1. Never, I repeat, never, stare into the sun while going in to bat. It is the worst thing a batsman can do. It totally maladjusts the pupil to batting conditions
2. You should rather focus your eyes on the sightboard
3. Avoid reading immediately before going out to bat
4. Conduct some basic vision exercises
5. Watch the bowler's hand and try to pick up the flight of the ball halfway down the wicket

Lawson put his own advice to profitable use; his batting average for that particular season improved from 15 to 32.

Appearance Maketh the Man

THE FIVE *HEAVIEST* CRICKETERS

1. W. Foulke, Derbyshire, 23 stone
2. Warwick Armstrong, Australia, 22 stone
3. D. Durston, Middlesex, 19.5 stone
4. George Brown, Hampshire and England, 18 stone
5. Dr W.G. Grace, Gloucestershire and England, 18 stone

– *The Encyclopaedia of Cricket* by Maurice Golesworthy

THE FIVE SMARTEST *DRESSERS* IN CRICKET ACCORDING TO RAVI SHASTRI

1. Imran Khan ('He can carry anything on him')
2. David Gower ('Very sober and English in appearance')
3. Tiger Pataudi ('Has set a high standard for himself. Whatever he wears suits him; the more formal the better')
4. Ian Botham ('By far the most outrageous dresser. He would wear what you'd expect no one to, and surprisingly it would look good on Ian')
5. Dilip Doshi ('Surprised? He takes a great care and interest in his wardrobe; has an incredibly good collection of suits')

FIVE AMAZING *LOOK ALIKES*

1. Greg Matthews – Stanley Laurel
2. Viv Richards – Joe Frazier; some feel he looks like Floyd Patterson
3. Tauseef Ahmed – Lionel Richie
4. Clarrie Grimmett – Mahatma Gandhi (according to Bill O'Reilly)
5. Stan McCabe – Napoleon Bonaparte

ADDING *COLOUR* TO CRICKET

Coloured clothing was one of Kerry Packer's brainwaves when he started his breakaway 'circus'. Ten opinions on his highly successful marketing gimmick.

1. 'The Australian side looked like waiters in a Ruritanian musical comedy' (Trevor Bailey).
2. 'I cannot escape the feeling that I am watching rounders played by adults (?) in pyjamas' (Harold Larwood).
3. 'Why didn't they just dress them up as convicts and celebrate 1988 a year earlier' (Bill O'Reilly seeing the 'yacht crew' uniforms for the Benson and Hedges Challenge Tournament in Perth, 1986-87).
4. 'I think in this regard cricket is being prostituted' (Ashley Mallett).
5. 'Coloured gear is easier to clean' (Maryna Procter, wife of South African cricketer Mike).
6. 'It is a colour which carries strong homosexual overtones in the Caribbean' (Tony Cozier on the pink clothing of the West Indians).

7. '....flannelled fairies'
8. '....licorice allsorts'
9. '....pink panthers'
10. '....the fancy-dress travesty which seemingly featured all of cricket's worst qualities' (E.M. Wellings).

FIVE OCCASIONS WHEN PLAYERS TOOK THE FIELD IN *NON-CRICKETING* ATTIRE

1. In the match between MCC and Combined University in 1893, players were permitted to wear gloves because of the extreme cold.
2. For the third day's play in the match between Notts and Hampshire at Southampton in 1930, players came onto the field in overcoats. The batting side required only one run to win the match.
3. At Dewsbury in 1899, Derbyshire's players fielded in civvies during their game versus Yorkshire. Heavy rain had flooded their dressing room.
4. The ChelstonCricketClub at Torbay, Devon, equipped their wicketkeeper with lemon and black gloves for a game in 1972. The Chelston batsman played in blue and yellow striped pads.
5. Alfred Lyttleton once kept wicket for Middlesex vs. Gloucestershire in 1860, wearing a hard straw hat.

CRICKET'S *MACHO* MATCH!

The selectors of this unusual contest have, for once, decided to consider each player on face value only.

The Heart-throbs	*The Pin-up Boys*
1. Mohsin Khan	1. Majid Khan
2. Rameez Raja	2. Allan Lamb
3. David Gower	3. Viv Richards
4. Martin Crowe	4. Ian Chappell
5. Clive Lloyd	5. Dean Jones
6. Ravi Shastri	6. Ian Botham
7. Imran Khan	7. Lance Cairns
8. Peter Willey	8. Rod Marsh
9. Sadanand Vishwanath	9. Wasim Akram
10. Garth le Roux	10. Malcolm Marshall
11. Dennis Lillee	11. Terry Alderman

WHAT TWENTY CRICKETERS HAVE GONE TO *FANCY DRESS* BALLS AS

1. Denis Compton – As W.G. Grace on the 1950-51 ship journey to Australia
2. J.J. Warr – As Gussie Moran on the same voyage to Australia
3. Godfrey Evans – As Carmen Miranda with a borrowed gown and a basket of fruit on his head, while on board the same ship
4. David Gower – As a Cowboy, and later as Pontius Pilate
5. Mike Brearley – As the greengrocer from Galilee, a Pakistani *mulla* and an Indian sage
6. Graham Gooch – As Oliver Twist
7. Geoff Boycott – As Adam and K.S. Ranjitsinhji (The rumour before the latter occasion was that Boycott, in all probability, would turn up as himself)
8. Neil Foster – As an Indian lady in a *sari*
9. Paul Downton – As the commissionaire of a five-star Indian hotel
10. Allan Lamb – As an urchin, dressed in rags and splattered with mud
11. Phil Edmonds – As a jailbird, an Arab Sheikh with a pair of dark glasses and a cheque book in hand
12. Derek Randall – As a fairy queen
13. Doug Insole – As Inspector Closeau
14. Clive Radley – As an Indian
15. John Emburey – As a green lizard
16. Geoff Miller – As a Derbyshire miner
17. Bob Willis – As a blind umpire. He carried a white stick along with him
18. Philip de Freitas – As Diana Ross
19. Geoff Cook – As Bertie Wooster
20. Ian Botham – As a Playboy 'bunny'

TEN FAMOUS *BEARDS* IN CRICKET

1. W.G. Grace
2. J. Blackham
3. G. Bonnor
4. Greg Chappell
5. Mike Hendrick
6. Mike Brearley
7. Allan Border
8. B.S. Bedi
9. Abdul Qadir
10. Lord Harris

THIRTY-TWO FAMOUS *BESPECTACLED* CRICKETERS

1. Zaheer Abbas
2. Dilip Doshi
3. Gordon Greenidge
4. M.J.K.Smith
5. J.N. Crawford
6. Bill Bowes
7. Tommy Mitchell
8. Geoff Howarth
9. Maharaja of Vizianagaram
10. Geoff Cope
11. Geoff Boycott
12. Eddie Hemmings
13. Clive Lloyd
14. David Steele
15. Lawrence Rowe
16. Paul Allott
17. Dirk Wellham
18. Eddie Barlow (was so short sighted that he found it hard to focus behind the front wheel of his bicycle when going to school!)
19. Anshuman Gaekwad
20. Bishen Bedi
21. Pankaj Roy
22. Paul Gibb.
23. Peter van der Merwe.
24. Percy Mansell
25. Bob Christiani
26. C.V. Wight
27. Ray Phillips
28. Roy Marshall
29. Walter Hadlee
30. Murray Bennett
31. Percy Fender
32. Alf Valentine

PECULIAR THINGS THAT CRICKETERS HAVE *WORN*

1. Desmond Haynes wears a gold chain with 'Love, Life, Laugh' engraved on it
2. Viv Richards' good luck charm is a gold chain with a piece of black coral – shaped like a man's head – attached to it
3. Dennis Lillee wore a black armband during the Adelaide Test in 1983 in memory of his grand father who had died
4. During Channel Nine's World of Sport TV programme, Ian Chappell and his team of commentators wore black armbands after Australia's first innings collapse at Old Trafford in 1980
5. David Bairstow turned out for a New Year's Match in Bradford, to mark the start of his benefit year, in a thermal underwear
6. Cricketers Greg Matthews and Derek Pringle wear ear studs
7. West Indian fast bowler Wes Hall was never seen without a crucifix dangling round his neck
8. Mohinder Amarnath and Alan Knott have always carried a red handkerchief on their person while playing

9. Greg Chappell always wore a copper bracelet to ensure that he never got arthritis
10. F.C. de Saram was imprisoned in 1962 for conspiring to overthrow the government in Sri Lanka. When Colin Cowdrey and Billy Griffith visited him in his prison cell some years later, he was found wearing – of all things – a Harlequin tie

Ashes to Ashes

THE MOST *ENTERTAINING ASHES TEST*!

John Arlott selects two sides which would give the spectator his money's worth
Australia :
Lindsay Hassett, Charlie Macartney, Don Bradman, Stan McCabe, Keith Miller, Ken Mackay, Richie Benaud, Rod Marsh, Ray Lindwall, Jack Walsh and Arthur Mailey
England :
Jack Hobbs, Colin Milburn, Wally Hammond, Denis Compton, Ted Dexter, Ian Botham, Wilfred Rhodes, Maurice Tate, Godfrey Evans, Jim Laker and Frank Tyson

FIVE PRONOUNCEMENTS WHEN THE LEEDS ASHES TEST OF 1975 HAD TO BE *ABANDONED*

The TV flashed 'Match Abandoned Due To Vandalism of Pitch' after some men sneaked in on the night before the last day of the match, shovelled the pitch and poured oil on the wicket. The match was abandoned with the scores reading: England 288 and 291, Australia 135 and 220 for 3. Rain from noon to 4 p.m. on the fifth day would, perhaps, have produced a draw anyway.

1. 'One of history's more diabolical acts' (BBC commentator Peter West).
2. 'No Test match has received wider coverage'. (John Woodcock).
3. 'Blind, raging uncontrollable fury (Ian Woolridge).
4. 'All they had done was to hijack an aircraft that was going to Cuba anyway' (Ian Woolridge, drawing attention to the fact that the vandals did little good, since the match was heading for a draw).

5. 'GEOFF BOYCOTT IS INNOCENT, OK!' (A cartoon in the *Mail*) .

WHAT THE CRITICS SAID WHEN *BOB MASSIE* TOOK 16 FOR 137 VS ENGLAND AT LORD'S IN 1972.

1. 'Mauler Massie Wrecks England' (*Daily Mirror*) .
2. 'But who *is* Bob Massie?' (John Woodcock).
3. 'The swing is *so* late! (Richie Benaud) .
4. 'Massie went thataway. Or was it thisaway' (*Daily Express*).
5. 'So near a Massiecre' (*Sun*) .

THE *ASHES BOOKS*

(Several books have been written on the Ashes Tests, but we have restricted ourselves to 10, whose titles bear a certain resemblance to each other)

1. '*Ashes And Dust*' by Douglas Jardine
2. '*Ashes And Rubber*' by F.H. Haigh
3. '*Ashes At Stake*' by S.C. Caple
4. '*Ashes Go Home*' by C. White and Roy Webber
5. '*Ashes in Suspense*' by E.W. Swanton
6. '*Ashes To Ashes*' by R. Warner and L. Blair
7. '*Ashes To Hassett*' by J. Kay
8. '*Ashes Triumphant*' by B. Harris
9. '*The Ashes Thrown Away*' by E.M. Wellings
10. '*The Ashes Crown the Year*' by Jack Fingleton

SEVEN VIVID *ACCOUNTS* OF THE 1974-75 ASHES SERIES IN AUSTRALIA

Australia subjected England to a reversal of the Bodyline tactics perpetrated by Douglas Jardine in late 1932-33. Australia won 4-1 in the mid-Seventies and England's batsmen confessed that they had never been as sorely tried by quick bowling.

1. 'Coming fresh to this Test series is like walking into a pitched battle between the Mafia and the IRA' (Ian Woodridge) .
2. 'Never in the 98 years of Test cricket have batsmen been so grievously bruised and battered by ferocious, hostile short-pitched balls' (*Wisden*).
3. 'Thomson's mere emergence through the swing gate to start bowling was greeted by a roar barely gentler than the one which accompanied Foreman to the canvas in Kinshasha' (Ian

Woodridge).

4. 'In the dressing room when they got his clothing off it looked a very nasty injury, almost as if the ball had lodged right in his ribs and then been pulled back out again' (Mike Denness on John Edrich's injury).
5. 'Within seconds of his dismissal, the whole of (David) Lloyd's body was quivering. He was shell-shocked, suffering from the effects of never having to move around so quickly in all his life' (Mike Denness).
6. 'One of the MCC's side started a letter home recently: "Dear mum, I got a half volley the other day in the nets" ' (John Woodcock).
7. 'Have you ever tried hammering your hands with a sledgehammer once every minute for six hours? (Wicket keeper Rodney Marsh).

Batting and Batsmen

FOUR INSTANCES OF CRICKETERS BATTING WITH *ONE HAND* IN TESTS

1. Lionel Tennyson, England vs. Australia, Leeds, 1921
2. Colin Cowdrey, England vs. West Indies, Lord's, 1963
3. Malcolm Marshall, West Indies vs. England, Leeds, 1984
4. Paul Terry, England vs. West Indies, Old Trafford, 1984

THREE BATSMEN VIV RICHARDS *ENVIES*.

1. Sunil Gavaskar
2. Greg Chappell
3. Gordon Greenidge

THE THREE GREATEST *INNINGS* ASIF IQBAL HAS SEEN

1. Javed Miandad's 116 not out vs. India, Sharjah, Austral-Asia Cup, 1986
2. Viv Richards' 189 not out vs. England, Old Trafford, 1984
3. Majid Khan's century before lunch at Karachi vs. New Zealand, 1976

DAVID GOWER'S SIX DREAM *BATSMEN*

'Once you reach that calibre, you are together on a plane above all the rest'

1. Viv Richards
2. Barry Richards
3. Gordon Greenidge
4. Zaheer Abbas
5. Sunil Gavaskar
6. Clive Lloyd

– *With Time To Spare* by David Gower and Alan Lee

FIVE *STROKES* DULEEP MENDIS ALWAYS WANTED TO PLAY

1. A hook like Ian Chappell.
2. A flick off the toes like Viv Richards.
3. An off-drive like Greg Chappell.
4. A square cut like Gordon Greenidge.
5. And having a go at everything like Ian Botham.

FIVE WAYS OF *INTIMIDATING* A BOWLER

1. Say 'Well left' when you are beaten
2. Tap the spot on the pitch after you have been beaten by the cutter
3. Look towards the sky and whistle loudly when you are hit hard on the thigh
4. Move away, objecting to the movement in the crowd behind his arm just as he is about to bowl
5. 'Someone flashed a mirror at me', when you are dismissed

FIVE *INNINGS* DICKIE BIRD FEELS HE WAS PRIVILEGED TO SEE FROM 25 YARDS AWAY

1. Clive Lloyd's 102 against Australia in the 1975 Prudential Cup final at Lord's ('It had power, grace and flair. Tremendous stuff').
2. Viv Richards' 292 against England at The Oval, 1976
3. Alan Knott's 135 against Australia at Trent Bridge, 1977 ('England were 70 for six when he came in, I think. England finished with over 300 in the end.')
4. Collis King's 86 against England in the 1979 Prudential Cup final at Lord's. ('Everyone talks of Richards' 138 not out, but you should have seen this. It was the last word in power.')
5. Gary Sobers' 156 against England at Lord's in 1973.

FIVE SONGS *KRISH SRIKKANTH* SINGS BETWEEN DELIVERIES

(It keeps his concentration going, he says)

1. Bridge Over Troubled Waters (Simon and Garfunkel)
2. Reaching Out (Bee Gees)
3. I Can't tell You Why (Eagles)
4. A religious hymn in Tamil in praise of Lord Krishna
5. Name of the Game (Abba)

SIX BATSMEN CHETAN CHAUHAN *ADMIRES*

1. Viv Richards : 'Has an amazing eye which enables him to put a ball from outside the off stump to square leg'.
2. Geoff Boycott : 'Even on the last day of a Test he would go to the nets and bat for a full 45 minutes ' .
3. Zaheer Abbas : 'A tremendous timer of the ball'.
4. G. Vishwanath : 'Always had so much time to play his shots'.
5. David Gower : 'A bit tentative initially, but once he got his eye in, the bowlers were in trouble'.
6. Sunil Gavaskar : 'His judgement, while leaving deliveries, was superb'.

– *Sportsworld*

ENGLAND'S FIVE BEST *BATSMEN*

A survey was conducted by the *Sunday Times* in 1986 among 8 county captains and players. They had to name one batsman each, with no conditions attached.

Mike Gatting ... 8 votes	Allan Lamb ... 3
David Gower ... 7½	Dennis Amiss ... 2
Geoff Boycott ... 6	Robert Bailey ... 1½
Graham Gooch ... 5½	J. Whitaker ... 1½

(Wayne Larkins, Bill Athey, Ian Botham and Tim Robinson one each)

THE THREE BATSMEN IMRAN KHAN *HATES* BOWLING TO

1. Sunil Gavaskar ('His perfect technique makes him the most difficult batsman alive to dismiss').
2. Gordon Greenidge ('It is a misconception that he is only an attacking batsman at the expense of technique').
3. Geoff Boycott ('He hardly gave the bowler a chance, though in the later stages of his career he appeared to be a bit suspect

against genuine fast bowling').

TEN DIFFERENT VIEWS ON *BATTING*

1. 'Whenever I am hit on the body it sort of wakes me up. I get to concentrate better.' (Mohinder Amarnath)
2. 'Runs are a habit. One should cultivate it.' (Bob Simpson)
3. 'Remember that the bowler can deliver only one ball at a time.' (H. Sutcliffe)
4. 'Batting, like professional golf, is a game of percentages.' (Glenn Turner)
5. 'Batting is just a series of habits. If you get into good ones when you're young, you're lucky.' (Tom Graveney)
6. 'My idea of heaven is to bat against my own bowling.' (Lord Cobham)
7. 'Don't give anyone the remotest chance of getting you out if you can possibly avoid it. Then the runs will come.' (Geoff Boycott)
8. 'Some day you go out to bat, thinking everything feels right today. You hit the first ball right in the middle of the bat and think : 'Keep going, Sunshine, you are all right there!' Then, three balls later, you are out. Other days you go out there feeling like death and 3 hours later, you are still there. You think : "What's wrong? I am still here! I must feel like death more often"'. (David Gower)
9. 'Barry Richards told me that batting was a hard grind. He told me I had to learn not to enjoy it.' (Kim Hughes)
10. 'Your head has got to be still. If your head is bobbing all over the place, you lose your bearings and judgement.' (Viv Richards)

IF YOU ARE OUT FOR *ZERO* YOU SCORE A...

1. ... duck
2. ... duck's egg
3. ... blob
4. ... nought
5. ... full moon

Being Sunil Gavaskar

THE FIVE KINDS OF *LETTERS* THAT THE MAIL BRINGS IN FOR GAVASKAR EACH DAY

('At home alone I get 40 to 50 letters a week throughout the year. About the same quantity comes to the office, and almost an equal number to my parents' house. During the cricketing season I can get anything between 15-20 letters a day at each of these places, pushing the weekly average to more than 200.')

1. 'Keep going until you are 40 years old'.
2. 'Stop flirting with the ball outside the off stump'.
3. 'Keep going until you get 10,000 Test runs'.
4. 'Retire now in the best interests of the country'.
5. 'Bat a little faster in the one-day games'.

Note. Gavaskar adds : 'Right through my career I have made it a practice to answer all fan mail personally, in my own handwriting'.

– *Sunday*

THE FIVE *COMPLAINTS* OF MARSHNEIL GAVASKAR

Sunil Gavaskar's wife normally has a lot to say about her husband that's, well, not exactly complimentary.

1. My birthday is in January and Sunil is always away
2. Between the cricket and the ribbon-cutting he even goes to office
3. He wasn't even around when our son Rohan was born
4. In retrospect, I do feel it is quite something that he was actually there by my side on our wedding day
5. The first wedding anniversary that we spent together was actually our fourth. That too, only for a while, till he caught his flight

FOUR STRANGE *MESSAGES* THAT HE HAS RECEIVED

1. 'The Limeys have 007, Beatles and Boycott. The Yanks remember Elvis, and we only have you. Don't let us down. This is not an election campaign'.
2. 'I want to see a century from you at Bombay before I die. I have just two months to live'. (A cancer patient from Sangli, Maharashtra, 1976).

3. 'My son is your big fan, but of late he is not taking his medicines at all. He is getting hysterical and uncontrollable. I request you to kindly send him a letter of advice and encouragement'. (From the father of a paraplegic in Dombivli, a suburb of Bombay)
4. 'I hereby present you with my slippers for your performance against the West Indies.'

THREE *ROLES* HE PLAYED AS A BOY

1. Lord Krishna 2. A Kashmiri boy in fancy dress competitions
3. 'Chandu' in the popular Marathi play *'Shaštang Namaskar'*

***SUNIL GAVASKAR* ON HIS 36 NOT OUT IN 60 OVERS IN THE WORLD CUP, 1975**

In what must rate as the poorest individual one-day innings ever, Gavaskar was at the crease for all 60 overs bowled by England while reaching 36 not out. Who can excuse a performance like that, you may ask? Sunil Gavaskar, of course!

1. 'I didn't play 60 overs myself, that's obvious'.
2. 'I couldn't force the pace and couldn't get out even when I tried to'.
3. 'As soon as the ball was delivered, my feet would move to a position for a defensive shot'.
4. 'The awful noise made by the crowd didn't help my thinking'.

FIVE *TRIBUTES* TO THE LITTLE MASTER

1. Keith Miller, when asked how he would have bowled to Sunil Gavaskar, replied : 'I'd have stood in the slips and let others bowl'.
2. 'A pocket-sized battleship armed with an impenetrable defence and astonishing gunpowder. The bigger the battle, the better the performance'. (Colin Cowdery)
3. 'The Indian combined Boycott's steadiness and Greenidge's ability to keep the runs flowing'. (Ian Botham)
4. 'I would have considered it an honour to play cricket with him'. (Don Bradman)
5. 'I have a feeling that if he had been born English or Australian, many of the better judges would have been tempted to bracket him with Bradman.' (Len Hutton)

THE GOOD AND THE BAD SIDES OF *SUNIL GAVASKAR*

1. 'He is extremely modest; he goes to the extent of asking young cricketers as well as old-timers about flaws in his technique'. (Former India and Bombay opener Ramnath Parkar).
2. 'You get the impression that he is nowadays too engrossed in himself'. (Bishen Bedi).
3. 'If we, his contemporaries, had sacrificed even 1 per cent of what he did, we would have become great cricketers'. (Former Bombay player Milind Rege).
4. 'In the field Sunny does retain a little of the majesty of the Raj. He never dives'. (Peter Roebuck).
5. 'He should be banned from playing for India again'. (Congress (I) MLA from Bengal, Rajesh Khaitan, in a memorandum presented to the Chief Minister of the State after he refused to play in Calcutta in early 1987).

TEN CONFESSIONS OF *SUNIL GAVASKAR*

1. 'Some people call me the Little Monster'.
2. 'Srikkanth has this electrifying effect on me'.
3. 'I must confess that I do not like fans pushing into my room...there are many items of an intimate nature lying around'.
4. 'My parents tell me I had an absolutely awful temper as a child – so much so, that they took me to a child psychologist to have me checked'.
5. 'I am fond of young people and would go to great lengths to avoid hurting them'.
6. 'I am frankly terrified of dogs, even small and apparently gentle ones. I just can't stand them'.
7. 'I pray every morning before a photograph of Satya Sai Baba, and put a "*teeka*" on my forehead at the time'.
8. 'I have only one major regret – that I didn't win a few more tosses as captain'.
9. 'I have been travelling so much that there are thousands of unanswered fan letters piled up at home. Some people have been sent replies after more than a year'.
10. 'I have had the privilege of being booed at every Test centre in India'.

Bodyline

England's captain Douglas Jardine evolved a strategy (defined as 'Bodyline') to contain Don Bradman in the Ashes series of 1932-33. The plan clicked; Bradman's average was restricted to 56.57. However, Jardine's brainchild sparked off unprecedented criticism and continued to be debated more than 50 years later

FIVE OPINIONS ON THE FILM *BODYLINE* BY BILL O'REILLY

1. 'It finished in a jumbled hotch-potch of anachronisms, inaccuracies and impossibilities.'
2. 'One who came rubbing his hands expectantly, thumped the "off" button with an irritated swipe that might well have damaged the set.'
3. 'Bradman emerged much more successfully from this film than he did from the real-life show.'
4. 'The lovely little mummy's boy, Jardine, was overcome with joy when the portly Lord Harris (who, you would never have guessed, captained England three times), presented him with a bat on his ninth birthday in the halls of Bombay's Government House Harris left his home in Bombay in 1885, five years before that little cherub was born.'
5. 'No effort was made to depict the heroic nature of Bill Woodfull's contribution to the series.'

AND HAROLD LARWOOD ADDS...

'There wasn't the ill-feeling and swearing in 1932-33 that the film claims'.

TWELVE BOOKS ON THE *BODYLINE SERIES*, 1932-33

1. *Cricket Crisis* by Jack Fingleton
2. *Bodyline : the Novel* by Paul Wheeler
3. *The Bodyline Controversy* by Laurance le Quesne
4. *The Larwood Story* by K. Perkins
5. *Bradman and the Bodyline* by Edward Docker
6. *In Quest of the Ashes* by Douglas Jardine
7. *Bodyline?* by Harold Larwood
8. *Fight for the Ashes* by Jack Hobbs
9. *The Ashes At Stake* by S. Canynge Caple

10. *Anti-Bodyline* by A. Kippax and E. P. Barbour
11. *Body whine* by R. Blundell and W. Branson
12. *Cricket and Empire* by Ric Sissions and B. Stoddart

TEN THINGS THEY SAID OF THE CONTROVERSIAL *DOUGLAS JARDINE*

1. 'Hey, which one of you bastards has been calling this bastard a bastard?' (Jack Fingleton asking the Australian players after Jardine came into the Australian dressing room to complain about unparliamentary language).
2. 'One of the greatest men I ever met'. (Herbert Sutcliffe).
3. 'He possessed a nobility and natural authority which men will follow anywhere, however grumpily and unwillingly'. (Christopher Douglas).
4. 'In a battle on a cricket field, or anywhere else on the world, I should always want Jardine on my side'. (Herbert Sutcliffe).
5. 'If I were facing lions or tigers in a jungle, he'd be my first choice as companion'. (Hadley Verity).
6. 'His wiles would have been better employed combating Rommel in the desert than handing out military provisions in the Kipling *Raj* backwater'. (Dennis Castle).
7. 'Bodyline apart, I consider Jardine the most efficient, scientific and shrewdest Test captain I played with or against'. (Jack Fingleton).
8. 'Nobody ever played a rising ball better'. (Harold Larwood).
9. 'He was very hard on me. He bowled me in more matches than anybody else on that tour (1932-33)'. (Harold Larwood).
10. 'Hey, Sardine...' (Australian crowds).

SEVEN ARGUMENTS IN DEFENSE OF *BODYLINE*

1. 'Fast bowlers have unintentionally hit batsmen ever since the game was played, and will continue to do so as long as cricket continues. It is all very well to subscribe to all the sentimental nonsense that has been written on the subject "for the good of the game". What would the game be without a fast bowler whose main attribute is the power to make lethargic batsmen jump about a bit?' (Fred Root, England cricketer)
2. 'Although leg-theory shock tactics might be blamed for upsetting and disturbing the equilibrium of graceful and artistic cricket, they have also taught us to appreciate quiet

periods of play and the music of falling wickets'. (Arthur Mailey)

3. 'It seems generally accepted that the bowling called Bodyline was a sudden and isolated piece of cricketing tactics, which the MCC outlawed and thereby made an end of the matter forever. In fact, it was inevitable in the normal course of cricket history. The importance it assumed was largely due to the quality of both, the man who directed it and the man who executed it... Perhaps an equally important aspect lay in Australian conditions. The wickets there in the Twenties and early Thirties were much faster than in England, so that a good length was a foot shorter of the batsman than in England. Moreover, there was at the time a dearth of fast bowlers in Australia. Their batsmen – like the English bastmen who faced Lindwall and Miller in 1948 – were completely out of practice against such speed'. (John Arlott)
4. 'Bodyline certainly did some good in that it caused an alteration in the LBW law (which MCC agreed to at the time)'. (Don Bradman)
5. 'My leg-theory bowling is not Bodyline bowling. It is not more physically dangerous to the batsman than is any very fast bowling'. (Harold Larwood)
6. 'It was all my fault'. (Batsman Bert Oldfield after being hit on the head by Larwood)
7. 'There is no danger if the batsmen play forward'. (Herby Taylor)

(Researched by Dr Surapriya Mukherjee)

TEN OPINIONS ON *HAROLD LARWOOD*

The tragedy of Harold Larwood is that while his name will be associated with 'Bodyline' as long as the game is played, it could very well be at the expense of his reputation as a fast bowler.

1. 'Why mummy, he doesn't look like a murderer'. (An Australian child on seeing Larwood at the theatre during the Bodyline series, 1932-33)
2. 'Larwood fast? Why, s'welp me, he wouldn't knock a dint in a pound of butter on a hot day. Don't tell me he is fast'. (Ernie Jones, late 19th-century Australian fast bowler)
3. 'The truth is that Larwood was so fast and so skilful in the 1932-33 series that his figure would still have set a standard in

history had he contended himself with orthodox means of attack'. (Jack Fingleton)

4. 'Harold Larwood is too good a sportsman to blame anyone but himself, but I always think I was to some extent responsible'. (Fred Root , England Test bowler of the Twenties, who was a leading exponent of the leg-theory)
5. 'I had this interesting experience from batting against Larwood. The first dorsal interasseous muscle, between the thumb and the index finger, ached for a week batting against him, so severe was the concussion of the ball hitting the bat. I experienced this against no other fast bowler'. (Jack Fingleton)
6. 'He's too bloody fast for me'. (Alan Kippax, lbw to Larwood for 8 in the Bodyline series)
7. 'Although I never played with him, Larwood appeared to me the best fast bowler I ever saw'. (F. S. Jackson)

And three from Larwood's point of view...

8. 'I am still glad to this day that I never apologized'.
9. 'The word"Bodyline"was maliciously coined by a cute Australian journalist for the purpose of misleading'.
10. 'Would you have behaved in similar outrageous fashion to me had I been bowling for Australia? (to barrackers)'.

Books and Authors

FIVE *BOOKS* RICHARD STREETON WOULDN'T MIND BEING MAROONED ON AN ISLAND WITH

(The contributor reports cricket for *The Times,* London)
Leaving aside reference books – and I stress this because personally I can enjoy dipping into Barclay's *World of Cricket* or a Roy Webber or a Bill Frindall record book for hours — my own favourite books are :

1. *On Top Down Under* by Ray Robinson
2. *Brightly Fades The Don* by Jack Fingleton
3. *Cricket Between Two Wars* by Sir Pelham Warner
4. *Sort Of A Cricket Person* by E. W. Swanton
5. *History of Cricket* by Rowland Bowen

Any of the above authors' other works would be welcome, closely followed by any Cardus, Robertson–Glasgow or Fender books. I'd love to take either a 1939 or a 1947 *Wisden* with me too.

MY FAVOURITE *BOOK*

1. Sir Neville Cardus considered the book on Walter Hammond by Ronald Mason the best biography he had ever read.
2. In the opinion of Alan Gibson, the best cricket book he has read is Hugh de Selincourt's *The Cricket Match.*
3. Arthur Gibson's favourite book is *The Summer Game* by Sir Neville Cardus.
4. Ray Hattersely wrote, 'The very name of *Wisden* is indivisible from cricket. It is – together with *Hansard Debrett* and *Burke* – one of those words which stand metonymy on its head. The name of a person has turned into the name of an institution.'
5. According to Sir James Barrie, the best book ever written was *The Cricket Match* by Huge de Selincourt.
6. Among the books that Ian Botham would take to a desert island is Jack Fingleton's *The Immortal Victor Trumper.*
7. John Arlott considers C.L.R. James' *Beyond A Boundary Book* as the best book that he has ever read.
8. Sir Don Bradman feels that the best book he has read is *On Top Down Under* by Ray Robinson.

***UNUSUAL* TITLES OF CRICKET BOOKS**

1. *Kissing The Rod* by Percy Fender
2. *The Sun Has Got Its Hat On* by Derek Randall
3. *Another Bloody Day In Paradise* by Frank Keating
4. *By God's Decree* by Kapil Dev
5. *With Time To Spare* by David Gower
6. *On Top Down Under* by Ray Robinson
7. *Cricket Wallah* by Scyld Berry
8. *Give Me Arthur : The Biography of Arthur Shrewsbury* by Peter Wynne Thomas
9. *Four Chukkas to Australia* by Jack Fingleton
10. *My Dear Victorious Stod* by David Frith
11. *Ave a go, yer mug* by Richard Cashman
12. *It Never Rains* by Peter Roebuck
13. *High, Wide and Handsome* by Frank Keating

14. *Lambs To the Slaughter* by Graham Yallop
15. *Rowdy* by Ashley Mallett

FIFTEEN BOOKS WRITTEN BY *SIR NEVILLE CARDUS*

1. *Australian Summer*
2. *Autobiography*
3. *Cardus on Cricket*
4. *Close of Play*
5. *The Club Cricketer*
6. *Cricket*
7. *Cricket All The Year*
8. *Days in the Sun*
9. *A Cricketer's Book*
10. *The Essential Neville Cardus*
11. *Full Score*
12. *Good Days*
13. *Idle Thoughts On Cricket*
14. *Second Innings*
15. *The Summer Game*

TEN UNLIKELY CRICKET WRITERS

1. Sir James Barrie
2. Arthur Conan Doyle (a poem commemorating his getting WG Grace out)
3. PG Wodehouse
4. Sir Robert Menzies (a feature in *Wisden*'s centenary edition)
5. Bob Hawke (a foreword in *Bat and Pad,* a compilation of Australian cricket writings)
6. Sir Home Gordon
7. Charles Dickens
8. J. B. Priestly
9. A. G. Gardiner
10. C. P. Snow

THE COMMONEST TITLE FOR CRICKET *BOOKS*

'Cricket' (used by more than fifty different authors for their works).

FOUR CRICKETERS WHO WROTE BOOKS TITLED '*BOWLING*'

1. Alec Bedser
2. Bob Massie
3. M. S. Nichols
4. Pat Pocock

CRICKET BOOK WITH THE *LONGEST* TITLE

'*A Correct Account of all the Cricket Matches Which Have Been Played By the Mary-le-bone Club, and all other Principal Matches, From the Year 1786 to 1822 inclusive*' by Harry Bentley,1823.

CRICKET BOOKS WITH THE *SHORTEST* TITLES

1. *Zed* by Zaheer Abbas and David Foot, 1983
2. *Over* by Huge de Sélincourt, 1932
3. *Fred* by John Arlott, 1971
4. *Play* by J. M. Kilburn, 1937
5. *Play* by Dr N. L. Stevenson, 1946

Bowlers and Bowling

THE FIVE *BOWLERS* TONY GREIG RESPECTED THE MOST

1. Dennis Lillee
2. Andy Roberts
3. Jeff Thomson
4. John Snow
5. Mike Procter

The Men and The Game by Tony Greig

THE FIVE BEST *DELIVERIES* BISHEN BEDI HAS SEEN

1. Clive Lloyd bowled by Chandrasekhar, Calcutta, 1974-75
2. Tony Greig bowled by Michael Holding, The Oval, 1976
3. Gary Sobers bowled by Salim Durrani, Trinidad, 1970-71
4. Ken Barrington bowled by Chandrasekhar, Lord's, 1967
5. Clive Lloyd bowled by Dennis Lillee, Perth, 1971-72

SEVEN BOWLERS CALLED FOR *CHUCKING* IN A TEST MATCH

1. Ernie Jones, Australia vs England, Melbourne, 1897-98
2. Tony Lock, England vs West Indies, Kingston, 1953-54
3. G. Griffin, South Africa vs England, Lord's, 1960
4. Haseeb Ahsan, Pakistan vs India, Bombay, 1960-61
5. Ian Meckiff, Australia vs S. Africa, Brisbane, 1963-64
6. Abid Ali, India vs New Zealand, Christchurch, 1967-68
7. David Gower, England vs N. Zealand, Trent Bridge, 1986

SIX CLASSICAL BOWLERS' *STYLES* WORTH COPYING ACCORDING TO LEN HUTTON

1. Ray Lindwall
2. Keith Miller
3. Fred Trueman
4. Dennis Lillee
5. Alec Bedser
6. Gubby Allen

FOURTEEN CRICKETERS WHO BOWLED *PACE AND SPIN*

1. B. J. T. Bosanquet
2. Trevor Goddard
3. Karsan Ghavri
4. Warwick Armstrong
5. Alan Davidson
6. W. Voce
7. Gary Sobers
8. Learie Constantine
9. Rusi Surti
10. Tony Greig
11. Eknath Solkar
12. Dhiraj Parsana
13. Maurice Tate
14. Bhagwat Chandrasekhar ('His fast one was as fast as Thommo's maan,' said Viv Richards!)

FIVE BOWLERS VIV RICHARDS WOULD PREFER TO *AVOID*

1. Abdul Qadir
2. Dennis Lillee
3. Andy Roberts
4. Joel Garner
5. Malcolm Marshall

(Richards has had the good fortune of not having faced the last three)

FOUR SUGGESTIONS TO CURB *INTIMIDATORY BOWLING*

1. 'A longer pitch' (Ted Dexter).
2. 'A line across the pitch, placed according to its degree of bounce as decided by the umpires' (E. W. Swanton).
3. 'Only three bowlers should be allowed to run in more than, say, 10 yards' ('Bomber' Wells).
4. 'In future, batsmen should only be out caught if the ball has touched the blade – or the back – of the bat. Any ball caught off the gloves or the handle of the bat would not be out' (Suggested by *The Cricketer* magazine).

JEFF DUJON ON SIX BOWLERS HE HAS *KEPT* WICKETS TO

1. On Michael Holding : 'All silken till the ball left his hand'.
2. On Andy Roberts : 'Would swing the ball a mile'.
3. On Colin Croft : 'When he pitched the ball it would be on the middle stump and cut towards the slips'.
4. On Joel Garner : 'He could generate exceptional bounce from

very close to the bat'.
5. On Courtney Walsh : 'A blend of Croft and Marshall'.
6. On Malcolm Marshall : 'The most complete fast bowler I have kept to'.

FIVE FAST BOWLERS LEN PASCOE *ADMIRES*

1. Dennis Lillee
2. Andy Roberts
3. Michael Holding
4. Jeff Thomson
5. Refused to name

FOUR *MATHEMATICAL* ANALYSES OF JEFF THOMSON BOWLING TO ROY FREDERICKS, PERTH, 1975-76

1. It took 0.438 seconds for the ball to travel from the bowler's hand to the bat
2. The batsman had 0.30 seconds to react : see the ball predict its course and decide on the stroke
3. The batsman had 0.30 seconds for movement : to play his stroke
4. Fredericks would therefore have to start his reaction 0.162 seconds before Thomson had released the ball!

– *The Art Of Fast Bowling* by Dennis Lillee

FIVE PEOPLE ON *BOWLING*

1. 'The generalized result derived from studying 17 fast bowlers is that : the run up provides 19% of the action, leg and hip rotation 23%, trunk flexion and shoulder girdle rotation 11%, arm action 42% and hand flexion 42%'. (Robin Marlar)
2. 'Swing bowling is bowling in a corridor of uncertainty'. (Terry Alderman)
3. 'A lot of bowling is done in the mind'. (Bishen Bedi)
4. 'Pakistan produces more fast bowlers than we do in India because it is a Muslim country and Islam is a more aggressive philosophy than ours'. (Bishen Bedi)
5. 'First a wide and then a wicket'. (Tom Emmett)

PERFECTION IN FAST BOWLING ACCORDING TO DENNIS LILLEE

1. The breathtaking run-up of Wes Hall
2. The silk smooth delivery of Ray Lindwall
3. The blistering pace of Jeff Thomson

4. The firebrand aggression of Freddie Trueman
5. The scintillating swing of Alan Davidson
6. The devastating cut of John Snow
7. The nagging accuracy of Brian Statham
8. The lethal bouncer of Charlie Griffith
9. The demoralizing yorker of Andy Roberts
10. The unstinting stamina of Mike Procter
11. The sheer brilliance of Keith Miller

– *The Art Of Fast Bowling* by Dennis Lillee

WHAT SEVEN FAST BOWLERS CONCENTRATED ON FOR THEIR *FIRST DELIVERY*

1. 'I aimed to bowl the best and fastest ball in my armoury' (Frank Tyson).
2. 'I aimed for a good line and length, but always wished it was an unplayable ball' (Alan Connolly).
3. 'It was my best chance of surprising a batsman, so I went as straight and as fast as possible' (David Larter).
4. 'I went for line and length…it was dangerous to try anything else with stiff muscles' (Peter Loader).
5. 'Flat out, trying to get a wicket' (Harold Larwood).
6. 'The idea was not to give the batsman any free, widish balls for him to assess my pace and that of the wicket' (Peter Lever)
7. 'If I could land the first ball roughly where I wanted it, I knew I had started on a good note' (Dennis Lillee)

– *The Art Of Fast Bowling* by Dennis Lillee

SIX DIFFERENT VIEWS ON THE *BOUNCER*

1. 'If you can't get nine, ten and jack out without bouncing, you have no business playing Test cricket' (Fred Trueman).
2. 'I use the bumper to try and get the batsman on his back foot. Then I have a better chance of getting him lbw or hitting the stumps' (Imran Khan).
3. 'Why, maan, if I had hit him and killed him, I'd never have played cricket again' (Wes Hall when asked why he never bounced to Lindsay Kline in the Adelaide Test, 1960-61. The batsman held out with Ken Mackay for around two hours and saved the match for Australia'.
4. 'I thought it was an unwritten law that bowlers never bowled bouncers to bowlers' (Ewen Chatfield, in hospital, after

having been hit on the temple by Peter Lever).

5. 'Much of what the bowler bowled, frankly went over my head too' (Keith Miller, all-rounder-turned-journalist).
6. 'If the batsman gets above himself, put one past his whiskers now and then' (Sammy Woods).

THE ORDEAL OF FACING A *WEST INDIAN* FAST BOWLER

1. 'Like an impending visit by one's mother-in-law' (Ian Botham).
2. 'Resembles an Exocet missile' (Derek Pringle on the bouncer).
3. 'I've cleaned by teeth and gargled, just in case you have to give me the kiss of life' (Tailender Pat Pocock to physio Bernard Thomas).
4. 'England's twelve for the Oval Test, 1984, in the *Daily Mail* appeared as 'David Gower, J. Agnew, P. Allot, I. Bother...'
5. 'A queue of batsmen will be checking the strength of their helmets and the validity of their insurance policies' (C. M. Jenkins).

THREE BOWLERS WHOSE *ABILITY* IMRAN KHAN ENVIES

1. Dennis Lillee ('Day in and day out he was the most consistent bowler that I have ever seen').
2. Michael Holding ('For sheer variety there was none to match him').
3. Abdul Qadir ('Fortunately I have never had to face him. His control for a leg spinner is unbelievable').

FRANK TYSON'S COMMENTS ON FIVE CONTEMPORARY FAST BOWLERS

On Richard Hadlee : 'Has a lithe, whippy action quite like that of Brian Statham'.

On Joel Garner : 'Has alarming bounce from a good length and a devastating, toe-crushing yorker'.

On Ian Botham : 'Is willing to try any wicket-producing variation, which leads him to bowl some remarkable deliveries – and some rubbish!'

On Kapil Dev : 'Will probably go down in Test history as the best Indian quickie of all time.'

On Imran Khan : 'Has a boomerang inswinger – even with the old ball'

RUN-UP *SPEEDS* OF FOUR GREAT FAST BOWLERS

1. Dennis Lillee : 33.57 km.p.h.
2. Andy Roberts : 28.78 km.p.h.
3. Mike Holding : 28.10 km.p.h.
4. Jeff Thomson : 18.02 km.p.h.

– *The Art Of Fast Bowling* by Dennis Lillee

...AND THEIR BOWLING *SPEEDS*

	Release speed	Speed at batting end
Jeff Thomson	160.45 km.p.h.	129.92 km.p.h.
Andy Roberts	150.67 km.p.h.	129.89 km.p.h.
Mike Holding	148.54 km.p.h.	122.74 km.p.h.
Dennis Lillee	139.03 km.p.h.	115.92 km.p.h.

(This study was conducted by Tom Penrose, Brian Bransky and Daryl Foster at Perth, 1975-76)

– *The Art Of Fast Bowling* by Dennis Lillee

THE *MAGIC* OF SPINNERS AND SPIN BOWLING – EIGHT LINES IN APPRECIATION

1. 'Bedi's pace through the air, Chandrasekhar's off the pitch' (Kenneth Gregory on R. O. Schwarz).
2. 'There is nothing so fascinating in cricket as a duel between the top flight batsmen and the good leg spinner' (Sir Don Bradman).
3. 'It's such a different kind of contest and it's so easy to lose concentration. For example,Viv Richards bowled me in the Barbados Test when I was all set' (David Gower).
4. 'If I go forward I am stumped; if I go back I am lbw. I shall never know how to play you' (Lionel Tennyson to 'Tich' Freeman, the Kent leg spinner).
5. 'A spinner gets you out nicely, rather than blasts you out with your gloves in front of your face' (Glenn Turner).
6. 'The modern obsession with speed has deprived cricket of such wonderful sights as Grimmett vs Hammond, and the footwork and strokeplay which are the by-products' (Don Bradman).
7. '...ever watchful for the enticing ball that asks to be driven and proves not to be quite there' (E. W. Swanton on England leg spinner between the Wars, Ian Peebles).
8. 'Flight was his secret, flight and the curving line, now higher, now lower, tempting, inimical; every ball like every other ball,

yet somehow unlike; each over in collusion with the others, part of a plot. Every ball a decoy, a spy sent out to get the lie of the land; some balls simple, some complex, some easy, some difficult; and one of them – ah, which? – the master ball ' (Neville Cardus on Wilfred Rhodes) ·

FREAK *DELIVERIES*

1. Alfred Mynn, circa 1840, struck the long stop in the chest with six successive deliveries. The victim had to be taken home where he spat blood for a fortnight.
2. Jack Durston, playing in the second Ashes Test at Lord's in 1921, dropped the ball from his hand as his arm turned over. The ball rolled down the wicket and came to a stop. Durston rushed to pick it up but Warren Bardsley, the batsman, got there first and hit it for four.
3. Alan Moss once hit the sight screen at Sabina Park while on a tour of the West Indies, first bounce!
4. On Pakistan's tour of Australia in 1983-84, a delivery from Abdul Qadir slipped out of his hand and settled at short mid-on. Qadir strolled across and picked it up. Greg Ritchie, the batsman, insisted that the ball be placed at the very spot from where Qadir picked it up. It was replaced – and Ritchie hit it for four.
5. Mike Hendrick bowled Madan Lal in a Test in the 1974 series with a ball that uprooted the off and leg stumps, leaving the middle intact.
6. Legend is built around a ball by C. J. Kortright of Essex. Bowled in the late 19th century in a county fixture, the ball jumped off a responsive pitch and hit the sight screen behind the wicket keeper without a bounce!

Captains and Captaincy

THE FIVE COMMONEST *EXCUSES* OF A LOSING CAPTAIN

1. 'Not enough match practice'.
2. 'We played against 13 men'.
3. 'If only we had held that catch'.
4. 'We had the worst luck in the world'.
5. 'Our best players were out of town'.

ACCORDING TO TREVOR BAILEY, BAD *CAPTAINS* ARE USUALLY....

1. Excitable men
2. Dull, apathetic men
3. Bowling captains, with an aversion to seeing anybody else bowl but themselves

CHETAN CHAUHAN'S ASSESSMENT OF THE FIVE *CAPTAINS* HE PLAYED UNDER

1. Tiger Pataudi : 'Reserved, aloof, assertive and technically very sound'.
2. Ajit Wadekar : 'Simple man, he had little control over the team'.
3. S. Venkataraghavan : 'Nobody discussed things with him because he thought that whatever he said was right'.
4. Bishen Bedi : 'Somewhat a dictator, assertive and attacking; really built up team spirit'.
5. Sunil Gavaskar : 'Very defensive and sometimes lost his cool. Not assertive and could not control his team'.

– *Sportsworld*

SIX *CAPTAINS* ON CAPTAINCY

1. 'Captaincy is 90% luck and 10% skill – but for heaven's sake don't try it without that little 10%' (Richie Benaud).
2. 'What do they expect me to do ? Walk around in a t-shirt with "I'm in charge" on it' (David Gower, when the selectors were critical of his restrained style of captaincy).
3. 'It's not a crown, it's a coconut' (Mike Smith on the England captaincy).
4. 'Captaining a team is like playing chess – working out strategy, moving the pieces round the field, and trying not to lose pawns' (Mike Brearley).
5. 'Captaincy is a relationship' (Asif Iqbal).
6. 'The toughest job in sport' (David Hookes on the England captaincy).

THE FIVE *YOUNGEST* TEST CAPTAINS

1. Tiger Pataudi (India), 21 years 77 days, versus West Indies at Bridgetown in 1961-62.
2. Ian Craig (Australia), 22 years 194 days, versus South Africa

at Johannesburg, 1957.

3. M. Bissett (South Africa), 22 years 306 days, versus England at Johannesburg, 1899.
4. M. P. Bowden (England), 23 years 144 days, versus South Africa at Cape Town, 1889.
5. G. C. Grant (West Indies), 23 years 217 days, versus Australia at Adelaide, 1930.

RICHIE BENAUD'S FOUR GREATEST *CAPTAINS*

1. Keith Miller : 'The best captain I ever played under.'
2. Ian Chappell : 'The best ever to lead Australia.'
3. Mike Brearley : 'A clear thinker, courageous and... having that share of luck so essential for any successful captain.'
4. Ray Illingworth : 'A shrewd psychologist and one who left his team in no doubt as to what he required of them'.

– *On Reflection* by Richie Benaud

FIVE ENGLISH CRICKETERS ON THEIR FAVOURITE *CAPTAINS*

1. 'As a tactician, a leader, and in terms of personality, it was Norman Yardley' (Trevor Bailey).
2. 'Looking back, I would rather play under Percy Chapman – I enjoyed the game more' (Leslie Ames).
3. 'Tactically, in terms of cricketing brain, nobody could beat Len Hutton' (Fred Trueman).
4. 'Lord Hawke was the best I played under, because he always set the field just as I asked him' (Wilfred Rhodes).
5. 'I'd take things from him that I would clip other guys in the ear for' (Ian Botham on Mike Brearley).

TEN *QUALITIES* A SUCCESSFUL CAPTAIN SHOULD HAVE

According to Sir Pelham Warner, former captain of England. Having devoted his life to the promotion of the game, Sir Warner was widely acknowledged as the 'Prime Minister of Cricket'.

1. Knowledge of the game, its tactics and strategy and a readiness to study and profit by the teachings of history
2. Belief in his men – this is the most important – a 'crabbing', grousing captain is anathema
3. Good temper
4. Good manners
5. Tact

6. A temperament which, should an incident arise, will meet such an incident with a brain packed in ice and therefore incapable of explosion
7. A realization that there is something new to be learnt about cricket every day and a pride in his office which should produce a burning enthusiasm and a keen anxiety to do everything in his power not only for the welfare of his side, but also for the good name of cricket, both on and off the field
8. A capacity to work physically and mentally with his bowlers
9. He must ensure good discipline, because an undisciplined army is untrustworthy. He need not resort to drastic methods, but must gain the respect of his men, so that in all their actions they will always bear in mind the thought 'Would the captain approve?'
10. Finally, no aversion to consulting his most experienced lieutenants. After all, great generals work with, and consult, their chiefs of staff

– *The Cricketer International*

Characters

FIVE CRICKETERS TIGER PATAUDI ENJOYED *TALKING* TO THE MOST

1. Sir Frank Worrell (West Indies)
2. Peter Pollock (South Africa)
3. Sir Donald Bradman (Australia)
4. Rev. David Sheppard (England)
5. J. M. (Mamasaheb) Ghorpade (India)

FIVE CHARACTERS *SIR WILLIAM GOLDING* WOULD HAVE LOVED TO PORTRAY IN HIS NOVELS

The contributor, one of the world's leading contemporary writers, won the Nobel Prize for literature in 1983.

1. Jack Hobbs – 'A craftsman'.
2. Jim Laker – 'His taking 19 wickets out of 20 in a Test match was too much for me. Besides, I was a slow bowler myself'.
3. Frank Wolley – 'My wife's idol. I consult her in all matters non-literary'.

4. Kapil Dev – 'I watched him on television. He is very, very impressive'.
5. Ian Botham – 'A character'.

'A DOZEN *GAME CHARACTERS'* BY JOHN ARLOTT

1. William Clarke
2. Sammy Woods
3. Tom Wass
4. George Gunn
5. Jack Newman
6. Arthur Wellard
7. Haydn Davies
8. Roley Jenkins
9. Tony Lock
10. Ken Mackay
11. Colin Milburn
12. Derek Randall

– *Wisden Cricket Monthly*

FIVE CHARACTERISTIC *WORDS* IN GREG MATTHEWS' VOCABULARY

The unconventional touch of Greg Matthews extends also to his language. Interviewers have complained that his recordings are barely decipherable; as Bill O'Reilly put it, 'It is a brand of English that I have never heard, and I was a school teacher'.

1. 'Gigs' : for cricket matches
2. 'The man' : for Viv Richards
3. 'Sensaysh' : His favourite superlative
4. 'Sweet man' : for Bob Holland
5. 'Zucchini' : He claims to have invented the word because he liked the sound of it

THREE HONEST *UMPIRES*

1. Pakistani umpire Khalid Aziz retired after refusing to follow the official directive to cheat during home Tests against West Indies in 1980-81. He said : 'The person who wanted to influence me did not like me because I declined to accept this unwanted advice'.
2. Batting in England's second innings in the 1978-79 Perth Test, Geoff Boycott was caught for 4 off the bowling of Dymock. Umpire Tom Brooks ruled the batsman 'not out'. Boycott went on to make 23. The umpire realized his error and apologized to the Australian captain Yallop, saying: 'I am afraid my error has cooked it for you'. England won by 166 runs. Brooks retired soon afterwards.
3. England Test cricketer Derek Randall admitted after

umpiring a Notts match in 1977 : 'I kept making the wrong decisions; so they chucked me off and made me run the line'.

IN AWE OF *DR. W. G. GRACE*

It would be almost impossible not to associate cricket with the vast bulk of Dr. W. G. Grace. While he lived, Grace was a national institution of sorts, probably as recognizable in the England of those days as Willam Gladstone. Champion batsman, bowler, captain and hustler...it was the rare person who did not have an opinion on him...

1. 'No monument, no portrait, no book can adequately represent either the vitality of W.G. or his superb skill in the game he loved'. (Lord Hawke)
2. 'He turned the old one-stringed instrument into a many-chorded lyre'. (Ranji)
3. 'A beard like a Goth or a Vandal'. (Arthur Conan Doyle)
4. '...no one has by prowess and personality alike so long and so indisputably dominated the field...' (Harry Altham)
5. 'He was a non-such'. (Tom Emmett)
6. '...the kindest and most sympathetic cricketer I have played with'. (Lord Harris)
7. 'Had Grace born in ancient Greece, the *Iliad* would have been a different book'. (Bishop of Hereford)
8. 'W. G. discovered batting; he turned its many straight channels into one great winding river'. (Ranji)
9. 'Oh yes, he blocks the shooters, he blocks 'em to t'boundary'. (A. Shaw)
10. '...was just a great big schoolboy in everything he did'. (an old friend of W. G.'s)

...AND FOUR WHO WEREN'T QUITE IMPRESSED

1. 'He has one of the dirtiest necks I ever kept wicket behind'. (Viscount Cobham)
2. 'Grace overbowled me and ruined my health before I was 25'. (G. Jessop)
3. 'He was far more cheeky than I've been – he used to stay at the crease when he had been bowled'. (Kerry Packer)
4. 'What do you know about cricket, you old buffer?' (A young batsman after W.G. intervened in a local game in Kent and agreed with the umpire's decision that he was out lbw)

KEEPING *DR W G. GRACE* IN CHECK!

'The Society For The Improvement Of Things In General And The Diffusion Of Perfect Equality, at a meeting to be held shortly, will submit the following propositions...'

1. That W. G. Grace shall owe a couple of hundred or so before batting.
2. That his shoe spikes shall be turned inward.
3. That he shall be declared out whenever the umpire likes.
4. That he shall always be the eleventh player.
5. That he shall not be allowed to play at all.

– Arlott and Trueman On Cricket

SIX INSTANCES OF *VICTOR TRUMPER'S* GENEROSITY

1. During a visit to the Coliseum on the tour of England in 1902, Trumper noticed a young boy selling songsheets and shivering in the rain as the Australian cricketers were about to leave. He slipped away from the group, bought the poor lad's entire unsold stock and sent him home happy
2. When a group of poor young boys came to his shop one day to buy cricket gear, Trumper returned the odd collection of shillings and gave away the equipment free of cost
3. He refused to open a sports goods shop in Sydney because Australian cricketer Syd Gregory was in the same trade. Trumper went into the sports goods business only after Gregory had wound up his business
4. He refused to score off a bowler in a game in North England when he learned that the young man worked in a coal mine. He played out three maidens and later said : 'Oh I didn't want to spoil the child's chances of gaining an easier living than one from heaving coal'.
5. He agreed to use a kid's bat vs Canterbury at Christchurch in 1913-14. 'All right, I'll try,' he said. 'Hang on to this while I get back.' Herbie Collins tried to dissuade him but Trumper was adamant. 'I couldn't refuse the kiddie'. He went on to score 293 in 190 minutes
6. He sold the bat with which he had made 185 not out vs England at Sydney in 1903-04 to a gentleman saying : 'It cost me 45 shillings, but now it is second-hand. You can have it for a pound.'

TEN THINGS *GEORGE BROWN* ATTRACTED ATTENTION FOR...

(George Brown, Hampshire and England, was an all rounder in the truest sense of the word)

1. ...tearing a pack of cards with his bare hands
2. ...walking 64 miles from Cowley to Southampton for a trial, carrying his bat and all personal belongings on his shoulder
3. ...keeping wickets for England wearing motor cycling gauntlets
4. ...riding his motor cycle at a considerable speed down the steps to the Bournemouth promenade
5. ...taking 629 first-class wickets as a bowler
6. ...pulling his bat away and taking the ball from a fast bowler on his chest, saying 'He isn't fast'
7. ...sharing a three-figure stand for every Hampshire wicket except the sixth
8. ...seizing a well-known Yorkshire player by the front of his jacket with one hand and holding him over the well of a six-story spiral staircase
9. ...asking that his ashes be scattered over the ground at Southampton
10. ...hitting a ball over the wicket keeper's head for six after he had been sent in to bat at number ten in a game against Warwickshire at Southampton in 1926. Later he vented his fury by breaking his bat in two, handing one half to the umpire and batting with the other

TEN CRICKETERS *ON THEMSELVES*

1. 'I am like wine – getting better and better over the years.' (Syed Kirmani)
2. 'I probably started playing cricket in the cradle.' (Dilip Vengsarkar)
3. 'I want people not to talk to me on Sundays – I am not good company. Sundays have always been for relaxing, eating and playing golf.'(Martin Crowe)
4. 'Most people think that fast bowlers are dummies and idiots – and I've got tangible proof that I am not!' (Geoff Lawson after getting a Bachelor of Optometry degree)
5. 'I suppose me mom'll still speak to me.'(Kim Hughes after losing the Leeds Test in 1981 to England)

6. ‘Imran Khan told me if I concentrated on my batting I could become the best all rounder in the world.’ (Malcolm Marshall)
7. ‘It is the way I was born. My mother was told it might have had something to do with the way she used to carry my sister, who is a year older, when I was in the womb.’ (Gladstone Small on his lack of a prominent neck)
8. ‘Finest bloody fast bowler t’draw breath.’ (Fred Trueman)
9. ‘Yorkshire, my county, played me for my whistling and good behaviour, while England chose me to go in with Grace and give him confidence.’ (George Ulyett)
10. ‘Hobbs, Hammond and Broad; it doesn’t quite ring true, does it?’ (Chris Broad)

TEN MORE CRICKETERS ON *THEMSELVES*

1. ‘I married cricket’. (Dickie Bird, a bachelor)
2. ‘I have cut back on my intake of alcohol. I am having early nights before the game and generally, am looking after my body a bit...because I just want to play cricket and be rich and lazy’. (Rodney Hogg)
3. ‘When I first go out to field early in the morning, my only enemy is sleepiness’. (David Gower)
4. ‘I felt like an old maid defending her virginity’. (Douglas Jardine after scoring one run in 90 minutes during the Bodyline series)
5. ‘I never needed the googly.’ (Sydney Barnes).
6. ‘I love a dogfight’. (Herbert Sutcliffe)
7. ‘When I let the ball go, I am not sure which way it is going to move, in or out’. (Mike Hendrick)
8. ‘We oldies live only for the sake of our memories.’ (Mushtaq Ali)
9. ‘I can be friendly, but very stubborn and unfriendly if the selfish public usurp my privacy.’ (Viv Richards)
10. ‘If I do not play for 2 or 3 days my whole body starts aching’. (Kapil Dev)

Compliments

THE FLAMBOYANT *KEITH MILLER*

In 55 matches for Australia, this dashing cricketer took 170 wickets and scored 2958 runs.

1. 'Miller's frame would have done credit to an athlete of ancient Greece'. (Frank Tyson)
2. 'Bowling seemed to come so easily to him that he did not even have to bother to mark out his run-up'. (Jim Laker)
3. 'I once saw Miller bowling David Sheppard with a googly using the new ball in a match at Lord's'. (Fred Trueman)
4. '...a wartime pilot in Britain, capable of crashlanding at 11 am and joining in a game of cricket at noon'. (Christopher-Martin-Jenkins)
5. 'He used to just say one word : "Scatter". And that's what the fieldsmen did – they scattered to their positions'. (Bob Simpson)

VIV RICHARDS – BATSMAN OF OUR GENERATION ?

Five admirers doff their hats to the gum-chewing genius from Antigua.

1. 'Viv Richards is streets ahead of everybody' (Dilip Vengsarkar)
2. 'After all, Richards was Superman' (Graeme Wright)
3. 'The great thing he always does is to keep his head still – something all great players do, whether it is Jack Nicklaus, Steve Davis or Dusty Hare when he is kicking goals' (Tom Graveney)
4. 'When I am old I will boast that I played with Viv...quite simply, he is the greatest' (Ian Botham)
5. 'He is human. He does fail – but so rarely compared with others' (Mike Gatting)

TEN *COMPLIMENTS* PAID TO DENNIS LILLEE

1. 'The greatest.' (Richie Benaud)
2. 'Dennis will eat nine out of ten fast bowlers for breakfast.' (Len Pascoe)
3. 'I admire his killer instinct.' (Norman Cowans)
4. 'When the ball was coming through the air, you could actually

hear it whistling – wheesh!' (Malcolm Marshall)
5. 'The best bowler I've seen – on any wicket'. (Jeff Thomson)
6. 'My playing for Australia means that I will be putting my kit down next to the great Dennis Lillee'. (Greg Matthews)
7. 'The best in his trade'. (Clive Lloyd)
8. 'He is one of the few cricketers in the world who can inspire a team just by being there'. (Kim Hughes)
9. 'A certainty for any dream Test side that I may pick'. (Mike Gatting)
10. '...made things happen by sheer will power'. (Imran Khan)

... AND ONE WHO *THOUGHT* DIFFERENTLY

'Dennis has had the advantage of playing against many weak teams'. (Harold Larwood)

FIVE QUOTES IN PRAISE OF *RAY LINDWALL*

The boy, who used to bowl at paraffin tins in the street down which Bill O'Reilly made his way home, went on to take 228 wickets for Australia. Critics went as much into raptures about his 'run to the wicket' as 'the one which swung out late'.

1. 'If J. S. Bach had seen Ray Lindwall run up to bowl, he would have rewritten one of his Brandenburg concertos'. (Fred Trueman)
2. 'He was a ballet dancer in an era of straining, sweating, quick bowlers'. (Frank Tyson)
3. 'Poetry in motion'. (Sir Pelham Warner on his approach to the wicket)
4. 'He was the best bowler I ever played against'. (Len Hutton)
5. 'Perhaps the greatest fast bowler of all time'. (John Arlott)

AND THOUGH LINDWALL SCORED TWO TEST CENTURIES...

Keith Miller said : 'He'd be very nervous before he went out to bat. His gloves would be trembling'.

THE INCREDIBLY TALENTED *SIR GARFIELD SOBERS*

Gary Sobers could walk in to bat high up in the order, then start the new ball bowling attack, use the seam when it lost its shine and chip in as a left-arm orthodox or unorthodox spin bowler if the circumstances so required. After he had wheeled down his overs, he would walk off to slip or leg slip and captain the side from there!

1. 'We'll never see his like again'. (Basil D'Oliveira)
2. 'When I was a boy, my idol was Sobers – just seeing him walk out to bat made my day, he didn't have to score a run'. (Larry Gomes)
3. 'So many times to me he has been absolute batting perfection'. (Jack Fingleton)
4. 'Graced the fields like a leopard'. (Richie Benaud)

BARRY RICHARDS – A WASTED TALENT

Barry Richards had played only four Tests for South Africa when his country was expelled from the International Cricket Conference. He spent the rest of his life playing for Natal, South Australia, Hampshire, Gloucestershire and Packer's International team. He was lost to the world for having been born in the wrong country.

1. 'No more elegant player has taken the field in our time'. (Richie Benaud).
2. '...has undoubtedly been the biggest influence on my career'. (Greg Chappell).
3. 'People look at him and say : "That is a beautiful talent. Look how easy it is for him". Of course, they are wrong. He only makes it look easy. I know how hard he works'. (Bob Woolmer).
4. 'No matter how well he batted – and sometimes he batted like a being from heaven – there was nothing to gain, nowhere to go. Small wonder that he ran out of ambition'. (Mike Gatting).
5. '...finds the difficult business of batting quite absurdly easy and all that has prevented him from piling up records like a Bradman has been his tendency to be bored if his supreme talent is not being fully tested by the mere mortals bowling at him'. (Christopher Martin Jenkins).

TEN LINES IN AWE OF *VICTOR TRUMPER*

Possibly the greatest batsman produced by his country, Bradman included, Trumper left behind a mourning Australia when he died at the age of 37 in 1915. As late as the 1980s biographies were still going into print on this remarkably talented and modest cricketer.

1. 'When he walked out to bat every blade of grass bowed to him'. (Sir Pelham Warner)
2. 'I wasn't fit to lick Vic's boots'. (Clem Hill)
3. 'The most gallant and handsome batsman of them all'. (Neville Cardus)
4. 'Aye, aye, 'e was a good batter, was Victor'. (Wilfred Rhodes)
5. 'I felt the ball spinning from my fingers beautifully. I knew that the length and flight through the air were going to be just right. And then Victor hit me for fours off consecutive balls'. (Sid Pegler)
6. 'They used to talk of my "grand manner". Compared to Victor, I was like a cab-horse side by side with a thoroughbred Derby winner'. (Archie MacLaren)
7. '...the greatest batsman who ever lived'. (Jack Fingleton)
8. 'I kept him quiet, which was as good as bowling men out. You couldn't dictate to Trumper. He played as *he* liked, not as *you* liked'. (Sydney Barnes)
9. 'I should have been proud to carry his bag'. (Charlie Macartney)
10. 'I'd sooner bowl against Trumper on a good wicket. He tries too hard on a sticky'. (C. A. Llewellyn)

TEN ODES TO *RANJI*

Kumar Shri Ranjitsinhji, to give the Indian prince his full name, was perhaps the first Indian to capture the imagination of England. He played for Sussex and England and is widely acknowledged as one of the game's most enchanting batsman.

1. 'Prince of a little state but King of a great game'. (A. G. Gardiner)
2. 'His style was a remarkable instance of the way a man can express personal genius in a game, nay, not only personal genius but the genius of a whole race'. (Sir Neville Cardus)
3. 'He's a blooming conjuror'. (George Giffen)
4. 'The best ball I bowled in my life was one which hit Ranji on his pads'. (A Surrey bowler)
5. 'He moved as if he had no bones'. (C. B. Fry)
6. 'All other batsmen are labourers in comparison'. (A. G. Gardiner)
7. 'It is not in nature that there should be another Ranji'. (Sir Neville Cardus)

8. 'Did he really happen? Or was he perhaps a dream, all dreamed on some midsummer's night long ago'. (Sir Neville Cardus)
9. 'They would have admired Ranjitsinhji as a white batsman, but they worship him because he is black'. (Hon. R. H. Lyttleton)
10. '...made our bowlers look like a lot of schoolboys'. (Australian captain Joe Darling)

...PLUS ONE WHO THOUGHT DIFFERENTLY

'Ranji did absolutely nothing for Indian sport and sportsmen. To all our requests for aid, encouragement and advice Ranji gave but one answer : "Duleep and I are English cricketers".' (Anthony D'Mello)

TEN INCIDENTS OF EXTREME *POPULARITY*

1. Mohammed Azharuddin, an officer of the State Bank of India, helped collect Rs 260 million for the bank in Gujarat in 1986. Investors who deposited more than Rs 10,000 were presented with his autographed photograph
2. A survey conducted by PBL Marketing in Australia in 1981-82 revealed that when asked to name 5 Pakistanis, respondents could name only one – Imran Khan
3. Sir Robert Menzies, former Prime Minister of Australia, made a special trip from Canberra to Cronulla (a distance of 230 miles) by plane and car to see Arthur Mailey on his deathbed
4. Dennis Lillee had his telephone number delisted from the directory to avoid receiving innumerable calls.
5. The manufacturers of Gillette blades withdrew their sponsorship of one-day cricket in 1982 after 18 years of promoting the game, because they felt that the name 'Gillette' was being associated by people more with one-day cricket than with razor blades
6. The portrait of Sir Frank Worrell appeared on a Barbados currency note in 1975.
7. An English newspaper carried out a survey of 104 men and 109 women to see if they recognized famous faces. As many as 47% knew David Gower, while among the wrong answers were Bob Willis, Ian Botham and Steve Cram
8. 'If this letter reaches you, the post office thinks more of you

than I do'. The letter was addressed (and received) – 'Mike Denness, cricketer in Australia'

9. By a special decree of the Prime Minister Rajiv Gandhi, Ravi Shastri was exempted from paying the import duty on the car he won as 'Champion of Champions' in Australia, 1985. He would have had to pay around £ 50,000 as duty under the normal import rules otherwise
10. Yorkshire supporter Miss Phyllis Culpan, who died in November 1985, left £ 100,000 in her will to Geoff Boycott, who had been a friend since the mid-Sixties

Confessions

WAYNE DANIEL LONGS TO....

1. ...see the sun out when arriving at the ground
2. ...hear the captain tell him, 'Get the boots on, we are fielding'.
3. ...take the long walk to the wicket with the umpire throwing over a nice new ball

THE SECRET *FEARS* OF TEN CRICKETERS

1. Sunil Gavaskar – Dogs and snakes
2. Greg Chappell – Snakes
3. John Lever – Flying
4. Zaheer Abbas – The Almighty
5. Viv Richards – Driving on a straight motorway for hours and hours without a turn
6. Iqbal Qasim – World War III
7. Sikander Bakht – My wife.
8. Graham Gooch – Being run out on 99
9. A. Mallett – Spiders
10. John Snow – Becoming an umpire after retirement

FIVE *CONFESSIONS* BY ALAN KNOTT

1. 'You'd never believe it but I actually started as a quick bowler'.
2. 'I am terrified of letting four byes go down the leg side'.
3. 'I watch my diet ever since an American health expert advised me that for maximum energy output I should eat natural foods only'.

4. 'I am a little better down the leg side one-handed than diving in front of first slip'.
5. 'I'd love to be six inches or more taller'.

– *Cricket Conversations* by Peter Walker

FIVE CONVENTIONAL *EXPLANATIONS* OF THE UNCONVENTIONAL GREG MATTHEWS

1. Spiked hair ('My mother said that if I kept my hair short it would remain strong and last longer')
2. Sleeves rolled down ('This is to protect the scars on my elbows when I am diving about')
3. Buttoned collar ('I had problems with the skin around my neck due to overexposure to the sun')
4. Black Raybans sunglasses ('It is good for the eyes and saves the wrinkles')
5. Ear ring ('I like the visual')

HUMBLE *ADMISSIONS* BY THREE MEN WHO HAVE BROKEN BRADMAN'S RECORDS

1. 'His record will only be beaten when someone scores 30 centuries in 52 Tests'. (Sunil Gavaskar after scoring his 30th Test century. Bradman scored 29)
2. 'It is sacrilege to talk about overhauling Bradman'. (Greg Chappell after getting past Bradman's 6996 Test runs)
3. 'I am conscious of how few innings Sir Donald took, and I feel humble'. (John Inverarity after surpassing Sir Donald's aggregate in the Sheffield Shield)

GEOFF BOYCOTT ON GEOFF BOYCOTT

Observations. Tributes. Confessions.

1. 'There may be only a day or two each season when I don't have a net'.
2. 'Roy of the Rovers stuff'. (on his hundredth hundred at Leeds, 1977)
3. 'How do I make the ball reach the boundary?' (at the age of 12)
4. 'All I have ever wanted was to do my best for Yorkshire'.
5. 'If you offer me Raquel Welch and a century for England, I'd take the century each time.'
6. 'England want my runs but they don't want me'.

7. 'Why does Fred Trueman hate me?'
8. 'It is not an end to my ambition – I haven't played for England a third time yet'. (after scoring his 150th first-class century)
9. 'How I wish I could hit the ball as cleanly and effortlessly as you'. (to David Gower)
10. 'Leaving Yorkshire would be a divorce for me since I have been married to the county since I was 17'.

IMRAN KHAN ON IMRAN KHAN

1. 'I grew up with a complex about being ugly'.
2. 'I would like my wife to be of an independent mind; I relate to people with some depth in them and want to see my wife using her brains, rather than working in the kitchen'.
3. 'The fact that I am shy has been considered to be arrogance'.
4. 'As a Muslim, I pray every night for the strength to be honest in life, and beg for health and happiness'.
5. 'If I am seen deep in conversation with a pretty girl in a club, the gossip columnists automatically jump to the wrong conclusions'.
6. 'I am not a naturally confident person'.
7. 'I am concerned that the countries of the Third World are getting poorer with no sign of immediate help'.
8. 'I have lost count of the number of times I've been reported married or engaged'.
9. 'This lady killer image is a creation of the media'.
10. 'I am not motivated by money'.

MORE OF *IMRAN KHAN* ON IMRAN KHAN

1. '*Arre,* I'm a *paagal* (mad) Pathan...'
2. 'Basically, I'm an introvert'.
3. 'I feel terribly uncomfortable when all those girls gush over me'
4. 'I'm a very simple man'.
5. 'I'm not really a playboy'.

VIV RICHARDS IN THE *FIRST PERSON*

1. 'In Britain I have a dozen or so girls who mean a good deal more to me than a one-night stand'.
2. 'I am a salesman for cricket'.
3. 'Joe Frazier was my idol. I tried to be like him'.

4. 'I am not one who is going to lie and let people put rubbish on me. I am going to stand up for my rights'.
5. 'I know my brothers feel very proud of me but it would be nicer if I had a sister. You know, she'd go and tell her friends about me and what I've been...all those little things. I know it's a bit sentimental but...'

BARRY RICHARDS ON BARRY RICHARDS

1. 'Every batsman has his own particular mannerisms. Mine is to appear offhand and a little disinterested. Underneath I am as nervous as any other cricketer.'
2. 'Some players have come up to me and said :"I wish I could play like you". Frankly, I often wish I were someone else'.
3. 'I want the financial return for my skill. What's so immoral about that? I've a dread of insecurity and the spectre of poverty and the avoidance of it used to haunt me continually'.
4. 'I will not deny that the dollar-a-run incentive I played for out in Australia made me a better player'.
5. 'This is one question (about racial discrimination) that I resent from pressmen'.

– *Cricket Conversations* by Peter Walker

MY FIVE MOST *EMBARRASSING* MOMENTS

By Dickie Bird, easily the most respected umpire in the game.

1. Nature called and I had to run off one afternoon when England was playing West Indies at Old Trafford in 1984. I said, 'I am sorry, gentlemen...'
2. Graham Gooch took a swipe at leg spinner Bob Holland during the '85 Ashes series. It was the hardest shot that has ever hit me. I took it on the boot and my ankle was swollen like a football for days. Gooch wasn't very happy; he got only one run for what would have been a certain four!
3. With a name like mine there are quite a few shouts from the crowd, ('Birdbrain', 'Blackbird', 'Sparrow' and the like) when I come off for bad light.
4. When Ian Botham took off my usual white cap – a golf one – and started fielding with it.
5. During the Edgbaston Test between India and England in 1986, a young lady came up to the pitch, lifted the two bails and slipped them into her panties. There was nothing I could

do to retrieve the bails. Finally, I ran off the ground, summoned a policewoman, who, in turn, fished out the property of the TCCB! I wasn't sure where to look!

TEN HONEST *CONFESSIONS* BY IAN BOTHAM

1. 'Basically, I'm a homebird. Call me a male chauvinist pig, but all I want is to come home and Kath to cook me a nice meal'.
2. 'There's a lot more things in my life than a game of cricket'.
3. 'Most of my interests are based around men'.
4. 'I get bored with my own company. I like to talk sport, flying, horse-racing'.
5. 'I don't ask Kathy to face Mike Holding, so there's no reason why I should be changing nappies'.
6. 'The fact is that I have, at various times in the past, smoked pot'.
7. 'I seem to be plagued by people who want to make a name for themselves. I don't fancy living my life over my shoulder'.
8. 'I sometimes wish that every day lasted about six weeks. There's always so much to do'.
9. 'I'd just love to take them (Somerset) apart every time I come across them in 1987...I suggest Peter Roebuck stays in London, where he'll be a lot safer'.
10. 'I'd rather face Lillee with a rhubarb stick (than go to court again).

TEN COMMENTS IN THE FIRST PERSON

1. 'I'm the sort of bowler I like to bat against.' (Allan Border)
2. '(My) thinking in millions simplifies the arithmetic no end'. (Phil Edmonds)
3. 'For all I care, you can call me Mr Smith.' (Tiger Pataudi to Sussex officials when the Indian law took away his title of Nawab)
4. 'Times have made me a pessimistic person'. (Rodney Hogg)
5. 'I had a lot of style. During lunch I used to send my shirt to the *dhobi* (laundryman) for ironing'. (Mushtaq Ali)
6. 'Can you imagine, looking at my face, that I can be short-tempered?' (Chetan Sharma)
7. 'Although the World Cup (1983) will affect my studies to some extent, I will be taking my books with me'. (Geoff Lawson)
8. 'I can smell a good player from half a mile off and I can see the

bludger (idler) from the same distance'. (Bill O'Reilly)

9. 'I am never going to be a loser again'. (Richard Hadlee after failing his school-leaving examination)
10. 'The hangman's name is Larwood! I have never forgotten these words'. (Harold Larwood)

Controversy

INDIA *LOST* THE 1978 SERIES IN PAKISTAN BECAUSE...

1. 'Two days after the tour started, the boys started counting the days when they would go back home'.
2. 'Our phones were tapped'.
3. 'They spied on us'.
4. 'They were very hostile – the crowds, the players, the press'.
5. 'The atmosphere was not right. We didn't get turned on'.

(Unbelievable, but these were captain Bishen Bedi's reasons for losing the historic series 2-0)

– *Sportsweek*

THE SIX *CONSEQUENCES* OF THE UNDERARM INCIDENT

1. The flag flew at half-mast over the office of a big Australian insurance firm in Wellington
2. A DJ from Wellington asked listeners if they had heard of a new underarm deodorant : 'It's called Chappell and it stinks'.
3. In Adelaide, an advertisement in the *Adelaide Advertiser* proclaimed: 'Death – Australian cricket died of shame last ball before stumps, 1 February, 1981. C'mon Aussies, c'mon.'
4. A New Zealand newspaper carried on its front page a cartoon of Greg patting Trevor on the head and saying : 'The Chappells are good at cricket but we are even better at bowls, right Trev?'
5. In Auckland,T-shirts with 'Aussies Have An Underarm Problem' went on sale.
6. Another T-shirt logo read : 'Trevor Chappell's Underarm Stinks'.

FIVE INCIDENTS *BISHEN BEDI* WOULD LIKE TO FORGET

1. The Kingston Test vs West Indies, 1975-76, when the opposition fast bowlers bowled at the Indian batsman rather than at the stumps
2. The one-day game at Sahiwal in 1978 when the Pakistan fast bowlers repeatedly bowled bouncers when their side looked like losing the match. India conceded the game when the Pakistan umpires refused to call wides
3. Ian Chappell's atrocious behaviour at Northampton in 1975.
4. Two teams, both claiming to represent Delhi, arriving at the ground for a Ranji Trophy match
5. The Indian Board 'disciplining' and dropping me for a Test because of a routine television appearance during the 1974 tour of England. My comments on TV were in no way connected with the Indian team!

THREE EXPERTS' VIEWS ON THE *ALUMINIUM BAT*

Dennis Lillee, as is his wont, surprised everybody. He turned out to bat in a Test against England with an aluminium bat. After he had played a few balls with it, opposing captain Mike Brearley objected to its use on the ground that it was causing damage to the ball. Lillee threw away the willow (oops!) in anger and a replacement was quickly requisitioned.

1. 'Aluminium bats are more durable and cheaper than willow bats'. (Dennis Lillee)
2. 'I picked it up in the dressing room, and was not impressed by the balance or the "feel" of the thing'. (David Gower)
3. 'The traditional willow is getting more and more expensive, so perhaps Lillee's bat will reappear at some time in the future'. (Dickie Bird)

WHY SIX CRICKETERS SAID 'YES'/'NO' TO *SOUTH AFRICA*

1. 'I would have asked them to see the film *Gandhi* and then they would realize why I won't go to South Africa.' (Sunil Gavaskar)
2. 'You have just got to think of an amount as big as that; you could retire for the rest of your life on that figure'. (Kim Hughes, after he had been offered $ 400,000 for a three-year contract)
3. 'It gave me the opportunity of playing international cricket at

the top level again'. (Dennis Amiss)

4. 'I was naturally quite tempted – well, very tempted – they were giving me the opportunity of earning in one month what I might expect to make in the next six years just as a Northamptonshire player. But I said 'no' for a number of personal reasons'. (Geoff Cook)
5. 'I am a professional cricketer with family responsibilities and the right to play where and with whom I choose'. (Alvin Kallicharran who was among the first West Indians to opt to go to South Africa)
6. 'I've got nothing on my conscience. I am just here to play cricket'. (Peter Willey)

THE FIVE GREATEST *CONTROVERSIES* IN INDIAN CRICKET ACCORDING TO DICKY RUTNAGUR

1. 'The sending back of Lala Amarnath from the 1936 tour of England. Amarnath had used abusive language after he had been sent in to bat late in an unimportant county fixture. The captain and the manager were singularly unimpressed.'
2. 'The selection of Iftikhar Pataudi as captain for India's 1946 tour of England.'
3. 'Polly Umrigar's resignation from the captaincy in 1959 in the middle of the series against Australia.'
4. 'Kapil Dev's dropping from the Calcutta Test against England in 1984-85, ostensibly for having played a rash shot in the previous Test in Delhi which ultimately led to India's defeat.'
5. 'Bishen Bedi being omitted from the first Test versus West Indies in 1974-75 as a disciplinary measure for having appeared in a television interview in England that summer.'

STAR WARS

Five opinions on the much-written-about Sunil Gavaskar-Kapil Dev domestic feud

1. 'I think differences exist in every family. Why pick on a cricket team?' (Sunil Gavaskar)
2. 'We think in different ways (about cricket), but I do not think we fight.' (Kapil Dev)
3. 'The media has blown up the whole issue.' (N.K.P. Salve, former Indian Board president)
4. 'I have never seen the two getting into a single argument – and

I have managed them on four tours.' (Raj Singh Dungarpur)

5. 'The opinion that they are, in fact, good friends has been expressed by Mr Salve, but he has failed to explain why good friends need others to sort out their personal differences.' (Tiger Pataudi)

HOW THE WORLD *REACTED* WHEN ENGLISH 'REBELS' TOURED SOUTH AFRICA IN 1981-82

1. 'They are selling themselves for blood-covered krugerrands'. (Shadow Environment secretary, Gerald Kaufman)
2. 'We do not have the power to prevent our sportsmen and women visiting South Africa or anywhere else. If we did we would no longer be a free country'. (Margaret Thatcher)
3. 'Traders can do business with South Africa. Holidaymakers can go to soak up the sun. Families can emigrate to the land of apartheid. So why shouldn't batsmen...'. (*Daily Mail* editorial)
4. 'They have not thought of anyone else in the game but themselves. I feel they are being used as political pawns and have succumbed to greed'. (K. Turner, Northants secretary)
5. 'I thought the day I read the news of Packer's coup was my saddest. I was wrong. This is much worse'. (Jim Laker)
6. 'There is nothing wrong with Wayne and his friends playing cricket where they like'. (Mrs Jayne Larkins)
7. 'These men have risked their careers. They have taken a stand against hypocrisy'. (Joe Pamensky, President of the South African Cricket Union)
8. 'Legally, they're absolutely clean. And morally they're cleaner'. (South African cricketer Mike Procter)

WHAT THEY SAID WHEN DENNIS LILLEE *KICKED* JAVED MIANDAD, PERTH, 1981-82

1. 'The most disgraceful thing I have seen on a cricket field'. (Bob Simpson)
2. 'If the Board is prepared to do its job, Lillee is due for a long holiday'. (Bill O'Reilly)
3. 'There is a fund of affection and admiration for him – Lillee – among cricketers all over the world. But it is diminishing'. (Alan Gibson)
4. 'To kick the batsman when he wasn't looking was the act of a

spoiled, angry child.'(Ian Chappell)

5. 'Javed Miandad is no angel'. (Tony Greig)
6. 'Lillee should be suspended for the rest of the season. I really don't give a damn if it is his benefit season or not'. (Keith Miller)
7. 'I lifted my bat to ward him off and to tell him that if he hit me, I would hit him...he kept saying dirty words to me'. (Javed Miandad)
8. 'I believe in an eye for an eye if somebody starts it'. (Dennis Lillee)

TEN VERDICTS ON THE CONTROVERSIAL *GEOFF BOYCOTT*

1. 'To late comers to the ground, he would so to speak announce: "Mr Boycott regrets he is unable to bat today being ludicrously enough, already out".' (Frank Keating)
2. 'With Beethoven, as with Boycott, it is the business that matters – the score'.(Robin Marlar)
3. 'You have caused enough trouble already'. (Mrs Gandhi when they were introduced in New Delhi, 1981-82. The remark was a reference to the threat of cancellation of the series because Boycott, who had been included, regularly played cricket in South Africa)
4. 'I'd not speak against him – I don't think it would be right. But I don't think he was lily-white'. (Albert Speight, his mother's sister's husband)
5. 'He is very open with people he knows and trusts, almost the opposite of the public view of him'. (Alan Kilvington)
6. 'It was the breath of life for him to succeed'. (Brian Close)
7. 'I somehow could not imagine him in strawberry mousse flannels, batting at night against a white ball.' (Alan Lee)
8. 'I had a wonderful letter from Boycott, saying that it was entirely due to me that he was a good cricketer'. (Barbara Cartland)
9. 'Boycott propped at a bar is as incongruous as Mr Brezhnev genuflecting in St Peter's'. (Terry Brindle)
10. 'So farewell, Sir Geoffrey of the white rose country. You may lay down your trusty sword, remove your creaking armour, and spend the rest of your days watching old videos in your ivory tower'. (David Frith)

FOUR *CRITICISMS* OF TONY GREIG RUNNING OUT ALVIN KALLICHARRAN, PORT-OF-SPAIN, 1973-74.

After Derek Underwood had bowled the last ball of the day to Bernard Julien, non-striker Kallicharran started walking towards the pavilion. Since Julien had played the ball to silly point there had been no intention to run. Meanwhile, Greig picked up the ball and hit the stumps at the bowler's end with Kallicharran out of his crease. The latter was given out. It resulted in vehement criticism of Greig's play and the subsequent recall of Kallicharran.

1. '...the dirtiest trick I have seen on a sports field'. (Errol dos Santos, president of Queen's Park Club)
2. 'There was a real danger of the tour being cancelled if the meeting hadn't bent the rules'. (John Thicknesse)
3. '...why the decision to reinstate Kallicharran? It is a naked political move, a clear move to avoid at any cost troubles on or off the field'. (Ken Lawrence)
4. 'I found it hard to believe that such a competitive cricketer as Greig was not counting the balls of Underwood's over as keenly as everyone else'. (John Thicknesse)

SARFRAZ NAWAZ HIT THE HEADLINES FOR...

1. ... flying back to England during a Test series in Pakistan as part of a one-man protest against the payment that he was receiving.
2. ... threatening to reveal who supplied drugs to Ian Botham in Karachi
3. ... forgetting a few days later who supplied drugs to Ian Botham.
4. ... successfully appealing against Andrew Hilditch for handling the ball in a Test.
5. ... bowling a succession of bouncers at Jeff Thomson while playing for Northants.
6. ... doing the same against Joel Garner in the Gillette Cup final in 1979.
7. ... 'retiring' time and again and withdrawing the statement in the 'interests of Pakistan cricket'.
8. ... marrying a popular Pakistan film actress Rani
9. ... being sent back from a tour of Sri Lanka in the mid-seventies on disciplinary grounds.
10. ... openly accusing the Pakistan Board chief Nur Khan of trying to finish his career.

11. ... successfully being elected into the Pakistan Assembly.
12. ... accusing captain Asif Iqbal of having placed a sizeable bet during his last Test match.
13. ... being seriously beaten up by political rivals in 1987 before making certain 'sensational' disclosures in the Pakistan Assembly.

FIVE QUOTES ON THE SERIOUS BUSINESS OF *APARTHEID*

Apartheid, literally translated, means 'apartness'. South Africa was expelled in 1970 from the International Cricket Conference as a measure of international protest against racial discrimination in that country.

1. 'Martin Luther King was a pioneer who had a tough time early on. If we can do a fraction of the good he did, I am prepared for that'. ('Rebel' West Indian cricketer Lawrence Rowe)
2. 'I believe you have a just cause. Not for a moment am I supporting apartheid or our government but I am supporting what cricket has achieved in breaking down our repugnant constitutional barriers'. (South African cricketer Peter Pollock)
3. 'Apartheid will be scrapped. It is only a matter of 'when'. I am confident that the final political changes we are looking for are not far down the road'. (South African cricketer Ali Bacher)
4. 'Apartheid, which I deplore, is not a manifestation of my generation or even my father's; it is a product of wrong decisions taken 50 years ago'. (South African batsman Barry Richards)
5. 'Obviously I am anti-apartheid, but I reserve the right to tackle the problem in my own way. Surely if I can play in competition with white South Africans and do better than them, then this is a clear indication to the politicians out there that people of all colours can, and should compete on equal parts' (Gary Sobers, who was almost banned from playing for West Indies after touring Rhodesia in the early Seventies)

FIVE REMARKS WITH REFERENCE TO COLOUR AND *SOUTH AFRICA*

1. 'I only notice I am black when I am shaving'. (Frank Worrell)
2. 'I told Viv Richards that his presence in South Africa as a black superstar would help catalyze political and sporting changes, and he would thus assist in eradicating apartheid'. (Ali Bacher)

3. 'I'd never thought I'd ever have the chance of playing on a grass wicket let alone against whites'. (Basil D'Oliveira)
4. '...a sort of racial prejudice in reverse'. (Gordon Greenidge on the hostile reaction to him in the West Indies following his return to play for them in Tests. Since he had spent some years in England prior to that, Greenidge had qualified to play for the country of his adoption too)
5. 'One saw all too little of the black African; enough though to assure oneself that he had far better natural manners and a warmer sense of humour than his Afrikaaner master'. (E. W. Swanton)

THE PUBLIC VERDICT ON TOURING *SOUTH AFRICA*

1. After a 'rebel' West Indian team toured South Africa, a poll was conducted by the *Daily Gleaner* in April '83. As many as 68% of the respondents in Jamaica felt that the 'rebel' cricketers were justified in going.
2. According to a MORI poll in 1983, 91% of the respondents in Britain felt that the government had no right to prevent people from playing in South Africa.

WHAT THEY SAID WHEN TREVOR CHAPPELL BOWLED THE *UNDERARM*...

(New Zealand needed 6 to tie off the last ball in a WSC match in 1980-81, when captain Greg Chappell instructed his bowler and brother Trevor to bowl the last delivery along the ground to batsman Brain McKechnie. McKechnie was contained. Australia won. But the criticism of the incident was not restricted only to the international press; wicket keeper Rod Marsh shook his head and the frustrated batsman threw his bat to show what he thought of the tactical coup)

1. 'Australian cricket is today in disgrace and the country's reputation as a sporting nation is severely damaged'. *(The Age)*
2. 'It was an action which has since been described as shameful, spineless, disgraceful, cheerless and gutless'. *(The Australian)*
3. 'I suppose I would have had to,' said Harold Larwood, when asked what he would have done if ordered to bowl the same by his captain. 'But I should have felt humiliated.'
4. 'Greg reached an all-time low in win-at-all-costs

gamesmanship'. *(The Herald)*

5. 'There could not be a lonelier man in the cricket world than Greg Chappell.' *(The Times)*
6. 'He (Greg Chappell) did something very stupid.' (Tony Greig)
7. 'Just how far does the lure of the lolly go to deprive us of basic self respect?' (Bill O'Reilly)
8. 'I felt like crawling into a big hole and wished I had never played the great game'. (Keith Miller)
9. 'How much pride, brother, do you sacrifice to win $ 35,000?' (Ian Chappell)
10. 'We'd played our guts out and I wasn't going to see us forced into another game'. (Greg Chappell)
11. 'The chance of my hitting a six must have been one in thousands'. (Brian McKechnie)
12. 'How are you at bowling your underarms, Trevor?' (Greg Chappell)
13. 'Hullo, hullo, what have we here?' (Richie Benaud on TV)
14. 'An act of cowardice'. (Robert Muldoon, the then New Zealand Prime Minister)

Crickets Unusual Aspects

SEVEN SYNONYMS FOR *ONE-DAY* CRICKET

1. 'giggle cricket'
2. 'disco cricket'
3. 'the pajama game'
4. 'slap and tickle'
5. 'hit and run'
6. 'slather and whack'
7. 'whackit'

FIVE THINGS JONATHAN RICE *NEVER* THOUGHT HE'D SEE HAPPEN – BUT DID!

1. Intikhab Alam running a five
2. Trevor Bailey hitting a six
3. Mike Brearley bowling
4. 'Dog Stopped Play'
5. Helmets

– *Wisden Cricket Monthly*

NIGHT CRICKET IS A GOOD EXCUSE TO...

By Bob Willis

1. ...down a few cans of beer
2. ...look at the women
3. ...have a brawl if the fancy takes you
4. ...enjoy seeing the ball hit regularly into the crowd

THE FIVE MOST EXHILARATING *SIGHTS* IN CRICKET

1. K. Srikkanth pulling a fast bowler for six from outside the off stump
2. Abdul Qadir bowling a maiden in the last over of a limited-overs match
3. Viv Richards hitting a fast bowler over cover for six by going onto the backfoot and wide of the leg stump
4. Dennis charging in to 80,000 chanting 'Lillee' 'Lillee'.
5. Derek Randall at cover

SIXTEEN *FILMS* IN WHICH CRICKET GETS A MENTION

1. *Chariots of Fire* (1981)
2. *The Sea Wolves*
3. *The Great Escape* (1963)
4. *The Deep* (1977)
5. *Shakespeare Wallah* (1965)
6. *The Lady Vanishes* (1938 and 1970)
7. *The Final Test* (1953)
8. *'Blackmail'* (1929)
9. *Goodbye Mr Chips* (1939 and 1970)
10. *Rebecca* (1940)
11. *What's New Pussycat?* (1965)
12. *The Charge of the Light Brigade* (1968)
13. *The Go Between* (1970).
14. *Two Gentlemen Sharing* (1968)
15. *Kabhi Ajnabi The* (1984)
16. *Tom Brown's School Days* (1950)

– *Wisden Cricket Monthly*

FIVE THINGS THEY SAID ABOUT THE GAME

1. '...an eighteenth century feudal dream' (Derek Birley).
2. 'It's a funny game' (Brian Johnston) .
3. 'It is a game where everyone plays in braces, where the blacksmith is liable to be called away in mid-innings on an urgent job, and sometimes about the time when the light

begins to fail, a ball driven for four kills a rabbit on the boundary' (George Orwell)

4. 'Cricket is the greatest thing that God ever created' (Harold Pinter).
5. 'This is more than a game: a craft at least, a science possibly' (John Arlott).

IN THE *FITNESS* OF THINGS

How does cricket rate when compared to other activities?

	Stamina	Strength	Suppleness
Swimming	4	4	4
Jogging	4	2	2
Cricket	1	1	2
Housework	1	1	2
Ironing	3	3	2
Shopping	2	2	2

(The above chart was worked out by a doctor on sports medicine. The maximum rating is 4)

IS THIS ANOTHER REASON WHY *TESTS* ARE NOT WHAT THEY USED TO BE?

A survey of the diminishing over-rate down the years.

1. 133 balls per hour: England vs Australia, The Oval, 1926.
2. 121 balls per hour: England vs the West Indies, The Oval, 1939.
3. 115 balls per hour: England vs Australia, Leeds, 1948.
4. 97 balls per hour: England vs Australia, Lord's 1956.
5. 108 balls per hour: England vs West Indies,1966.
6. 88 balls per hour: England vs West Indies,1976.
7. 75 balls per hour: Bowled by West Indies in the first innings vs England, The Oval, 1980.

– *Wisden Cricket Monthly*

TOO MUCH *CRICKET?*

Five viewpoints on whether the game is being 'over-killed' in India.

1. 'I do not think we are playing too much cricket. We are professional cricketers who earn our livelihood by playing. How then can I say that we are playing too much?' (Kapil Dev)
2. 'We might just protest under the Labour Act!' (Dilip

Vengsarkar)

3. 'I am never home for my kids' birthdays. In fact, I have not spent the last eight Christmases at home'. (Roger Binny)
4. 'I think by playing more cricket, the game gains and no one loses'. (S. Sriraman, the Indian Board president)
5. 'From the Indian point of view, money has to be generated to pay certain overdrafts. This is for stadia built – and to be built. Players therefore get worn out; it undermines the value of international cricket and one day the spectators will be driven off'. (Raj Singh Dungarpur)

WHAT'S 'IN'

1. Nicknames
2. Ghost writing
3. TV replays
4. Sledging
5. 'Fives' after every dismissal

...AND WHAT'S 'OUT'!

1. Spin bowling
2. Blazers
3. 'Walking'
4. Potbellies
5. 'Please' and 'thank you'

SIX *PROPOSALS* BY CHRISTOPHER MARTIN-JENKINS TO THE ICC TO MAKE CRICKET LESS DANGEROUS

1. A white line to be painted 15 feet in front of each popping crease. Any ball not pitching on the batsman's side of the line should be called and signalled a no-ball by the square leg umpire
2. Extend the pitch by four feet at either end. The bowler's front foot should land behind, or cutting, the bowling crease (level with the stumps) rather than the popping crease as at present
3. A bastsman may only be out 'caught' if the ball has hit the blade of the bat, not the handle or the glove
4. The number of off-side fielders behind the wicket should be limited to five
5. Cricket should be played with a durable ball, created of man-made substances, which swings, spins, and bounces like a leather ball but which, being less solid or hard, is also less dangerous
6. Tests and one-day Internationals should be played on artificial pitches where the bounce is true and the pace sufficient to enable batsmen to play strokes with confidence and skilful bowlers of all types to prosper

– The Cricketer International

TEN INTERESTING OBSERVATIONS OF HOW IT WAS *THEN – AND NOW*

1. 'The game has lost its glory. I don't know what W.G. Grace or Ranji would say if they came out of their graves'. (Mushtaq Ali).
2. 'The champion of an era would have adapted himself to be a champion in any era'. (Sir Don Bradman).
3. 'Looking around the present first-class scene, there are a few too many transistor-listening, aimlessly-wandering young men in the game'. (Ray Illingworth).
4. 'Cricketers are getting too selfish'. (Basil D'Oliveira).
5. 'In 1946-47 Hammond's team travelled fewer than 7,000 miles inside Australia for 87 playing days. The 1986-87 England party covered around 17,000 miles inside Australia to play on only 64 days'. (E. M. Wellings).
6. 'It's much harder bowling to the top players today than when I first started'. (Norman Gifford).
7. 'Fifty per cent of backplay has gone. The front foot gets stuck up the wicket automatically'. (Arthur Milton).
8. 'When I first started, the batsman would leave the ball alone outside the off stump for the first two hours of the innings'. (Alan Knott).
9. 'These damned faceless helmets which make all players look machine-made from an assembly line; one looks the same as the other; blazers have given way to track suits; now a cricketer off the field could be a speedway rider or an all-in wrestler, or both'. (Gordon Ross).
10. 'Given a choice between commercial capital and traditions, I would line up with the fuddy duddies every time'. (Doug Insole).

TEN *VERSIONS* OF HOW TIMES HAVE CHANGED

1. 'Don't be surprised if a lanky man in a yellow coat (Tony Greig) comes onto the Lord's pitch soon to poke and prod it. All is now sacred when done in the name of pop, crackle and squeak, it seems, but take my advice that when you see a village game, pull in and watch it. There might not be much more'. (Jack Fingleton).
2. 'Both the game and the players are too defensive'. (Herbert Sutcliffe).

3. 'What has happened in cricket has been to me, at least, an unforgettable and unforgiveable nightmare'. (Jack Fingleton).
4. 'Modern cricket has become stereotyped'. (Peter Philpott).
5. 'They say we want four-day cricket. I tell them we played 4-day cricket – 20 overs an hour – for 3 days. Now it would be 15 overs an hour for four – exactly the same thing'. (Alec Bedser).
6. 'I wish the present-day batsmen would use their feet more and jump down the pitch'. (Sarah Trumper, wife of Australian cricketer Victor, in 1963).
7. 'Even when we got Bradman out we didn't go around hugging. We just rested while the next bloke came along'. (Harold Larwood).
8. 'At one time you only had the bowler and the wicket keeper asking. Now they will shout from cover. In many cases they do it deliberately to stop the batsmen from running'. (An anonymous Test veteran).
9. 'Cricket, as I have known and admired it, has gone…it is the day-and-night of the big buck'. (Jack Fingleton).
10. 'It is pretty certain that if I were young today, I wouldn't become devoted to first-class cricket and wish to write about it. Since around 1960, cricket, in the organized form in which it was presented to the public, has been changed so much that W. G. Grace would not know it was cricket at all'. (Sir Neville Cardus).

TEN EVERLASTING *VIEWS* ON CRICKET

1. 'Cricket will soon be bowled out by other pastimes'. (An article in 1793).
2. 'No one invented cricket. Like almost everything else, cricket evolved'. (Andrew Lang).
3. 'Hail Cricket! Manly British game!
First of all sports! Be first alike in Fame!' – James Dance
4. 'Cricket is not a good game if you are not good at it. If you are out for nought, you've done nothing all day, then you are not much good in the evening either'. (Mike Brearley).
5. 'It's a thinking game is cricket. If tha' doesn't use thi' brains tha' might as well give up'. (Wilfred Rhodes).
6. 'Heaven (as the Bishop said of the strawberry) might doubtless have devised a better diversion, but certainly no

better has been invented than that which grew up on the village greens of England'. (Andrew Lang).

7. 'Cricket is an idea. It was an idea of the gods'. (James Barrie).
8. 'Cricket has imperishable memories and indestructible traditions, and the lover of cricket enters into them and makes them his own'. (Lord Birkett).
9. '...it's more than a game. It's an institution'. (Thomas Hughes in *Tom Brown's School Days*).
10. 'Cricket has made me a better man'. (Chetan Chauhan).

TEN PEOPLE WHO DON'T CARE MUCH FOR *ONE-DAY CRICKET*

1. Brian Close: 'After spending the whole week trying to get our players think positively, on the seventh day I had to ask them to do almost everything against the cricketing commonsense I'd been preaching for the previous six'.
2. Pakistani broadcaster Omar Kureishi: 'A cow born in a stable does not become a horse'. (while stressing that one-day cricket is not the 'real' game).
3. Ashley Mallett: 'I tend to think of these matches as hit-and-miss, tip-and-run"circus"games'.
4. Greg Chappell: 'I can hardly remember an innings I have played in one-day cricket, but there are several I can remember playing in Test matches'.
5. Bob Wyatt: 'Limited-overs cricket does not in any way help batting'.
6. Norman Preston, former editor of *Wisden*: 'Both batsmen and bowlers are denied the opportunity to develop naturally in the one-day game'.
7. Ian Peebles: 'Once a premium is put on stifling, as against despatching a batsman, all manner of fallacious practices must follow'.
8. Tony Pawson: '...improves some basically sound batsmen, ruins more by undermining technique'.
9. Raj Singh Dungarpur: 'Replacing Test cricket with one-day cricket would be like having Cockney as the official language of England in place of the language that is taught in the universities and spoken in the House of Commons'.
10. Allan Border: 'To be honest, one-day cricket is purely a TV game aimed at the general public. It is not really for the

players at all. Test cricket is what the game is all about and what the players and the purists really love....There is a possibility that your ability as a player may well be analysed by future generations on your one-day statistics. That's the day I dread most'.

Cricketers

FIVE CRICKETERS DAVID FRITH HAS ALWAYS WANTED TO *INTERVIEW*

1. AE Stoddard
2. V. Trumper
3. W.G. Grace
4. William Lambert
5. Archie Jackson

DAVID GOWER – THE WORLD'S *GREATEST* AMBIDEXTERIST

1. He bats left-handed
2. Bowls right arm
3. Deals cards with his left hand
4. Hammers a nail with the right
5. Brushes his teeth with either!

FIVE PAIRS OF CRICKETING *TWINS*

1. Alec and Eric Bedser, Surrey
2. F.G. and W.H. Stephens, Warwickshire
3. J.S. and W.H. Denton, Northants
4. A.D.E. and A.W.S. Rippon, Somerset
5. Joan and Barbara Blaker from Eltham

TWELVE ENGLISH CRICKETERS WHO ALSO PLAYED *FOOTBALL* FOR THEIR COUNTRY

1. J. Arnold
2. A Ducat
3. R.E. Foster
4. C.B. Fry
5. L.H. Gay
6. W. Gunn
7. H.T. Hardinge
8. A. Lyttleton
9. H. Makepeace
10. C.A. Milton
11. J. Sharp
12. W. Watson

THIRTEEN CRICKETER-*DOCTORS*

1. Ali Bacher (South Africa)
2. W.G. Grace (England)
3. Dilawar Husain (India)
4. R.L. Park (Australia)
5. Jehangir Khan (India)
6. E.M. Grace (England)
7. J.E. Barrett (Australia)
8. H.V. Hordern (Australia)
9. P.C. Charlton (Australia)
10. O.E. Nothling (Australia)
11. R.B. Minnett (Australia)
12. C.B. Clarke (West Indies)
13. H.J.H. Scott (Australia)

THIRTEEN *CRICKETERS* WHO BOWLED WITH THEIR CAPS ON

1. Wilfred Rhodes
2. Sydney Barnes
3. G.H. Simpson-Hayward
4. Warwick Armstrong
5. Fred Spofforth
6. Sonny Ramadhin
7. Clarrie Grimmett
8. B.J.T. Bosanquet
9. George Hirst
10. Hugh Trumble
11. A.E. Trott
12. Geoff Boycott
13. Greg Matthews

THE OTHER SIDE OF *DILIP VENGSARKAR*

By Manali Vengsarkar

1. 'Small things like shabbiness or unkempt children bother him'.
2. 'Dilip hates to shop around. His policy is "You have to decide beforehand what you want, in what colour and design".'
3. 'He used to get a lot of embarrassing fan mail, but these days its mostly "*rakhis*".'
4. 'He is a very organized person. He has to be–he's been living out of a suitcase for the last 10 years'.
5. 'He has always wanted to be captain of the Indian team'.

–Gentleman

GOD'S *FORGOTTEN* CRICKETERS

This is the title of a book by South African author Andre Odendaal featuring 16 of his country's greatest cricketers deprived of international competition. Believe it or not, three of those chosen were coloured. They were :

1. Baboo Ebrahim
2. Tieffie Barnes
3. Edward Hubane

HOW FIVE CRICKETERS KEPT/KEEP IN *TRIM*

1. Dennis Amiss slipped a disc at the age of 17 while playing football. He has to take precautionary loosening-up exercises to reduce stiffness in his back daily.
2. Greg Ritchie worked overtime in the gym, cut down on soft drinks, beer and red meat and came down from 89 kg to 79 kg before the '82-83 season in Australia. He later admitted : 'It was even tougher than scoring a century in Pakistan'.
3. 'I like *yoga* because there isn't the tension normally associated with muscular exercises. The mind seems to get inside the body and tells you which muscle to move. It relaxes the muscles instead of straining them,' confessed Alan Knott.
4. 'I did 100 sit-ups a day for four months before playing in England,' confessed Malcolm Marshall.
5. Bill O'Reilly was a fitness fanatic. He boasted: 'In the 10 years I was in the centre, I was so fit I could have won the Melbourne Cup'.

MIKE BREARLEY, THE CRICKETER *INTELLECTUAL*

Ten opinions on the man

1. 'He is the brightest man I have met, too bright perhaps to enjoy the earthy atmosphere of the players' bar' (Bob Willis).
2. 'The fellow with a degree in people' (Rodney Hogg).
3. 'He would have made an exceptional Trades Union negotiator' (Trevor Bailey).
4. 'The best England captain that I have seen...' (Jim Laker).
5. 'The most formidable brain that has ever been applied to the problem of winning matches' (Jim Laker).
6. 'A brain as sharp as barbed wire...' (Christopher Martin-Jenkins).
7. 'I knew how to write and he knew cricket' (Dudley Doust, co-author).
8. '...there were those of his detractors who considered him to be a little too "socialistic" in his outlook on life to be in charge of an English eleven whatever that might mean ' (Richie Benaud).
9. 'Mike's qualities were many, but one of the best was his ability to remember how a particular batsman liked to play and where he liked to hit the ball; if the bowlers didn't know, Mike would tell them where to bowl' (Mike Gatting).

10. 'I'd have liked to stick on him' (Phil Edmonds).

ELEVEN *DREAM STARTS*

1. Stan Callaway scored 207 for New South Wales vs Queensland in 1914-15. It turned out to be his only first-class innings
2. Joe Solomon scored a century in each of his first three innings in first-class cricket; 114 not out for British Guiana vs Jamaica, 108 vs Barbados; 121 for West Indies vs Pakistan in 1957-58
3. G.R. Vishwanath scored 230 on his first-class debut for Mysore against Andhra and 137 in his first Test for India vs. Australia in 1969-70
4. Dirk Wellham scored a hundred for New South Wales on his first-class debut and 103 for Australia in his first Test against England in 1981
5. Mohammed Azharuddin scored hundreds in his first three Test matches for India – at Calcutta, Madras and Kanpur vs England in 1984-85
6. Bob Massie took 16 for 137 on his Test debut for Australia against England at Lord's in 1972
7. Mike Selvey found himself in the England team to play West Indies at Old Trafford in 1976 because of injuries to the front-line bowlers. He picked up the wickets of Roy Fredericks, Viv Richards and Alvin Kallicharran in the first 20 balls he bowled in Test cricket
8. Lawrence Rowe scored 214 and 100 not out on his Test debut against New Zealand at Kingston, 1971-72
9. Yajurvinder Singh, playing his first Test for India at Bangalore against England in 1976-77, took seven catches at short leg. He equalled the innings and match record for catches by non wicket keepers held by Greg Chappell
10. Sunil Gavaskar scored 774 runs in his first Test series – against West Indies in 1970-71
11. Narendra Hirwani took 16 wickets in his debut Test at Madras against West Indies, 1987-88

ELEVEN CRICKETERS WHO FACED *SUSPENSIONS*

1. Saeed Ahmed...was suspended for life, at home and abroad, for abusing members of the Pakistan Board during the 1969-70 Pakistan-New Zealand series. He subsequently apologized and the ban was lifted. Later in the 1972-73 series in Australia,

he was asked to return to Pakistan following his refusal to open the innings. He defied the official ruling and stayed back. When Saeed Ahmed finally returned, he was banned for life on charges of gross indiscipline

2. Jeff Thomson...was suspended from soccer after punching a referee while playing for a church team in Sydney at the age of 17
3. Viv Richards...was suspended for two years after his impulsive gestures in a Leewards Islands match had sparked off trouble, leading to his recall to the crease
4. Tony Greig...was suspended for two months in 1978 for his attack on Boycott in a newspaper article. As a consequence, he also lost the Sussex captaincy
5. Ian Chappell...was suspended for three weeks for swearing at umpire Bob Marshall during the South Australia-Tasmania match at Davenport in 1979-80. On his return, he was reported on a further two counts of misconduct by umpire Graham McLeod in the game against England for South Australia in Adelaide. He faced a further suspension of six weeks
6. Rodney Hogg...was suspended for one match for kicking down the stumps in a Melbourne district game in 1984-85
7. Shaun Graf...was suspended for three matches for a similar offence and obscene language in 1984-85
8. Steve Fitchett...was suspended for five matches for refusing to leave the wicket in a Melbourne district match in 1984-85
9. Ian Botham...was banned from playing for England for more than two months till 31 July 1986 following his confession that he had smoked pot
10. Dennis Lillee...was ruled out for a couple of first-class games after he had kicked Javed Miandad in a Test at Perth in 1981-82
11. Dilip Vengsarkar...was suspended for six months from international and national cricket by the BCCI for reporting India's matches in 1987-88

Cricketers on Cricketers

TEN CRICKETERS ON ONE *ANOTHER*

1. 'He has a degree in people' – Rodney Hogg on Mike Brearley.
2. 'You should have seen Ranji. He could see the stitches (on the ball)' – Wilfred Rhodes on Ranji's eyesight while batting.
3. 'Every time he sees an Australian he goes mad' – Sir Pelham Warner on Douglas Jardine.
4. 'God's gift to Indian cricket' – Sunil Gavaskar on Mohammed Azharuddin.
5. 'Give me Arthur (Shrewsbury) – and any other nine' – W. G. Grace.
6. '...came off the pitch like the crack of doom' – Walter Hammond on Amar Singh.
7. 'It was like batting against the World eleven at one end and Ilford Second eleven at the other' – An anonymous England batsman on Richard Hadlee and the other New Zealand bowlers.
8. 'Brave bugger' – Ian Chappell on John Edrich.
9. 'The most aggressive Indian I've seen' – Tony Greig on Kapil Dev.
10. 'He's escorting the ball to the boundary' – Richie Benaud on Dilip Doshi.

MORE OF CRICKETERS ON CRICKETERS

1. 'He was a superb competitor, never complained on the field and never apologized' – Greg Chappell on John Snow
2. 'That man is a god' – Arun Lal on Ravi Shastri
3. 'Watching Gower bat is one of life's pleasures' – Peter Roebuck
4. 'He'll hit the first two deliveries for boundaries and you're thinking to yourself, "It's a bloody long time to the end of the over".' – Brian Brain on Gordon Greenidge
5. 'It's possible to scare some batsmen, but not Peter Willey. You've got to beat him with pure pace to get him out' – Michael Holding
6. 'A most gracious opponent' – Greg Chappell on Bob Willis
7. 'Kim Hughes comes in the best traditions of classical batsmanship' – Jack Fingleton

8. 'He is not interested in anything but showing up the opposition' – Tony Lewis on Majid Khan
9. 'With only a slightly different psychomatic constitution, Chris Old could have been one of cricket's great players' – Mike Brearley
10. 'A man who would enjoy the Klondyke or a Mansion House dinner' – C. B. Fry on Bill Murdoch

TEN MORE *CRICKETERS* ON THEIR MEN IN TRADE

1. 'A dove' – Arthur Mailey on Victor Trumper.
2. 'A cross-batted village-greener' – Gerry Weigall on Maurice Leyland.
3. 'The Artful Dodger' – Mike Selvey on Alan Knott.
4. 'He just belts the hell out of everything he can reach' – Jack Ryder, Bradman's first Test captain on the prodigy.
5. 'Hutton's chief fault lies in his lack of aggression' – Don Bradman.
6. 'He's really slippery' – Wes Hall on Malcolm Marshall.
7. 'Spectacular, brilliant and even sounder when he got tired of picking himself off the floor' – Jim Laker on Rohan Kanhai.
8. 'The extraordinary thing about Alec Bedser was that he bowled an inswinger with a very side-on action which was the hallmark of the outswinger' – Fred Trueman.
9. 'His concentration was such that when facing slow bowlers, he would actually watch the ball spinning in the air and play it accordingly' – Jim Laker on Ken Barrington.
10. 'He is the only cricketer I know who takes the *Financial Times* in to breakfast every morning' – David Gower on Phil Edmonds.

THE AMAZING *JOEL GARNER*

Five cricketers on the 'Big Bird'.

1. 'You could never tell if he was out late by just looking at his eyes: they are always red and look like road maps' (Clive Lloyd).
2. 'Once or twice I swear I saw him nodding off between deliveries' (Imran Khan).
3. 'He is the sort of bloke who takes you for a walk on the sunny side' (Dennis Lillee).
4. 'I distinctively remember that I did not see the first four balls

at all – I just heard them whizzing past' (Asif Iqbal).

5. 'I felt he was too huge a man to be successful with women. But during the WSC I had the opportunity to observe his success off the field at close quarters....he had so many admirers that the only time he found time to rest was during the match' (Imran Khan).

FIVE CRICKETERS ALAN KNOTT *ADMIRES*

1. John Snow : 'The best bowler I've kept to. Every time he bowled a bouncer it was right on target'.
2. Jeff Thomson : 'The quickest bowler I've seen. The sort who could produce a ball to bowl even Sobers if he had 150 on the board!'
3. Ashley Mallet : 'The most under-rated bowler, who always played in the shadows of his country's fine fast bowlers'.
4. Brian Close : 'I never came across any player so completely sure that he was right'.
5. Ray Illingworth : '...understood the needs of his players'.

– *Cricket Conversations* by Peter Walker

CRICKETERS ON CRICKETERS

1. 'With him you could hear the "thing" spinning' – C. F. Walters on Clarrie Grimmett.
2. 'The most disciplined and most professional cricketer' – Kim Hughes on Roger Harper.
3. 'He would have won the prize for the whitest body after four months on tour in Australia. He just doesn't like the heat' – David Gower on Chris Old.
4. 'His bat had no edges' –Fred Trueman on Len Hutton.
5. 'One look at his forefinger tells you why he was the biggest spinner of the ball in his time' – Jim Laker on Lance Gibbs.
6. 'How good would this magnificent batsman have been with 20/20 vision' – Richie Benaud on Zaheer Abbas.
7. 'A Nourse, a Nourse! My kingdom for a Nourse!' – Sir Pelham Warner on Dudley Nourse.
8. 'He resembles England's Sir Anthony Eden in far more ways than one' – Keith Miller and R.S. Whittington on Peter May.
9. 'He is a king player, always in control' – Maninder Singh on Allan Border.
10. 'Not a captain's backside, mind you, too full of strange

theories, and his mind on the day's race card, but on his day what a player!' – Ray Illingworth on Ted Dexter.

FIVE CRICKETERS' VIEWS ON *DEREK RANDALL*, THE CLOWN PRINCE OF CRICKET

Few contemporary cricketers are as fidgety, absent minded or comical as Derek Randall (of Nottinghamshire and England). Besides, even though he only makes sporadic appearances for his country, he is acknowledged as perhaps the best cover in the modern game.

1. 'He's hopping about, waiting...watching, panicking if he sees a ball beat the bat. You'd think he's never played the game before' (Richard Hadlee).
2. 'I once saw a remarkable party piece from him in a benefit match for Mike Brearley. A guy hit a skier 60 feet up in the air, and Randall got underneath it, put his hands behind his back and caught it' (Bob Willis).
3. 'I've never seen a so-called recognized opening bat play a shot like that in my life. It looked more like a Woody Allen sketch' (Fred Trueman on Randall's frantic effort to get out of the way of a Lillee bouncer).
4. 'If everyone was like you, Arkle, there'd be no wars – there'd just be total chaos' (Ken Barrington).
5. 'Randall annoys me a lot. He's always trying to get my goat. Always saying something stupid' (Rodney Hogg).

...AND TWO VIEWS OF *RANDALL* ON RANDALL

1. 'I'm all bones and no meat'.
2. 'Bill Taylor, one of the Notts lads, reckons that when they finished putting everybody together they used all the spare parts to make me. He could be right'.

THE *FATHER* OF MODERN CRICKET?

Has any single cricketer had a greater influence on cricket from 1975 to the mid-Eighties than Clive Lloyd? He was awarded a doctorate from a university in England and his country's highest honours. Five people speak about him.

1. '...a one-man generation' (*Sportsworld*).
2. 'He, surely, is the finest post-War fieldsman; his nearest rival would be the Rhodesian Colin Bland' (John Arlott).

3. 'Never a great captain' (Bob Willis).
4. 'He met Lillee's bouncers with a swishing hook of the bat, just as if he was scything the head off a cobra with a samurai sword' (Tony Lewis on Lloyd's unforgettable 102 in the Prudential Cup final, 1975).
5. 'He is one of those men who can make opponents tremble simply by the swaggering way he steps out to the middle' (Mike Gatting).

IN APPRECIATION OF *LEN HUTTON*

Five opinions on one of England's greatest opening batsmen

1. 'He could change his mind twice and then play his third-choice stroke perfectly' (Fred Trueman).
2. 'There is nothing that we can teach this lad' (His coach George Hirst).
3. 'He was head and shoulders above any English player of my time' (Ray Illingworth).
4. 'A marvel–the discovery of a generation' (Herbert Sutcliffe).
5. 'He doesn't commit crudities. The "wrong" stroke at times–yes, because of an error of judgement. But never an uninstructed stroke' (Neville Cardus).

SPEAKING FRANKLY ABOUT *ROD MARSH*

1. 'If he missed a Test through injury or illness, dismay would be felt across 3,000 miles from Perth to Surfers Paradise' (Ray Robinson)
2. 'He cannot catch a cold on a beach even when dressed in a bikini on a cold day' (Syd Barnes)
3. 'He's fat, he's round, he bounces off the ground' (chant by Australia's supporters)
4. 'He's part of cricket history. His name is there forever' (His golfer brother Graham Marsh)
5. 'He's the sort of bloke who'd walk into a hardware store, see a spade and say :"That's a spade"(John Benaud)
6. 'If Rodney Marsh had been a Yorkshireman playing between the Wars, he would have been as much immortalized by Neville Cardus as was Emmott Robinson' (Irving Rosenwater)
7. 'I am very lucky in the leg department, as mine were the result of a transplant from the trunks of two healthy *jarrah* trees' (Rod Marsh)

FIVE ENGLISH CRICKETERS AS SEEN BY *FRANCES EDMONDS*

'If you called any England cricketer an intellectual today, he'd have you up for libel,' writes Frances Edmonds. Mrs Edmonds is the wife of England bowler Phil and author of *Another Bloody Tour,* an account of England's ill-fated 1985-86 tour of the West Indies .

1. Ian Botham : 'You would have to pay me a lot more than 40 Grand to sleep with him, what a nauseating prospect'.
2. Phil Edmonds : 'He has the reputation of being awkward and arrogant, mainly because he is awkward and arrogant'.
3. Paul Allott : 'A Botham clone, only slimmer and brighter. Who isn't? '
4. Graham Gooch : 'Plays cricket fairly well'.
5. On Mike Brearley's *Art of Captaincy* : '...that book of ex-cathedra pronouncements'.

FIVE *OBSERVATIONS* BY IMRAN KHAN ON FELLOW CRICKETERS

1. 'I remember Mick Jagger once describing how he got interested in cricket; it was the sight of Dennis Lillee roaring up in his full glory. I had felt the same way about Lillee'.
2. 'The best way to get Viv Richards out is by boring him'.
3. 'Gavaskar is a more refined version of Geoff Boycott'.
4. 'I consider Sarfraz (Nawaz) to have one of the best cricket brains I have known: he taught me more about swing bowling than anybody'.
5. 'Javed (Miandad) does not take constructive criticism terribly well'.

JEFF THOMSON–THE FASTEST BOWLER OF OUR TIME?

Four people on record.

1. Phil Wilkins : 'He stands 6 ft 1 in and weighs 14½ stone, a broad-shouldered raw-boned, mean-gutted fellow you'd back to win a prize fight'.
2. Greg Chappell : 'Thommo gets my quote as the quickest and most dangerous of them all'.
3. Clive Lloyd : 'The best thing to do when playing him is to get down to the other end'.

4. Harold Larwood : 'He was too erratic to make any impression'.

THE COLOURFUL *BISHEN BEDI* PROMPTED SIX OBSERVERS TO SAY....

1. 'There is much more under the left-hand Sikh's mini-turban *patka* than a coil of hair, a comb and a perspiring scalp' (Ray Robinson)
2. 'My dream match would be to see Bishen Bedi at one end and Ray Lindwall at the other' (Jim Laker)
3. 'It's more a sleek catspaw pad up the wicket' (Peter Walker on Bedi's runup)
4. 'Bishen Bedi could land the ball on a tea leaf' (Ray Robinson)
5. 'Has the classical loop and he gives the ball a real rip, he has a quicker ball, a drifter, a big spin ball and an arm ball... he can bowl you four different deliveries right on the spot every over' (Tony Greig)
6. 'I've always thought that a great clockmaker would have been proud to have set Bedi in motion — a mechanism finely balanced, cogs rolling silently and hands sweeping in smooth arcs around the face' (Tony Lewis)

WHAT FIVE PEOPLE THINK OF THE *CHARISMATIC* IMRAN KHAN

1. 'The Prince of Princes. The modern-day Miller' (Richie Benaud)
2. 'Imran is a one-man selection committee' (Zaheer Abbas)
3. 'If he's as quick as Lillee, then Lillee must have been bowling at half-pace' (Gary Sobers reacting to Press acclaim after Imran's bowling in Australia, 1976-77).
4. 'A thinking man's cricketer' (Mike Gatting)
5. 'I'd like to die in his arms' (A female admirer)

THREE THINGS THEY SAID OF *DENNIS LILLEE*

1. 'He is as meek as a kitten' (Mrs Shirley Lillee, Dennis' mother).
2. 'In real life there are a few more home-loving, domesticated husbands as Dennis' (His wife)
3. '...he is tough and beautifully primitive – in the same category as John Wayne and Muhammad Ali. He is a typical brute in

real life...he doesn't want to be domesticated...he feels vulnerable in women's company...he has a caveman love-making style and can be included amongst the eight sexiest males of the world' (A London newspaper).

THE *CRITIC* ON THE CRICKETER

1. '...like some amiable Paddington bear' – John Arlott on Clive Lloyd.
2. 'He's always smiling, but if I could bat like he does I would be laughing in my sleep' – a TV commentator on Viv Richards.
3. 'David Steele looked like everyone's idea of a bank clerk going to war' – Clive Taylor of the *Sun*.
4. 'Wally Hammond did not walk to the wicket, he strode' – Denzil Batchelor.
5. 'His square cut was like a Dervish swordsman whirling for the neck' – Frank Keating on Everton Weekes.
6. 'So many times to me he has been absolute batting perfection' – Jack Fingleton on Gary Sobers.
7. 'His batsmanship was often that of a spendthrift with doubloons to throw away to the herd of fielding opposition' – Neville Cardus on Archie MacLaren.
8. 'Learie Constantine is probably the only all-rounder in cricket who could win his place in a Test side by fielding alone' – CLR James.
9. 'Imran Khan once told me that Javed Miandad had the outlook of a street-fighter and I daresay his passions rather than his commonsense are always about to take over when he is in charge' – Henry Blofeld.
10. 'The Indian boys are the best behaved lot in the world' – N.K.P. Salve.

CRITICISMS OF THE ENIGMATIC GEOFF BOYCOTT

1. 'If Barber was cricketing poetry, Boycott and his lot were blank verse' (Frank Cook).
2. 'Where the fast bowling is,Boycott isn't' (Tony Greig).
3. 'I sent someone in to try to run him out because he was making no effort to score. That was the first real indication I had had of just how selfish a player he was. He was 21 at that time' (Robin Feather, former captain of Yorkshire Colts).
4. 'My personal objection to Boycott as a batsman in comparison

with the other 'greats' that he was hoping to emulate and surpass was that, by and large, he was a one-pace player' (Richard Hutton).

5. 'What a shame "Fiery" Boycott could not wait for his MOM award and the acclaim of his fans, who had waited so patiently for their hero to appear. But Geoffrey had to catch a train to Middlesborough and left before the end of the game. I suppose he would have retired if he had been batting and called for a substitute if we had fielded second' (Bob Willis).
6. 'Flexibility, the sublime quality, was absent. Consequently, his obstinate self-justification made matters worse' (David Frith).
7. 'His batting became more frugal, his life more remote as the false God beckoned. And when he got his heaven, he must have been shattered to find that there was no one there but he alone' (Tony Lewis).
8. 'The good people of St Vincent, who have suffered a volcanic eruption in 1979 and a hurricane last August, will be spared a long innings by Boycott' (Michael Melford, 1980-81).
9. 'For all his greatness, he could never pick the outswinger of a left-arm and over-the-wicket bowler' (Bishen Bedi).
10. 'Boycott occasionally bats with the joviality of an undertaker' (Alex Bannister).

... *And one in his defence*

'I know some of the younger players are glad to see him go, but they've never seen him out in the middle in Australia, batting against the quicks for hour after hour' (Derek Underwood after Boycott had been sent back from India, 1984-85).

Deaths

FIVE CRICKETERS WHO DIED IN A MENTAL *ASYLUM*

1. G. H. S. Trott (Australia)
2. Johnny Briggs (England)
3. P. G. McShane (Australia)
4. W. E. Midwinter (Australia)
5. J. W. Zulch (South Africa)

WHAT FIVE CRICKETERS WERE DOING WHEN THEY *DIED*

1. Iftikhar Ali Pataudi – ...playing polo when he suffered a heart attack

2. Bill Woodfull – ...playing golf when he suffered a fatal heart attack
3. Bill Murdoch – ...watching a Test between Australia and South Africa at Melbourne, 1910-11
4. Charles Bannerman – ...returning from watching the day's events at the Kensington Racecourse in 1930
5. Johnny Douglas – ...trying to save his father aboard a sinking ship in 1930

TWELVE CRICKETERS WHO COMMITTED *SUICIDE*

1. Syd Barnes (Australia)
2. Tom Richardson (England)
3. A. E. Trott (Australia)
4. Jim Burke (Australia)
5. A. E. Stoddart (England)
6. G. H. Cresswell (New Zealand)
7. Baqa Jalani (India)
8. A. E. Relf (England)
9. W. H. Scotton (England)
10. A. Shrewsbury (England)
11. C. A. Faulkner (S. Africa)
12. V. M. Tancred (S. Africa)

SIX FATAL ENTRIES BY *NON-CRICKETERS* ONTO THE PLAYING AREA

1. A bird was killed by a Greg Chappell delivery in midpitch in the match between Western Australia and South Australia in 1969. The delivery deflected and bowled batsman John Inverarity, but the umpire declared it a no-ball
2. G. A. Smithson drove a ball which killed a bird hopping along the boundary during the Leicestershire-Worcestershire match at Worcester in 1953
3. George Brown of Brighton bowled a ball which eluded the wicketkeeper and the long stop. It hit a dog near the boundary on its head. The animal died instantly
4. A pigeon which came in the way of a powerful drive by D. Ramsamooj during the Northants-Surrey match at The Oval died on the spot
5. Dr Jehangir Khan, father of Pakistan Test player Majid, killed a sparrow while bowling to T. N. Pearce for Combined University against MCC in 1936. The ball and the bird it killed are both preserved in the Lord's museum.
6. C. J. Knott's delivery killed a butterfly in flight during the Hampshire-Gloucestershire game at Portsmouth in 1951

FATAL *ILLNESSES* OF CRICKETERS

1. Sir Frank Worrell (West Indies) – leukaemia
2. K. Wadsworth (N. Zealand) – cancer
3. L. Amar Singh (India) – pneumonia
4. W. Murdoch (Australia and England) – apoplectic fit
5. J. Selvy (England) – paralysis
6. H. B. Cameron (S. Africa) – enteric fever
7. G. A. Kempis (S. Africa) – fever
8. Roy Kilner (England) – enteric fever
9. Archie Jackson (Australia) – tuberculosis
10. R. E. Foster (England) – diabetes
11. G. F. Grace (England) – pneumonia
12. A. O. Jones (England) – tuberculosis
13. G. A. Lohmann (England) – tuberculosis
14. J. T. Brown – congestion of the brain
15. Fred Morley (England) – congestion and dropsy
16. Victor Trumper (Australia) – Bright's disease

FIFTEEN CRICKETERS WHO DIED UNNATURAL *DEATHS*

1. E. A. Macdonald (Australia) – run over by a speeding car
2. C. A. Absalom (England) – a crane dumped a cargo of sugar on him
3. Leslie Hylton (West Indies) – hanged for the murder of his wife
4. M. Bowden (England) – fell heavily from his cart and died in a mud hut in Rhodesia in 1892. A man with a gun kept watch over his body lest it be eaten by lions. Bowden was buried in a coffin knocked together out of whisky cases
5. Jack Iddon (England) – killed in a car accident
6. W. W. Whysall (England) – fell on a dance floor, injured his elbow and died of septicaemia
7. O. E. Whyne (South Africa) – lost at sea while yachting
8. Bob Crisp (South Africa) – last seen paddling a canoe around a Greak island
9. T. A. Ward (South Africa) – electrocuted while working in a gold mine
10. Stan McCabe (Australia) – fell from a cliff near his home in Sydney
11. William Bruce (Australia) – drowned
12. Johnny Douglas (England) – Drowned at sea when his ship

capsized

13. Collie Smith (West Indies) – succumbed to injuries in a car crash
14. G. B. Street (England) – died in a motor cycling accident
15. T. Campbell (South Africa)-crushed to death between two railway bogies

TEN *DEATHS* WHILE THE MATCH WAS STILL ON

1. Melbourne club cricketer Roger Payne, 50, of Beaumaris died after being hit on the chest in 1977
2. George Summers was hit by a delivery at Lord's in 1870. He died a few days later
3. Frederick, son of King George II, died at the age of 44 in 1751 after being hit by a cricket ball in Buckinghamshire. An internal abscess burst and suffocated him
4. Two schoolboy cricketers were killed in Melbourne in separate accidents on 2 February 1980 while fielding close to the wicket. The Victorian President of the National Safety Council called for protective helmets in all matches
5. Charles Grace, W. G.'s son, died while playing the game
6. A young boy, Ian Thompson, died after being hit on the head by a ball while walking in Greenway Recreation Ground, Taunton, 1986
7. Morris Woolley, 49, captain and opening batsman for Thoresby Colliery, Notts, died after deflecting a ball onto his head in a match in May 1982. A blood vessel in his brain ruptured and caused a haemorrhage
8. Anisur Rahman, 19, was killed after being hit on the chest while passing a boy's match in New Karachi
9. Aqeel Ahmed was struck on the head by a bouncer in an inter-Districts match at Mirpurkhas in Sind Province in 1980. He succumbed to the injury
10. Brian Crawford, 20, opening batsman for Dandenong Methodist Cricket Club, died after being struck on the temple while batting in a game outside Melbourne in 1976. He was rushed to hospital but died 4½ hours later

Don Bradman

MY SIX *GREATEST* TEST MATCHES BY DON BRADMAN

1. Leeds 1938
2. Melbourne, 1932-33
3. Lords, 1930
4. Nottingham, 1934
5. Sydney, 1947
6. Leeds, 1948

(All the matches mentioned were between England and Australia).

– *Farewell to Cricket* by Don Bradman

TWELVE BOOKS ON *DON BRADMAN*

1. *Bradman* by Johnnie Moyes
2. *Bradman* by G. N. Natu
3. *Bradman* by S. L. Chitnis
4. *Don Bradman* by Flicker Productions
5. *Don Bradman* by P. Lindsay
6. *Sir Donald Bradman* by A Davis
7. *Bradman The Great* by B. J. Wakley
8. *The Bradman Book* by 'Outfield'
9. *Don Bradman's Book* by Don Bradman
10. *Farewell To Cricket* by Don Bradman
11. *My Cricketing Life* by Don Bradman
12. *Brightly Fades The Don* by Jack Fingleton

TEN *TRIBUTES* TO THE INCOMPARABLE DON BRADMAN

Despite being widely acknowledged as the greatest batsman of all time, Don Bradman finished with four runs short of 7000 and .06 short of a Test average of 100. The 'catch' lies in the fact that he played only 52 Tests over 20 years for Australia and scored the most hundreds – 29 – until Gavaskar surpassed it with his effort in 1983.

1. 'The only batsman who gave me an inferiority complex' (Jim Laker).
2. 'The Don – head of the world's family of batsmen' (Richie Benaud)
3. 'A solitary man with a solitary aim' (R. C. Robertson-Glasgow).
4. 'I felt like a little boy in front of him' (Fred Trueman).
5. 'The player I would have most loved to bat with' (Geoff Boycott).

6. 'His only concern about the seam was apparently to flatten it at once ' (Neville Cardus).
7. '"Plum" Warner told reporters privately that Don was the only batsman he had seen who could square cut me from right over the stumps...and he was right' (Harold Larwood).
8. 'In the many pictures that I have stored in my mind from the "burnt-out Junes" of 40 years, there is none more dramatic or compelling than of Bradman's small, serenely moving figure in its big-peaked green cap coming out of the pavilion shadows into the sunshine, with the concentration, ardour and apprehension of surrounding thousands centred upon him, and the destiny of a Test match in his hands' (Harry Altham).
9. 'If, as often happens, people say "Oh, but he hasn't the charm of McCabe or the mercury of Macartney or the dignity of Hammond", the objection is a little unintelligent, as though a lion were being criticized for lacking the delicacy of a gazelle, the worrying tenacity of the terrier, and the disdainful elegance of a swan or a camel' (Neville Cardus).
10. '...as much in the grip of his superb machine as he is master of it' (Neville Cardus).

...AND OTHERS WITH A DIFFERENT POINT OF VIEW

1. 'In short, he was shockingly mean' (Ian Woolridge).
2. 'Think of how many runs he would have scored had he held the bat properly ' (Bill Andrews on Bradman's unconventional grip).
3. 'Bradman isn't worth $ 300,000' (Kerry Packer).
4. 'Bradman's size is a handicap. It compels him to make cross-bat shots which, while they are effective, are not so beautiful to watch ' (Arthur Mailey).
5. 'Bradman was too frightened' (Harold Larwood, 1932-33).

FIVE IMPRESSIONS OF THE *DON*

By Jack Fingleton (Fingleton, who later turned journalist, played much of his cricket between the Wars with, and under, Bradman)

1. 'Bowlers bowled to him as Bradman made them'.
2. 'The greatest personality to walk a cricket field'.
3. 'Today, from Adelaide, he holds about as many business directorates as he still holds cricket records'.
4. 'Anyone who saw him bat would scoff at the suggestion that

modern captaincy is now so gifted that it would have nobbled him'.

5. 'He was the genius absolute. To bat with him was an education and a revelation'.

Dream Teams

MIKE GATTING'S UNBEATABLE *LIMITED-OVERS SIDE*

'It would be a dream of mine to lead this team onto Lord's one sunny June day. I would not be short on confidence...'

1. Barry Richards ('Sometimes he batted like a being from heaven').
2. Graham Gooch ('If Barry Richards was number one in the Seventies, Graham Gooch takes the title for the Eighties').
3. Viv Richards ('He does things his own way; at times, he can look casual, even lazily uninterested, at the crease, but in all probability the illusion is simply part of the Richards repertoire').
4. Allan Border ('The best number four batsman in the world today').
5. Clive Lloyd ('A man of awesome presence and no obvious nerves – my captain').
6. Ian Botham ('By nature he is a winner, a guy who never accepts the inevitability of defeat').
7. Imran Khan ('In many senses a thinking man's cricketer').
8. Alan Knott ('The best wicket keeper of my lifetime and perhaps – who can say? – the best of all time').
9. Derek Underwood ('By instinct a negative, mean bowler').
10. John Emburey ('The best off spinner of his generation').
11. Malcolm Marshall ('By common consent – and personal experience – the quickest bowler in the world today').
12. Michael Holding ('With that silky smooth run-up, I always get the impression that he is assessing his options and applying a deal of psychology to the waiting batsman').
13. Joel Garner ('Despite his deceptively casual lope to the wicket, Garner can bowl as sharply as anyone when he is in the mood').

– *'Limited-overs'* by Mike Gatting

JOHN ARLOTT'S DREAM *PAKISTAN ELEVEN*

1. Hanif Mohammed (captain).
2. Majid Khan.
3. Zaheer Abbas.
4. Mushtaq Mohammed.
5. Asif Iqbal.
6. Saeed Ahmed/Javed Miandad.
7. Imtiaz Ahmed.
8. Imran Khan.
9. Intikhab Alam.
10. Fazal Mahmood.
11. Sarfraz Nawaz.

– *Wisden Cricket Monthly*

JOHN ARLOTT'S FAVOURITE *AUSTRALIAN ELEVEN*

1. Arthur Morris
2. Colin Macdonald
3. Don Bradman
4. Stan McCabe
5. Keith Miller
6. Vic Jackson
7. Ray Lindwall
8. Jack Walsh
9. Bert Oldfield
10. Arthur Mailey
11. Bill Johnston
12. Craig Serjeant

– *Wisden Cricket Monthly*

ALEC BEDSER'S ALL-TIME BEST *AUSTRALIAN* ELEVEN

1. Arthur Morris
2. Bob Simpson
3. Don Bradman (captain)
4. Lindsay Hassett
5. Greg Chappell
6. Neil Harvey
7. Keith Miller
8. Richie Benaud
9. Don Tallon
10. Ray Lindwall
11. Dennis Lillee

12th man : Alan Davidson.

– *Cricket Choice* by Alec Bedser

SIR NEVILLE CARDUS' *ALL TIME ELEVEN*

('Of those who have won affection and thrilled our understanding of the fine art of cricket')

1. Jack Hobbs
2. Victor Trumper
3. Ranji
4. Wally Hammond
5. Frank Woolley
6. Denis Compton
7. C. A. Faulkner
8. Jock Cameron
9. Keith Miller
10. Maurice Tate
11. Sydney Barnes

IAN BOTHAM'S *TEAM* OF THE SEVENTIES

1. Graham Gooch
2. Sunil Gavaskar
3. Vivian Richards
4. David Gower
5. Greg Chappell (captain)
6. Ian Botham
7. Imran Khan
8. Alan Knott
9. Dennis Lillee
10. Jeff Thomson
11. Derek Underwood

THE BEST ALL–TIME *CAMBRIDGE ELEVEN*

By J.G.W. Davies

1. K. Duleepsinhji (1925-28)
2. F. S. Jackson (1890-93)
3. Ranji (1893)
4. Peter May (1950-52)
5. Ted Dexter (1956-58)
6. Gilbert Jessop (1896-99)
7. Trevor Bailey (1947-48)
8. R. W. V. Robins (1926-28)
9. Derryck Murray (1965-66)
10. Gubby Allen (1922-23)
11. Ken Farnes (1931-33)

– *The Cricketer International*

JOHN ARLOTT'S TEAM OF THE MOST *WATCHABLE* CRICKETERS

1. Jack Hobbs
2. Wilfred Rhodes
3. Viv Richards
4. George Brown
5. Keith Miller
6. Ted Dexter
7. Mike Brearley
8. Ian Botham
9. L. N. Constantine
10. Jim Laker
11. Doug Wright
12. Wes Hall

TONY GREIG'S *WORLD* ELEVEN (CIRCA 1976)

1. Barry Richards
2. Geoff Boycott
3. Clive Lloyd
4. Gary Sobers (captain)
5. Graeme Pollock
6. Mike Procter
7. Alan Knott
8. John Snow
9. Andy Roberts
10. Bishen Bedi
11. B. Chandrasekhar

A TEAM OF CRICKETING *KNIGHTS*

The list includes only those who were knighted for their services to the game.

1. Francis E. Lacey, 1926
2. Frederick Toone, 1928
3. Pelham Warner, 1937
4. Don Bradman, 1949

5. Jack Hobbs, 1953
6. H. D. G. Leveson Gower, 1953
7. Len Hutton, 1956
8. Frank Worrell, 1964
9. Neville Cardus, 1967
10. Gary Sobers, 1975
11. Gubby Allen, 1986

CRICKET IN *HEAVEN*

E. W. Swanton selects his side to take on W.G. Grace's team in heaven

1. Jack Hobbs
2. Wilfred Rhodes
3. Walter Hammond
4. Frank Woolley
5. Stan McCabe
6. Frank Worrell
7. George Hirst
8. Learie Constantine
9. Maurice Tate
10. Bert Oldfield
11. Sydney Barnes

12th man : Duleep or P. Chapman

***DAVID FRITH'*S 'COLOURFAST AND SHRINKPROOF ELEVEN'**

Frith, currently the editor of *Wisden Cricket Monthly,* selects an Australian side of 'non-conformists, entertainers all'.

1. Syd Barnes
2. Jim Burke
3. C.G. Macartney
4. K. Miller
5. K. Mackay
6. A. E. Trott
7. S. M. J. Woods
8. Rod Marsh
9. Tibby Cotter
10. A. Coningham
11. A. Mailey

– *The Cricketer International*

ALEC WAUGH'S *TEAM* OF CRICKET WRITERS

1. W. A. Darlington
2. Herbert Farjeon
3. J. C. Snaith
4. Arthur Conan Doyle (captain)
5. Nigel Balchin
6. P. G. Wodehouse
7. Clifford Bax
8. Hugh de Selincourt
9. Reginald Berkeley
10. Hesketh Pritchard
11. Rupert Brooke

GORDON ROSS'S BEST *WEST INDIAN SIDE* OF ALL TIME

1. Gordon Greenidge
2. Frank Worrell
3. Everton Weekes
4. Clyde Walcott

5. Viv Richards
6. Clive Lloyd
7. Gary Sobers
8. Wes Hall
9. Andy Roberts
10. Sonny Ramadhin
11. Alf Valentine

DAVID FRITH'S *FANTASY* MATCH

Heaven's XI (chosen from cricketers who have passed on) :

1. W. G. Grace
2. Jack Hobbs
3. K. Ranjitsinhji
4. Walter Hammond
5. C. G. Macartney
6. Frank Woolley
7. Bertie Oldfield
8. Tom Richardson
9. W. Rhodes
10. Jim Laker
11. C. J. Kortright (who, incidentally, never played a single Test!)

The Living XI :

1. Len Hutton
2. G. Greenidge
3. Don Bradman
4. Ian Chappell
5. David Gower
6. Ian Botham
7. Leslie Ames
8. Bishen Bedi
9. Dennis Lillee
10. Jeff Thomson
11. B. S. Chandrasekhar

(If any batsman is unavailable, put in S. M. Gavaskar. If any bowler is unavailable, put in G. Sobers, whose batting might come in handy!)

THE BEST ALL-TIME *OXFORD* ELEVEN

By Huwe Richard

1. CB Fry (1892-95)
2. Colin Cowdrey (1952-54)
3. M. Donnelly (1946-47)
4. RE Foster (1897-1900)
5. D. Jardine (1920, 21, 23)
6. Imran Khan (1973-75)
7. A. Kardar (1947-49)
8. A. C. Smith (captain, 1958-60)
9. F. H. E. Cunliffe (1895-98)
10. H. O. Whitby (1884-87)
11. I. Peebles (1930)

– *The Cricketer International*

***WORLD* ELEVEN 1921-1971**

While choosing their teams, selectors (Gubby Allen, Les Ames, Bill O'Reilly and Jack Fingleton) listed a total of 35 cricketers. The following nine found a place in each of their lists.

1. Don Bradman
2. Denis Compton
3. Walter Hammond
4. George Headley
5. Jack Hobbs
6. Len Hutton
7. Ray Lindwall
8. Gary Sobers
9. Maurice Tate

– *The Cricketer International*

M. L. JAISIMHA'S DREAM *INDIAN* LIMITED-OVERS ELEVEN

The contributor has restricted himself to the cricketers he has seen. This, he rues, has compelled him to omit players like Mushtaq Ali, Amar Singh, C. K. Nayudu and Mohammed Nissar.

1. Krish Srikkanth ('I have hardly seen anyone hit the ball harder').
2. Sunil Gavaskar ('My captain. The ideal foil to Srikkanth too').
3. Dilip Vengsarkar ('This choice of mine might raise a few eyebrows').
4. Mohinder Amarnath ('The right man to hold the fort').
5. Tiger Pataudi ('He would be about 40 runs on even before he went in to bat').
6. Polly Umrigar ('An emotional choice really because I played much of my cricket with him').
7. Kapil Dev ('What can one say of him?').
8. Roger Binny / Eknath Solkar ('Depending on the day, I would choose between them').
9. Abid Ali ('A highly inspired cricketer').
10. Salim Durrani ('The ideal man to have if you needed 30 in 3 overs').
11. E. Prasanna ('More reliable than Chandra, I think').
12. Farokh Engineer ('What a man to have opening your innings, provided Srikkanth was resting ! ')

– *Sportsworld*

BOB WILLIS' **WORLD ELEVEN OF THE SEVENTIES**

('A team to represent the World against another planet. A 5-day Test to be played on a good wicket').

1. Geoff Boycott ('Geoff has greater powers of concentration than any other player I have seen').
2. Sunil Gavaskar ('Sunny has extraordinary power for such a

small man').

3. Viv Richards ('Without doubt the batsman of the Seventies. Bats with that constant deadpan expression, as though nothing could ever disturb him').
4. Greg Chappell ('The most consistent batsman in my career').
5. Clive Lloyd ('Among the greatest of run plunderers').
6. Gary Sobers ('Can have no real rival as the best all-round cricketer ever').
7. Ian Botham ('Ian has a raw and aggressive talent which one normally does not associate with English players').
8. Alan Knott ('Knotty at his peak was very hard to better').
9. Andy Roberts ('He gets my vote ahead of Snow and Thomson').
10. Dennis Lillee ('To my mind, the best bowler who has ever lived').
11. Lance Gibbs ('Greater control than other spinners').

THE BEST-EVER INDIAN *ELEVEN*

Selected by Raj Singh Dungarpur, cricket administrator in India and manager on several occasions.

1. Vijay Merchant
2. Sunil Gavaskar
3. Vijay Manjrekar
4. Vijay Hazare
5. G. R. Vishwanath
6. CK Nayudu (captain)
7. Vinoo Mankad
8. Kapil Dev
9. Syed Kirmani
10. L. Amar Singh
11. Subhash Gupte

12th man : Eknath Solkar

RAVI SHASTRI'S WORLD *ELEVEN* OF 1995

1. Richie Richardson
2. Krish Srikkanth
3. Mohammed Azharuddin
4. Martin Crowe
5. A. Gurusinghe
6. Ravi Shastri (surprised?)
7. P. de Freitas
8. Kiran More
9. Wasim Akram
10. Courtney Walsh
11. Anthony Gray
12. Maninder Singh

TIGER PATAUDI'S UNBEATABLE INDIA-PAKISTAN *ELEVEN*

(Thankfully, for the rest of cricketing world, the two countries do not field a joint team.)

1. Hanif Mohammed
2. Sunil Gavaskar
3. Zaheer Abbas
4. G. R. Vishwanath
5. Javed Miandad
6. Kapil Dev
7. Imran Khan
8. Wasim Bari
9. Fazal Mahmood
10. Bishen Bedi
11. B. S. Chandrasekhar

12th man : E. Solkar (who else?)

JACK FINGLETON'S CAST FOR A DREAM TOURNAMENT THE ALL-TIME BEST WEST INDIAN TEAM

Frank Worrell (captain), Gary Sobers, Clyde Walcott, George Headley, Rohan Kanhai, Viv Richards, Learie Constantine, Sonny Ramadhin, Andy Roberts, Lance Gibbs and Wes Hall.

... THE ENGLISH TEAM

Dr W. G. Grace (captain), Len Hutton, Jack Hobbs, Walter Hammond, Denis Compton, Peter May, Godfrey Evans, Harold Larwood, Sydney Barnes, Wilfred Rhodes and George Hirst.

... THE AUSTRALIAN TEAM

Sir Don Bradman (captain), Bill Ponsford, Victor Trumper, Stan McCabe, Greg Chappell, Hugh Trumble, Don Tallon, Bill O'Reilly, Clarrie Grimmett, Dennis Lillee and Ray Lindwall.

... THE SOUTH AFRICAN TEAM

Dr Ali Bacher (captain), H. B. Cameron, Graeme Pollock, Barry Richards, Dudley Nourse, Herby Taylor, Hugh Tayfield, P. Heine, J. Blackenburg, G. A. Faulkner, R. Schwarz.

... THE UMPIRES

Frank Chester and George Hele.

... FAVOURITE CRICKET WRITERS TO REPORT THE MATCHES

Sir Neville Cardus, Ian Peebles and Robertson–Glasgow.

... AND MESSENGERS

The World press.

– *Batting From Memory by* Jack Fingleton

SIR NEVILLE CARDUS' IDEAL ENGLAND *ELEVEN* (CIRCA 1974)

1. Jack Hobbs
2. Herbert Sutcliffe
3. George Gunn
4. Walter Hammond
5. Denis Compton
6. A. MacLaren (captain)
7. Frank Woolley
8. Len Braund
9. Leslie Ames
10. Wilfred Rhodes
11. Tom Richardson

Should the team go to Australia, the additions would be Ted Dexter, Maurice Leyland, Cecil Parkin, Hedley Verity and Godfrey Evans.

– *The Cricketer International*

STARS AND *STARS*

A selection of the best elevens of all time based on their star signs.

Aries Eleven (21 March-20 April)

1. Glenn Turner
2. Dennis Amiss
3. David Gower
4. A. Kallicharran
5. Vinoo Mankad
6. George Giffen
7. Polly Umrigar
8. Alan Knott
9. Malcolm Marshall
10. Syd Barnes
11. Bill Lockwood

12th man : Colin Bland

Taurus Eleven (21 April-20 May)

1. Jack Fingleton
2. C. G. Greenidge
3. Ted Dexter
4. Peter Burge
5. Gilbert Jessop
6. C. B. Fry
7. Derryck Murray
8. Hugh Trumble
9. A. Watkins
10. Hedley Verity
11. B.S. Chadrasekhar

12th man : Alf Valentine

Gemini Eleven (21 May-20 June)

1. Glenn Turner
2. George Headley
3. Denis Compton
4. Walter Hammond
5. Frank Woolley
6. Tom Graveney
7. Khokhan Sen
8. R. Illingworth
9. Brian Statham
10. Maurice Tate
11. Bob Willis

12th man : Alan Davidson

Cancer Eleven (21 June-20 July)

1. Len Hutton
2. S. Gavaskar
3. W. G. Grace
4. John Edrich
5. Zaheer Abbas
6. Stan McCabe
7. H. B. Cameron
8. R. Hadlee
9. Tony Lock
10. Alec Bedser
11. Dennis Lillee

12th man : Graham McKenzie

Leo Eleven (21 July-21 August)

1. Barry Richards
2. Eddie Barlow
3. Greg Chappell
4. A. Border
5. Frank Worrell
6. Gary Sobers
7. Godfrey Evans
8. Jack Gregory
9. Trevor Goddard
10. Jeff Thomson
11. Doug Wright

12th man : Tom Richardson

Virgo Eleven (22 August-22 September)

1. Lindsay Hassett
2. Archie Jackson
3. Ranjitsinhji
4. Don Bradman
5. Clive Lloyd
6. Mike Procter
7. D. Lindsay
8. L. Constantine
9. Abdul Qadir
10. G. Hirst
11. F. Spofforth

12th man : Martin Crowe

Libra Eleven (23 September-22 October)

1. Majid Khan
2. Geoff Boycott
3. Neil Harvey
4. Bill Ponsford
5. Martin Donnelly
6. R. Benaud
7. Jim Parks
8. R. Lindwall
9. John Snow
10. B. S. Bedi
11. Lance Gibbs

12th man : V. Manjrekar

Scorpio Eleven (23 October-22 November)

1. V. Trumper
2. W. Rhodes
3. D. Jardine
4. A. D. Nourse
5. F. S. Jackson
6. Mushtaq Mohammed
7. Rod Marsh
8. Ken Mackay
9. Peter Loader
10. Harold Larwood
11. C.T.B. Turner

Sagittarius Eleven (23 November-20 December)

1. Herbert Sutcliffe
2. Jack Hobbs
3. K. Barrington
4. A. C. MacLaren
5. Keith Miller
6. Ian Botham
7. Imran Khan
8. Trevor Bailey
9. Leslie Ames
10. Fred Titmus
11. Bill O'Reilly

12th man : Joel Garner

Capricorn Eleven (21 December-19 January)

1. Hanif Mohammed
2. Arthur Morris
3. Peter May
4. Colin Cowdrey
5. Rohan Kanhai
6. C. Walcott
7. Kapil Dev
8. J. Waite
9. C. Grimmett
10. A. Mailey
11. Wayne Daniel

12th man : Tiger Pataudi

Aquarian Eleven (20 January-19 February)

1. Herbie Collins
2. Bob Simpson
3. E. Hendren
4. G. Vishwanath
5. Kim Hughes
6. M. A. Noble
7. Don Tallon
8. Fred Trueman
9. A. Roberts
10. Mike Holding
11. Jim Laker

12th man : M. Azharuddin

Pisces Eleven (20th February-20 March)

1. David Sheppard
2. G. Pollock
3. Viv Richards
4. E. Weekes
5. Brian Close
6. F. Engineer
7. E. Peate
8. N. Adcock
9. J. Gleeson
10. Rodney Hogg
11. P. Edmonds

12th man : E. Solkar

Equipment

NINE STAGES IN THE *EVOLUTION* OF THE BAT

1. Piece of stick
2. Club
3. Battes
4. Curved bat
5. Batten bat
6. Skyscraper
7. Shouldered bat
8. Spliced bat
9. The present day versions (scooped at the back, the aluminium variety, the shoulder shaved, and the perforated one)

– *Barclay's World of Cricket*

FIVE DIFFERENT TYPES OF *HELMETS* USED BY CRICKETERS

1. Grid Iron (used by Ian Botham when fielding close)
2. Grand Prix (jutting peak type, worn by Clive Rice)
3. Bikie (the sort used by Dennis Amiss and Barry Richards in 1977)
4. Star Wars (the sort used by Ian Davis)
5. Bider (peaked, fibreglass shell, looking like a riding hat with jaw protection and perspex face guards)

SEVEN *SYNONYMS* FOR THE CRICKET BALL

1. 'cherry'
2. 'plum'
3. 'leather'
4. 'bird of crimson leather'
5. 'the fatal missive'
6. 'the ascending pellet'
7. 'the flying orb'

SIX UNUSUAL PROTECTIVE DEVICES WORN ON THE *HEAD*

1. A 3-peaked cap designed by Patsy Hendren's wife to combat Learie Constantine, while he bowled to her husband at Lord's in 1933
2. Richard Daft went in to bat with a towel wrapped around his head after the previous batsman (G. Summers) had been hit. This occurred in a Notts-Yorkshire game in 1870. The injured batsman was to succumb to his injuries
3. George Brown of Hampshire used a crash helmet when Larwood and Voce were bowling during a county fixture in the

Twenties

4. Though the use of a sola topee was not unheard of during the early years of Test cricket in India, Mohinder Amarnath used one as late as 1979-80 at Bombay. He was tempted into hooking, made a mess of it and finished on top of his stumps.
5. Mike Brearley used a skull cap inserted under his England cap in the Ashes series of 1977. Gavaskar and Srikkanth were to use modified versions some years later
6. The first man to wear a helmet in a Test match was Graham Yallop, who used it against the West Indies in 1977-78. It resembled an astronaut's head gear, complete with a visor

THE *HELMET*

Five arguments

In favour of...

1. Saves you the trouble of combing your hair
2. Very economical – can be used on your motor bike as well
3. Does not fly off during a quick single
4. You can well argue 'It wasn't me' after you have scored a duck
5. The verbal abuse by close-in fielders doesn't reach your ears

Against...

1. You can't always hear your partner's call
2. You are deprived of a souvenir – your colleagues cannot sign on it
3. The bowler comes in even faster – he knows you're chicken
4. Because you cannot hear the verbal intimidation, the chap at silly point thinks you're too dumb to retaliate
5. It can get hot up there

SIX DISSENTING *VOICES* ON THE USE OF HELMETS

1. Denis Compton : 'I suspect the modern Zombie-like mode of helmet-wearing will get a fair thrashing'.
2. Andrew Caro, former chief of PBL Marketing: 'It seemed to suggest that Hell's Angels had inherited the cricket field'.
3. Tony Lewis: 'Batting in special headgear is foreign to the game's concept. By a stretch of imagination you can envisage a sort of Rollerball situation, a battle to death'.
4. Sir Donald Bradman: 'I find it sad that helmets have made their appearance because they detract from a player's

personality'.

5. Frank Eric McElhone, one of Victor Trumper's teammates: 'Helmets are a reversal of everything we know and love in cricket'.
6. Trevor Bailey: 'Helmets are so impersonal you cannot make one batsman out from the other'.

...AND THREE IN FAVOUR OF THEIR USE

1. Derek Pringle: 'I owed it to the taxpayers who had contributed towards my four years of higher education. They wouldn't take kindly to seeing a reconstituted government grant leak out all over the wicket'.
2. Gerald Brodribb: 'The value of the helmet is evident when, as seen, in the fourth Test of the 1984 series, a batsman like Fowler gets a fearful blow on the head, strong enough to dent the helmet'.
3. Mike Brearley: 'Why do miners wear helmets and building workers, too?'

Fielding/Wicket Keeping

IF I AM *KEEPING* BADLY, IT IS BECAUSE...

By Bob Taylor

1. Lack of concentration
2. Standing up too soon
3. Snatching at the ball

SANDEEP PATIL'S FIVE BEST *FIELDERS*

Patil, not the best of fielders, retired prematurely from the game.

1. Eknath Solkar
2. Derek Randall
3. David Gower
4. Mohd. Azharuddin
5. Tiger Pataudi

FIVE *BATSMEN* EKNATH SOLKAR HATED FIELDING CLOSE TO

'They hit so hard...'

1. Ian Chappell
2. Clive Lloyd
3. Rohan Kanhai
4. Gary Sobers
5. Viv Richards

AND THE TWO MOST *DANGEROUS* BATSMEN

Roy Fredericks and Gordon Greenidge ('They used to attempt to pull or sweep off almost every ball').

– Sportsworld

MY FIVE GREATEST *CATCHES* ACCORDING TO EKNATH SOLKAR

1. Catching Doug Walters off the bowling of Prasanna, Delhi, 1969-70
2. Catching Keith Stackpole off Venkataraghavan, Madras, 1969-70
3. Catching Alan Knott off Venkataraghavan, The Oval, 1971
4. Catching Clive Lloyd off Chandrasekhar, Bangalore, 1974-75
5. Catching Mike Denness off Chandrasekhar, Calcutta, 1972-73

– Sportsworld

TREVOR *BAILEY'S* SEVEN DO'S AND DON'T'S WHILE FIELDING

1. Always return the ball to the wicket keeper, unless there is a chance of a run out at the other end
2. Try to throw full tosses into the wicket keeper's hand just over the top of the stumps; aim for as flat a trajectory as possible
3. Don't run with the ball before throwing in as it wastes valuable time
4. Most overthrows could be prevented if the appropriate fieldsman backed up
5. When stopping a ball try to get as much as your body as possible behind the hands as a second line of defence
6. Never snatch at a catch. Let it enter the natural cup formed by the hands and 'give' in the direction the ball is travelling
7. Close-to-the-wicket fielders must get down and stay down as the ball is bowled; the others must be moving in

– Gillette Book Of Cricket And Football

DEREK RANDALL'S FIVE TIPS TO *FIELDERS*

1. Try and anticipate the batsman's every move
2. Try to get to know individual players' habits and mannerisms. For example, Geoff Cook and Graeme Wood always look for

a quick single at the start of an innings. For Vishwanath you had to stand deeper at gully because he liked playing shots in that area

3. Fielders are made, not born. So work on your fielding as hard as on the other departments of the game
4. Early training season; long runs, sprints and exercises to maintain your stamina will help your fielding a great deal
5. When standing at slip, expect every ball to come at you at catching height

– *The Sun Has Got Its Hat On* by Derek Randall

FIVE FREAK *CATCHES* PEOPLE STILL TALK ABOUT

1. During the second Test between Australia and India at Kanpur in 1959, Nari Contractor pulled Alan Davidson. Neil Harvey, standing at short leg, turned and ducked. The ball ended up between Harvey's thighs
2. Playing for Surrey against Hampshire in 1947, Alf Gover moved to short leg on completing his over. Gover was still in the process of putting on his sweater when Jim Laker began bowling from the other end to Rodney Exton. The batsman played it to short leg. It hit Gover between the legs above the knees. In a reflex action, the fielder kept his knees together, completing the catch
3. John Edrich got a thick edge from a delivery off Bedi. The ball hit wicket keeper Engineer on the body and was dropping to the ground, when Engineer flicked it into the air with his left foot to effect a remarkable catch
4. Perhaps the most celebrated catch of cricket history was taken at the Oval in 1880. Batsman Bonnor of Australia skied a ball and was well into the third run when Fred Grace, brother of WG, circled under it and held on
5. S. Callaway, in a game between Otago and Southland at Dunedin in 1909-10,drove a ball back at the bowler H. Scott. It hit the latter on the head, went up 60 feet in the air for short leg to come and complete the dismissal

AND JUST ONE MORE...

Graham Gooch starred in an unusual dismissal at Leeds against India in 1986. Maninder Singh edged a ball from Dilley which Gooch dropped. The alert wicket keeper Bruce French tried to hold the rebound – but failed. While the ball popped out of French's gloves, Gooch kicked it up with his foot and completed the catch at the third combined attempt

Grounds

THE THREE FAVOURITE *GROUNDS* OF IAN BOTHAM

1. Ascot
2. New Market
3. Doncaster

(Fooled you there again, didn't he!)

UNFORGETTABLE MEMORIES OF *EDEN GARDENS*

By Debashis Bandopadhyay, a journalist, who has not missed an international match at the ground for the last 30 years.

1. Alec Bedser twice throwing down the wickets from long-on in an exhibition match in the mid-Fifties.
2. In another exhibition game, Gary Sobers' Eleven was in trouble. Sobers was playing an extremely patient knock. Jaisimha, standing at mid-on, motioned his arms above his head as a signal for Sobers to hit a six. Sobers did just that – over Jaisimha's head next ball. Then retreated back into his defensive shell.
3. Hall and Griffith coming out of the shadows of the mahogany trees at Eden Gardens some 20 years back ...I can still recall Hall's spikes glinting in the early evening sun.
4. Coming straight from college and lining up outside the stadium...in those days a daily ticket used to cost us Rs 2. My brother and I used to stay up all night outside the ground to play cards, breaking the branches of trees and lighting a fire to keep ourselves warm in the winter night. The most frustrating thing is that after keeping vigil for the entire night, we would then be hustled out of our places, way up in the queue, by local toughs, freshly risen from a good night's sleep.
5. During the India-Pakistan Test in 1986-87, the 80,000 present stood up to applaud local lad Arun Lal on 3 separate occasions – only to learn that each time Lal had run leg byes and failed to get his second fifty in the game. Lal did get his half century later, and the crowd was on its feet for a fourth time.

THE AURA OF *LORD'S* – THE MECCA OF THE GAME : FIVE AWED OPINIONS

1. 'Lord's is as much part of the London scene as Buckingham Palace, the House of Commons, the National Gallery, the red double-decker buses and so on…' (Jack Fingleton).
2. 'History modelled in turf and building'. (J. M. Kilburn).
3. 'Lord's is the cathedral of cricket, The Oval low-church' (Richard Gordon).
4. 'Sir, now I know this country is finished. On Saturday with Australia playing, I asked a London cabbie to take me to Lord's, and had to show him the way' (A letter to *The Times*, London).
5. 'One walks with cricket's past, present and the future at Lord's' (Jack Fingleton).

… AND FIVE DISGUSTED ONES

1. 'The ground was sloping from one end to another, there were a lot of people at the gates and at the pavilion entrance. Everybody was too snobbish. I just didn't vibe with it' (Sunil Gavaskar).
2. 'The MCC should change their name to MCP (Leading Indian woman cricketer Diana Eduljee, on being refused entry to the Lord's pavilion during a Test match).
3. 'If the only answer is disappointment, you are in very good company; the young Jack Hobbs thought it was an awful place' (Matthew Engel).
4. '…but for incivility, lack of co-operation and plain bloody-mindedness from the staff, inadequate or patronizing announcements, and for giving you the feeling that you are not wanted, there is nowhere to touch Lord's' (A letter in the *Sunday Times* in 1982).
5. 'For a start (as two distinguished lady doctors have discovered in recent years, having been called in to treat patients and then humiliatingly hustled out) 50 per cent of the human race is excluded from entry to the pavilion at birth' (Matthew Engel).

Habits, Hobbies, Idiosyncracies, Preferences and Superstitions

IAN BOTHAM'S *MUSICAL* PREFERENCES

1. Dire Straits
2. Super Tramp
3. Meat Loaf
4. Rod Stewart
5. Barbara Streisand

SEVEN *VEGETARIAN CRICKETERS*

1. Warren Bardsley (Australia)
2. Tom Horan (Australia)
3. Dilip Doshi (India)
4. K. Srikkanth (India)
5. K. Jayantilal (India)
6. Vijay Merchant (India)
7. Yashpal Sharma (India)

MY FAVOURITE *MOVIE*

1. Allan Border – *The Sting*
2. Viv Richards – *The Learning Tree*
3. Graham Yallop – *Raiders of the Lost Ark*
4. Ewen Chatfield – *The Guns of Navarone*
5. Martin Crowe – *Kelly's Heroes*
6. Greg Chappell – 'I haven't had time to go to the movies for a long time'.

HOW *MIKE BREARLEY* SPENT THE WINTER OF 1982 (after retirement)

1. 'Continuing my qualifications as a psychoanalyst.'
2. 'Teaching part time at Westminster School.'
3. 'Writing a book on captaincy.'
4. 'Listening to Test Match Special on the radio until I fell asleep.'

FIVE CRICKETERS WHO REFUSE(D) TO PART WITH THEIR BATS

1. Geoff Marsh goes to bed with it
2. Daniel Day and John Bowyer of Surrey were buried with their bats
3. James Broadridge of Sussex would take it along on walks
4. Ted Wainwright of Yorkshire used to sleep with it

CHETAN CHAUHAN'S FIVE DO'S AND DON'T'S

1. No sex during a Test
2. No liquor during a Test
3. No late nights during a Test
4. Play as straight as possible
5. Psyche the mind to just stay in the middle

CRICKETERS' *FAVOURITE* FILM STARS

1. Raman Lamba – Clint Eastwood
2. M. Azharuddin – Amitabh Bachchan
3. K. Srikkanth – Kamalhasan/Sridevi
4. Roger Binny – Steve McQueen
5. Chetan Sharma – Anil Kapoor/Jayaprada ('I hope she is reading this')
6. Raju Kulkarni – Amitabh Bachchan
7. Chandrakant Pandit – Kamalhasan
8. Dilip Vengsarkar – Amitabh Bachchan
9. Mohinder Amarnath – Sanjeev Kumar/Rekha
10. Maninder Singh – Amitabh Bachchan/Rekha

– *Femina*

LITERARY PREFERENCES OF SIX ENGLAND CRICKETERS ON THE CARIBBEAN TOUR OF 1980-81.

1. David Gower – The *Daily Telegraph/The Times* crosswords
2. Paul Downton – *The Thornbirds*
3. John Emburey – *Bowled Over* by Frank Keating
4. Geoff Boycott – *Shogun;* Chancellor Manuscript by Robert Ludlum; and *The Thornbirds*
5. Graham Gooch – *The Devil's Alternative; The Island* by Peter Benchley
6. Ian Botham – *Derek and Clive* by Dudley Moore and Peter Cook; *Dirty Movies;* and *McVicar* by McVicar

SIX THINGS DEREK RANDALL TELLS HIMSELF IN THE *MIDDLE*

1. 'Come on, Rags, get stuck in'
2. 'Don't take any chances'
3. 'Get forward, get forward'
4. 'Get behind the ball'
5. 'Take your time, slow and easy. You idiot, Rags. Come on, come on, come on England'
6. 'Wake up, Rags. Concentrate. Concentrate, you idiot'

VIZZY'S *ODDITIES* ON THE 1936 TOUR OF ENGLAND

Maharaja Sir Vijaya Vizianagaram, to give Vizzy his full name, was India's captain for the 1936 series.

1. Carried 36 items of personal luggage to England
2. Was accompanied by two servants who slept on the floor by the door of his bedroom
3. His wardrobe included dozens of silk shirts.
4. Had his shirts ironed during each interval
5. Carried with him a large-sized hookah which he smoked in bed

FIVE *WAYS* WAYNE DANIEL RELAXES

1. Reading everything about Formula I motor racing
2. Reading thrillers
3. Going to the pictures
4. Listening to pop music – the Eagles are fine
5. A 15-minute sleep in the physio's office after having been in the field all day

FIVE *WOMEN* RAVI SHASTRI WOULD LOVE TO SPEND AN EVENING WITH

(It would not be possible to list the number of girls who would dream of spending an evening with the Indian all-rounder, so we had to do it the other way around. Eat your hearts out, girls!)

1. Gabriela Sabatini, Argentina's teenaged tennis star
2. Lydia de Vega, champion sprinter and actress from the Philippines
3. Brooke Shields
4. Whitney Houston
5. Ursula Andress.

TEN CRICKETERS *ENJOY*...

1. Bruce French – mountaineering
2. Kevin Curran – tiger-fishing in the Zambezi
3. Keith Fletcher – shooting partridge
4. M. Azharuddin – watching 'Different Strokes'
5. Maninder Singh – writing a letter to his sweetheart
6. Allan Border – winning money off Greg Chappell
7. Rodney Hogg – running and Australian Rules football

8. Graham Gooch – girls eating bananas
9. Ian Botham – the end of a tour
10. Chandrakant Pandit – reading the *Ramayana*

WHAT EIGHT CRICKETERS CAN'T *STAND*

1. Len Pascoe – 'Knowalls'
2. Graeme Wood – 'Air travel'
3. Greg Chappell – 'Strikes by ABC staff ; blacking out cricket telecasts'
4. Kim Hughes – 'Fickle sports fans'
5. Ewen Chatfield – 'Doing the dishes'
6. Dirk Wellham – 'Noise and crowds'
7. John Dyson – 'Garlic, ear-bashers and autograph hunters who are rude'
8. Martin Crowe – 'Inconsistent umpiring, thoughtless media and smoking'

TEN EATING *HABITS* OF DAVID GOWER

1. 'The thought of Chinese food appeals me'
2. 'I like herbs and spices in omelettes'
3. 'I love roasts and steak'
4. 'Formal dinners are not my scene'
5. 'I have restricted myself to attempts to cook chips'
6. 'I am quite good at mashed potatoes'
7. 'Anything too hot will instantly turn me off'
8. 'One of my favourite dishes is Malay satay'
9. 'I am particularly partial to *Pouilly Fuisse* or a German wine'
10. 'To finish a meal, there can be nothing better than a glass of port'

– *With Time To Spare* by David Gower and Alan Lee

EIGHT *SUPERSTITIOUS* BATSMEN WHO ALWAYS PUT THEIR LEFT PAD ON FIRST

1. Jack Hobbs
2. Len Hutton
3. Ken Barrington
4. Greg Chappell
5. Martyn Moxon
6. Martin Crowe
7. Tim Robinson
8. Dipak Patel

...AND TWO WHO ALWAYS PUT THEIR RIGHT ONE ON FIRST

1. Graeme Pollock
2. John Dyson

TEN CRICKETERS WHO SMOKE(D) A *PIPE*

1. Bob Taylor
2. Dennis Amiss
3. Ross Edwards
4. Lionel Tennyson
5. Fred Titmus
6. Freddie Brown
7. Billy Griffith
8. Walter Hadlee
9. Jack Fingleton
10. Warwick Armstrong

SECRETS OF GREG CHAPPELL'S SUCCESS IN HIS OWN WORDS

1. 'I like to sit by myself before I go out to bat'.
2. 'I try to play very, very straight when I just go in'.
3. 'I keep saying to myself something repetitious as: "Watch the ball, watch the ball"'.
4. 'I exchange the time of day with the umpires. It's a form of relaxation really'.

WHAT TEN CRICKETERS LIKE TO DO IN THEIR *SPARE* TIME

1. Krish Srikkanth – sleep
2. Chetan Sharma – watch 'Buniyaad' and listen to old Hindi songs
3. Ewen Chatfield – gardening
4. Phil Edmonds – read *The Financial Times*
5. Jonathan Agnew – game viewing in Zimbabwe.
6. Les Taylor – fox hunting
7. Dirk Wellham – read History and English literature.
8. Dilip Vengsarkar – go on long drives.
9. Raju Kulkarni – watch 'Top of the Pops'
10. Roger Binny – watch 'Sons and Daughters' on TV

TEN *ODDITIES* OF BATSMEN AT THE CREASE

1. Sunil Gavaskar (India) – rubbed his sweat on the face of his bat
2. Carlisle Best (West Indies)– gives a ball-to-ball commentary
3. Lawrence Rowe (West Indies) – whistled loudly to get over his nervousness
4. Krish Srikkanth (India) – often walks to the square leg umpire between balls and sings songs
5. Mike Brearley (England) – was humming a cello passage from Rasoumoffsky quartets while facing Jeff Thomson in 1977
6. G. R. Vishwanath – used to look at the chain round his neck

between balls
7. Eric Rowan – would conduct his own commentary
8. Derek Randall – chatters to himself
9. Phil Mead – would glance around the field, tug his cap and shuffle his feet before crouching in his stance
10. David Bairstow – bangs his bat on the ground thrice and fiddles with his gloves an equal number of times

MOHINDER AMARNATH'S *CODE OF CONDUCT*

1. Play straight
2. Leave all deliveries outside the off stump
3. Try and stay at the wicket for as long as possible
4. Avoid the cut whether on zero or on 100
5. I tell myself 'I am not going to get out this ball' before each delivery

– *Sportsworld*

CRICKETERS' *HOBBIES*

1. Wes Hall – collecting gold chains
2. Qasim Omar – collecting post cards
3. Dilip Doshi – collecting video cassettes of cricket matches
4. Doug Walters – playing cards
5. Bill Lawry – reading Phantom comics and racing pigeons
6. Jeff Thomson – fishing and growing orchids
7. Ian Botham – parasailing, hand gliding and ballooning
8. Javed Miandad – producing perfect imitations of signatures of Pakistani team-mates
9. Martin Kent – collecting wine glasses
10. Mike Brearley – collecting dreams. He writes them down each morning in a log book which he keeps at the side of his bed

WHAT TEN CRICKETERS WOULD LOVE TO *EAT*

1. Ewen Chatfield – Weiner Schnitze
2. Dilip Vengsarkar – Bombay Duck
3. Greg Chappell – Spaghetti Bolognaise
4. Roger Binny – Beef steak
5. Viv Richards – Pepper Pot, a West Indian dish that contains a variety of meat, vegetables and red pepper
6. Allan Border – anything with garlic
7. Graham Gooch – Boeuf Wellington
8. Martin Crowe – Rogan Josh

9. Sunil Gavaskar – fried pomfret
10. Ian Botham – Kabanois

THE TEN ODDITIES OF *ALAN KNOTT*

1. He used to tape his pad to his trousers, doing away with the middle strap and buckle
2. Taped the ends of both his sleeves
3. Against fast bowling, he changed his batting grip, so as to have his top hand behind the handle, enabling him to hold his hands in front of his face and keep the bat straight
4. He never ate cheese and meat at the same meal
5. Drank little and avoided parties
6. Was very fussy about getting in eight hours of sleep
7. Used to set aside a couple of hours for ablutions and exercises before breakfast each morning
8. Had his car-seat remodelled after he had hurt his neck in two car accidents
9. Would leave the ground in India with three sweaters, an anorak with the hood up, and dark glasses as a precaution against catching a cold
10. Was a yoga fanatic

FIVE *CRICKETERS* WHO OPENED THE BATTING, KEPT WICKETS AND BOWLED IN THE SAME TEST.

1. The Hon. Alfred Lyttleton in 1884 versus Australia at The Oval.
2. W. G. Grace in 1884 versus Australia at The Oval.
3. F. L. Mooney in 1953-54 versus South Africa at Port Elizabeth.
4. W. Ferguson in 1953-54 versus England at Port-of-Spain.
5. Taslim Arif in 1979-80 versus Australia at Lahore.

FAVOURITE *SINGERS* OF TEN CRICKETERS

1. Bob Taylor – Frank Sinatra
2. Faoud Bacchus – Donna Summers
3. Wasim Bari – Lata Mangeshkar, Mehdi Hassan
4. Haroon Rashid – Taslim Arif
5. Sunil Gavaskar – Jagjit Singh
6. Zaheer Abbas – Noorjehan
7. Graham Yallop – Olivia-Newton John

8. Allan Border – The Beatles
9. Bob Willis – Bob Dylan
10. Kapil Dev – Mohinder Amarnath

ODD *QUIRKS* OF NINE CRICKETERS ON THE FIELD

1. Victor Trumper – Never used a grip on his bat handle
2. Jack Gregory – Never wore gloves while batting
3. Eknath Solkar – Never wore an abdomen guard while fielding at short leg for a significant part of his career; was forced to wear one at the insistance of his captain Tiger Pataudi
4. Glenn Turner – Preferred wearing a towel tucked down the inside of his right thigh if the ball was moving around considerably
5. Clive Lloyd – Regularly used a bat weighing almost three pounds with six grips rolled over the bat handle
6. Arthur Richardson – Liked to play with a heavy bat with cowhide fastened around it
7. Greg Matthews – Always plays with his collar buttoned and sleeves rolled down
8. Victor Trumper – Rolled his sleeves a couple of folds upwards from his wrists
9. Alan Kippax – Imitated Victor Trumper

TEN ODDITIES THAT CAN ONLY HAPPEN IN CLUB CRICKET

By Lt Col A.T. 'Bobbie' Burlton

1. Arriving late, and sometimes without an apology, to the captain
2. Not immediately reporting your arrival to the captain
3. Wearing dirty gear
4. The fielding side preceding the umpires onto the ground
5. Kicking the ball
6. A fielder, having dropped a catch or being responsible for an expensive bit of his fielding, not apologizing to the captain and the bowler concerned
7. A batsman picking up the ball even at the request of a fielder; he has no right to ask you to break the laws
8. A fielder throwing a sweater or a cap to the umpire, without so much as a by-your-leave
9. The wearing of wrist-watches

10. Unkempt hair…it is by no means unusual to see the youngsters scampering off for a run and, rather than risk losing it *en route*, clutching their cap with their disengaged hand

– *The Cricketer International*

DAVID GOWER'S *DESERT ISLAND* DISCS

1. Handel's 'The Arrival Of The Queen Of Sheba'.
2. Elton John's 'Goodbye Yellow Brick Road'.
3. Genesis' 'I Know What I Like In Your Wardrobe'.
4. Beethoven's 'Emperor Concerto'.
5. Supertramp's 'Breakfast In America'.
6. Dire Straits' 'Tunnel Of Love'.
7. Al Stewart's 'On The Border'.
8. Vaughan Williams' 'The Fantasy On A Theme' by Thomas Tallis.

Note. Gower would prefer the Beethoven record with the best wine, an encyclopaedia and a VCR with a cassette of 'Rumpole Of The Bailey'.

– *Wisden Cricket Monthly*

FIVE CRICKETERS WITH A PREDILECTION FOR *ALCOHOL*

1. Bobby Peel came to play for Yorkshire one day in 1897 under the influence of alcohol. He urinated on the pitch and was banned from playing for his county again
2. Suffering from an attack of malaria in the 1920-21 series vs England. Warwick Armstrong went out to play an innings after fortifying himself with two 'stiff' whiskies. He scored a century
3. Billy Barnes was often warned not to come to county matches for Notts drunk. He staggered to the crease during one such occasion against Middlesex at Lord's. He scored a hundred in two hours, saved the match for his side, but was later hauled up on disciplinary grounds. He is said to have astonished the committee members by saying: 'How many of you gentlemen could make a hundred, drunk *or* sober?'
4. Captain G.H.S. Trott asked C.E. McLeod to have a glass of unidentified liquid as an antidote for nervousness before the latter went out to bat against England at Melbourne in 1897-98. It was only after the teetotaller McLeod had scored a

hundred did Trott reveal that he had given the young man a peg of whisky

5. A man fond of his drink, Sammy Woods would invite friends to a long walk over the countryside in Somerset. He would venture out a day previous to the engagement and bury bottles of drink at selected sites. The following day as the walk became tiring, Woods would from time to time attempt to sniff his favourite drink in the air and boast to his audience that he could unearth refreshments within minutes. He would then proceed to dig at the appointed spots and produce bottles for his astonished guests.

SUPERSTITIOUS CRICKETERS

1. Asif Iqbal — used the same bat and trouser which proved lucky.
2. Mohinder Amarnath — carries a red handkerchief in his pocket.
3. Jonathan Agnew — never uses a bowling marker.
4. K. Srikkanth — prostrates himself in front of his grandparents before every match; the extra 'K' in his surname was added on astrological advice.
5. Eldine Baptiste — is superstitious about the numbers 13 and 49.
6. Umpire Don Shepherd — raises one leg whenever a side is on 222.
7. David Bairstow — does everything in threes: pats the ground thrice; fiddles with his gloves thrice
8. Derek Pringle — circles the stumps at each end with his bat.
9. Alan Knott — always touched the bails at the batting end before facing the first ball; his lucky handkerchief stayed in his pocket and his favourite teddy bear in the kit bag !
10. Mike Selvey and Greg Thomas — prefer not to play in August.
11. Athol Rowan — stayed in bed on every Friday the 13th
12. Allan Lamb — tried to wear the batting shirt in which he was last successful.
13. Sunil Gavaskar — wore something new for each match; walked to the right of his partner when going out to bat.
14. G. R. Vishwanath — looked at the chain round his neck before each ball
15. Keith Miller — Disliked the score 87 (13 short of 100)

16. Trevor Bailey — considered wearing a cap unlucky
17. Doug Walters — remembered which locker he occupied at a ground and went to it again
18. Ron Archer — never looked at the scoreboard
19. Ken Mackey — wore his left sock and left boot first, and walked out on the left side of his batting partner.
20. Greg Chappell — did not whiten his pads in 1977
21. Joe Darling and Victor Trumper — stuck to an old pair of trousers which were considered lucky
22. Wes Hall — always wore a crucifix round his neck
23. Colin Cowdrey — remained naked in the dressing room except for a blue England cap
24. Norman O'Neill — always wore an old pair of yellow socks
25. Ken Barrington — got out from the right side of the bed; repeated an exact number of strokes while brushing his teeth
26. Viv Richards — chews gum on the field
27. Allan Border — does not shave during a Test or Shield match.
28. Derek Pringle — does not read newspapers during a game
29. Jonathan Addison — too numerous to mention
30. David East and Clive Rice — are wary of the number 111
31. David Capel — never eats duck before a game; did so once and recorded the only 'pair' of his career.
32. Zaheer Abbas — believed somebody had put a magic spell on him during Pakistan's tour of India in 1979-80; did not cross the incoming batsman when going out to bat
33. Richard Hadlee — facing a hattrick
34. Mike Whitney — always kisses the ball before bowling the first delivery of the match
35. Shaun Graf — never moves from where he is sitting when the batsman preceding him is at the crease
36. England players, 1978-79 — lifted their feet off the ground as on antidote to the score being 111

Compiled by Dr Surapriya Mukherjee

Handicaps

SIX CRICKETERS WHO WERE/ARE *ASTHMATICS*

1. A. J. Watkins (England)
2. Rodney Hogg (Australia)
3. Eddie Hemmings (England)
4. E. G. Arnold (England)
5. J. T. Brown (England)
6. Chris Tavare (England)

FOUR CRICKETERS WHO WENT BLIND IN LATER LIFE

1. Percy Fender
2. Wilfred Rhodes
3. Phil Mead
4. Samuel Morris

THREE INNINGS THAT WERE PLAYED WITH A HIGH BODY *TEMPERATURE*

1. Javed Miandad scored 66 in the Jalandhar Test against India in 1983. 'My head was spinning out there in the middle', said Miandad. He rated it as his best Test innings till then.
2. Dean Jones vomited several times, changed shirts and had tablets brought out to him in the middle in the Madras Test, 1986-87. He scored 210. The match was tied.
3. Tony Greig, batting with a body temperature of 104°F, scored 103 in Calcutta, 1976-77. England won the match by 10 wickets.

FOUR CRICKETERS WHO PLAYED DESPITE THE LOSS OF AN *EYE*

1. Ranji, who lost an eye in a shooting accident in 1915
2. E. P. Nupen of South Africa lost an eye as a youngster, while knocking two hammers together. A splinter flew off, handicapping 'Buster' Nupen for life. He went on to become one of the greatest fast-medium bowlers South Africa ever had on matting
3. Tiger Pataudi was injured in a car accident in 1961. He lost his right eye
4. Colin Milburn was involved in a car mishap and lost the sight in his left eye

ELEVEN FACTORS THAT ADD TO *DENNIS LILLEE*'S GREATNESS

1. He suffered from general soreness in the foot throughout his career
2. He often played with bruised heels
3. He often complained of skin peeling off from underneath his big toe
4. He suffered from soreness in the shin as well as under the ribs
5. He had a hernia problem
6. ...and ricks in the neck

7. He had a serious attack of bursitis during the sixth Test against MCC in 1974-75
8. He had severe back trouble during the series against Rest of the World in 1971-72
9. The back injury recurred in the third Test against Pakistan in 1972-73
10. He incurred a stress fracture of the lumber vertebrae during the first Test against West Indies in 1972-73
11. His back problem kept him out of the 1977 Ashes series in England

NINE *HANDICAPPED* CRICKETERS

1, 2, 3, 4. Tiger Pataudi, E. P. Nupen, Colin Milburn and Ranji – blind in one eye

5. Len Hutton – his left arm was shortened by 2 inches in a World War II injury
6. Azeem Hafeez – four fingers of his right hand were chopped off in an accident early in his life
7. B. Chandrasekhar - his right arm is withered due to an acute attack of poliomyelitis as a 5-year-old. He usually threw in with his left
8. Eddie Paynter – lost the tops of a couple of fingers on his right hand in an accident
9. Fred Titmus – had four toes of his foot chopped off by the propeller of a boat on the tour of West Indies in 1968-69

TEN CRICKETERS WHO USE(D) *CONTACT LENSES*

1. Paul Allott
2. Martyn Moxon
3. Eddie Hemmings
4. Chris Tavare
5. Geoff Boycott
6. Zaheer Abbas
7. Derek Pringle
8. Lawrence Rowe
9. Anshuman Gaekwad
10. Clive Lloyd

AILMENTS TWENTY-THREE CRICKETERS SUFFER / SUFFERED FROM

1. Geoff Howarth – migraine
2. Viv Richards – pterygium (film of skin growing over the eyes) because of exposure to sunlight over long periods
3. Rodney Hogg – schewermann's disease (degenerative condition of the vertebrae)

4. Johnny Briggs – epilepsy
5. E. M. Grace – inflamed knee joints
6. George Lohmann – respiratory trouble and tuberculosis
7. Archie MacLaren – lumbago
8. V. Trumper – Bright's disease
9. J. T. Brown – 'congestion of the brain'
10. E. G. Arnold – chronic bronchitis
11. D. D. Blythe – epilepsy
12. C. G. Borde – arthritis
13. C. Blythe – epilepsy
14. Lawrence Rowe – an allergy to grass
15. Majid Khan – a bad back. He had to sleep on the floor or insert boards under the mattress
16. Bill Ponsford – colour blindness
17. B. S. Chandrasekhar – polimyelitis
18. Chris Tavare – hayfever
19. Bruce Francis – migraine
20. K. S. Ranjitsinhji – hayfever
21. Greg Chappell – partial face paralysis
22. E. L. McCormick – lumbago
23. Chris Old – 'everything', according to Mike Brearley

Have a Laugh!

HAVE A *LAUGH!*

1. In Sydney two blondes walked up to Joel Garner and asked him: 'Hey Joel, you're 6 ft 8 in., are you proportionate all over?' The 'Big Bird' looked embarrassed, but replied with eyes downcast : 'Of course not. If I was I would be 8 ft 6 in.'
2. Richard Ellison: 'Why am I called "Plank"?'
   Chris Cowdrey : "Exactly"

FIVE REASONS WHY I DON'T WANT TO BE A *TEST CRICKETER*

By Norman Taylor, a 22-year-old unemployed London youth.

1. I wasn't taught sleaging at school
2. Am frightened of flying

3. Too illiterate to write a column
4. My father wants me to become a bus conducter
5. I agree with him

FIVE REASONS WHY I DONT' WANT TO BE A *TEST* CRICKETER

By Patrick Baptiste, an Australian enthusiast and bank employee.

1. Streakers embarrass me
2. I'd get into a tax problem with so much money going around
3. I am not a West Indian
4. I will expect favours in return from female autograph hunters
5. My bank won't give me leave

A CODE OF *PENALTIES*

By Stephen Gospage

1. Bad throwing – 4 points and a one week course from Geoff Boycott on how to do it properly
2. Intimidatory close fielding – 3 points and a golden chance as one of Fagin's boys in the new film version of *Oliver*
3. Protesting to umpires – 2 points and a chance to listen to 3,600 spins of 'What kind of fool am I?' by Rohan Kanhai
4. Timewasting – 1 point and a chance to do one week's community work helping infants undo their shoelaces before bedtime at 6.30

– The Cricketer International

FIVE *REASONS* WHY I DON'T WANT TO PLAY TEST CRICKET

By 'Binks', a colleague of ours, who complains that cricket puts him to sleep. He has promised us that this is the only cricket book he'll read!

1. Malcolm Marshall
2. Joel Garner
3. Michael Holding.
4. Imran Khan
5. Can't handle the promiscuity that goes with the job.

UNHAPPINESS IS...

By E. J. Brack

...going to the toilet and missing a wicket

...having to go shopping with your wife when the Test is on television

...getting up in the middle of the night only to discover that England have already lost by an innings

...being captain of England

...trying to bowl fast in Pakistan

...being Bob Willis' hairdresser

...being Chris Old's doctor

...doing Derek Randall's laundry

...bowling round the wicket at Swaroop Kishen's end

– *Wisden Cricket Monthly*

IT IS MOST *LIKELY* THAT YOU'LL FIND...

...Bob Willis at a Bob Dylan concert

...Ian Botham in a confessional/courtroom

...Duleep Mendis in a sauna bath

...Chris Old in hospital

...Richie Benaud in your drawing room

...Don Bradman in the record book

...Sarfraz Nawaz in the headlines

...Sunil Gavaskar at the crease

...Graeme Wood at the wrong end

...Stuart Surridge on playing equipment

IT'S *UNLIKELY* THAT YOU WILL FIND...

Geoff Boycott at a nudist beach

Gus Logie on a basketball court

Gary Sobers at nets

Mohammed Azharuddin on a barstool

Ian Botham at Sunday morning Mass

Bruce Reid at a slimming centre

Rev. David Sheppard at King's Cross

B.S. Chandrasekhar at the crease

Viv Richards in South Africa

Joel Garner bringing home the Derby winner

And any contemporary Test cricketer at home!

THE FIVE MOST DIFFICULT *JOBS* IN CRICKET ACCORDING TO JONATHAN RICE

1. Captaining Derbyshire
2. Spelling the Sri Lankan Test eleven
3. Out-talking Henry Blofeld
4. Losing to Warwickshire
5. Acting as Ian Botham's insurance broker

– Wisden Cricket Monthly

'*WHAT*'S ON IN LONDON?' ACCORDING TO JONATHAN RICE

1. 'No Bouncers Please, We're British' by Ray Cooney, Mike Gatting, Andy Lloyd and Paul Terry
2. 'Bats' by Andrew Lloyd-Webber and Duncan Fearnley, based on the poems on John Snow
3. 'The Leg Trap' by Agatha Christie and Douglas Jardine
4. 'Les Miserables' by Herbert Kretzmer and Robin Marlar about the Lord's Test, India vs England, 1986
5. 'A Little Night Cricket' by Stephen Sondheim and Kerry Packer, about WSC
6. 'Out of Africa', starring Robert Redford as Allan Lamb and Meryl Streep as Zola Budd
7. 'Saturday Night Fever' (film version of 'The Pyjama Game', starring John Travolta as Richie Benaud and the Bee Gees as the entire Sri Lankan eleven)

– Wisden Cricket Monthly

SHAKESPEARE IN CRICKET?

1. 'Who loses and who wins? Who's in? Who's out?' (*King Lear,* Act V Scene III).
2. 'Yet if you be out sir, I can mend you' (*Julius Caesar,* Act I Scene I).
3. 'And there have sat the livelong day with patient expectation' (*Julius Caesar,* Act I Scene I).
4. 'Then leave him out. Indeed he is not fit' (*Julius Ceasar,* Act II Scene I).
5. 'Now bid me run' (*Julius Caesar,* Act II Scene I).
6. 'Bring me to the test' (*Hamlet,* Act III Scene IV).
7. 'Have I caught thee?' (*Merry Wives Of Windsor,* Act I Scene III).
8. 'A very good bowler' (*Love's Labour Lost,* Act V Scene II).

9. 'Like greyhounds in the slips' (*Henry V,* Act III Scene I).
10. 'Our play is done' (*Twelfth Night,* Act V Scene I).
11. 'Gone and hath nothing' (*Romeo and Juliet,* Act III Scene I).
12. 'Scants us with a single' (*Troilus and Cressida,* Act IV Scene IV).
13. *'Doubly redoubled strokes'* (*Macbeth,* Act I Scene II).
14. 'Play such fantastic tricks' – the pitch. (*Measure for Measure,* Act II, Scene II).
15. 'Pack when it begins to rain'. (*King Lear,* Act II Scene IV).
16. 'Out!' (*A Midsummer Night's Dream,* Act III Scene II).
17. 'This was the most unkindest cut of all' (*Julius Caesar,* Act III Scene II)

NINE INSTANCES OF KEN BARRINGTON'S *MALAPROPISMS*

The lovable batsman and later manager of England abroad, was a master of the unintended word. He was referred to as Mr Malaprop in cricket circles in later years.

1. 'You were simply caught in *two-man's* land'. (When Brian Rose went half back and half forward before getting out)
2. 'The people wouldn't let old Forbes Burnham (Prime Minister of Guyana) deprive them of their cricket; 10,000 to watch a practice match today; it'd be a real *evolution* if he tried it'.
3. 'It's pretty *inoculous*'.
4. 'I look like one of those guardsmen outside Buckingham Palace. What is it they 'ave on their 'eads? *Fuzzbies* or something?'
5. 'It's coming down like *pea-pods*'. (When it was raining hard)
6. 'It was a great performance in anyone's cup of tea'. (On Robin Jackman's bowling)
7. 'I kipped really well, I slept like a lark'.
8. 'High-philosophy bullets'.
9. 'Smog-or-gasbord'. (For 'smorgasbord')

FOUR OF THE WITTIEST CRICKET *LIMERICKS*

1. The one which won the prize in a competition conducted by *The Times*

   'A cricketer bowling for Sarum,
   Said: "Them whose 'ave pads better wear 'em,
   But wear 'em instead

Not on the legs but their 'ead.
'Cos I aims not to bowl 'em but scare 'em" '

2. 'A cavalier batsman called Lillee
Was facing the bowling of Dilley.
He swung his tin bat,
But to cries of "Howzat?"
Was Lillee caught Willey bowled Dilley.'

3. By Mrs M. W. Johnston:
'Said a gallant young batsman called Gatting:
"Please excuse me of ratting;
But I've broken nose and thumb,
And been hit on the bum,
So it's rather put paid to my batting." '

4. By Gilbert Jessop, legendary hitter:
'Upon the piano she lbs (pounds)
Makes most deafening sbs
And the uproar that reigns
The policeman compleigns
Keeps him nightly awake on his rbs.'

A DOZEN CRICKETING *PUNS*

1. 'I'm GARNER wash that man right out of my hair'.
2. 'The LLOYD'S my shepherd'.
3. 'Amazing GRACE'.
4. 'Try a little ten-DENNESS'.
5. 'AMISS you since you went away'.
6. 'Thank 'EVANS for little girls'.
7. 'Happy days ZAHEER again'.
8. 'Keep BRIGHT onto the end of the road'.
9. 'Don't DILLEY-dalley on the way'.
10. 'KANHAI forget you?'
11. 'ASIF it could make a difference'.
12. 'HUGHES are my heart's delight'.

'FELIX'S,' *TONGUE-IN-CHEEK* AWARDS FOR 1980

1. 'The Charlie Griffith Remembrance Award for the Most Staggering Act of Humanity: D. K. Lillee for picking up wounded seagulls. Prize' a life subscription to the Zoo, and a chance to meet its latest and most sensational disc jockey.
2. 'The Vidal Sassoon Award for Refusal to succumb to

Prevailing Fashion' : Derek Underwood, for not growing a beard or moustache. Prize: two tickets to Elton John's next concert. (Ineligible: G. Boycott – extra hair located elsewhere; G. Dilley – does not yet own a razor)

3. 'The Gibbs-Ramadhin Nostalgia Award for Spin Bowlers': Derek Parry, for actually achieving selection for West Indies in a representative match. Prize: signed copy of J. K. Lever's forthcoming book *Carrying Drinks Can Be Fun.*
4. 'The D. R. Jardine Special Memorial Award': J. M. Brearley, for managing to become the most unpopular Pommie of the lot, apparently for being an 'intellectual' (though official enquiries have not yet ruled out his beard as proximate cause). Prize: V-signed copy of the new book *Multisyllabic Australian* (The Hill Publishers, Sydney, 2 pages).
5. 'The Lords Harris and Hawke Award for Most Uncharacteristic Act of Intelligence and Foresight': the TCCB, for refusing to put the Ashes at stake. Prize: a plastic replica of the Wisden Trophy (since England are unlikely to regain that for at least 12 generations).

– *Wisden Cricket Monthly*

Ian Botham

KATHY BOTHAM ON HER HUSBAND

1. 'I quite enjoy my independence. When Ian's been home for a few days I am quite glad to see the back of him. He takes up so much time'.
2. 'The point is I haven't got Ian very much. I have shared him with others for 10 years'.
3. 'I think our marriage has stayed out of the divorce courts because we are apart so much'.

FIVE BITS OF *ADVICE* TO IAN BOTHAM

By E.J. Brack

1. Stop buying newspapers
2. Stop reading newspapers
3. Stop talking to newspapers
4. Stop writing for newspapers
5. Stop giving newspapers cheap copy

–Wisden Cricket Monthly

FIVE *REASONS* WHY IAN BOTHAM SHOULD HAVE REFUSED THE ENGLISH CAPTAINCY

Brian Close knows Ian Botham better than most by virtue of his playing for Somerset in Botham's early years. He was among the handful who felt that Botham should have refused the captaincy when he was given the job in 1980. The 'experts' were to come later, much later. Said Close to Botham:

1. 'Your own form will suffer. You are too much of an action-man to be able to stand back and take an objective view of your players' performance'.
2. 'Your batting will suffer because your concentration will go when you start thinking about long-term captaincy problems'.
3. 'When you are bowling you will be asking yourself: "Should I be trying someone else?" And again, you will lose your concentration'.
4. 'The results will be bad and you'll have the media on your back and you won't like that'.
5. 'You'll have the most miserable time of your life'.

TEN THINGS IAN BOTHAM *DID/DOES*

1. Smokes incessantly before a Test match
2. Landed a 31 kg sailfish while gamefishing off the Queensland coast, 1986-87
3. Chased Ian Chappell out of a bar while playing for Melbourne University, 1976-77
4. Manhandled journalist Henry Blofeld at Nassau airport, Bahamas, April 1981
5. Was involved in a fight with Rodney Hogg at a waterside pub under the shadow of the Harbour Bridge, 1983
6. Defied a call by the TCCB to discontinue his column in the *Sun,* June 1983
7. Ignored TCCB's appeal to stop playing soccer for Scunthorpe United to avoid injury before the tour of Pakistan and New Zealand, 1983-84
8. Brawled with a young sailor on the street, December 1980
9. Bashed up a policeman during his charity walk from John O' Groats to Land's End in 1985
10. Infuriated his guests during a benefit dinner at Cambridge in April 1984. Botham walked out after eating the first course but picked up a cheque worth £ 5000

TEN *ACCUSATIONS* AGAINST IAN BOTHAM

Spokesmen of insurance companies have been overlooked in this survey.

1. 'Ian Botham is all mouth' (Jeff Thomson).
2. 'He is a cricketing anarchist. He respects no rules, bows to no circumstances – nor does he show his younger team-mates that he wants his team to do well'. (Peter Roebuck).
3. 'If Botham is an English folk hero, as was claimed in *(The Observer,* then this must be an alarming time for the nation' (David Miller).
4. 'I've known him for 14 years, ever since we played together in the Somerset under-15 team. Already he was a brash, daring youngster, willing to have a go at various activities, attempted by most of us later in life' (Peter Roebuck).
5. 'In so many ways, Ian Botham is a product of modern society with its many imperfections' (Don Mosey).
6. 'You two are nothing but wasters. You'll make nothing of your careers. You'll just drift away. You'll be the people

society wants to forget' (Headmaster to Botham and a schoolfriend).

7. 'For a start off, you (Ian) are not good enough for Kathryn. And you Kathy, will ruin his career. You're both too young' (Brian Close to Botham and his wife before they got married).
8. 'This fellow is the most over-rated player I've seen. He looks too heavy and the way he's been bowling he wouldn't burst a paperbag. I know he's got a lot of runs in his career but from what I have seen, he bats like I used to. The only difference is that I went in at number 10' (Harold Larwood).
9. 'We have a complete mad man out here' (Phil Edmonds to his wife on the phone while on the tour of Pakistan and New Zealand, 1977-78).
10. 'Ian is not easy to live with' (Kathy Botham).

WHAT TEN PEOPLE *THINK* OF IAN BOTHAM

1. 'He is a lonely man, perhaps the loneliest I've ever met' (Somerset colleague Peter Roebuck).
2. 'Ian has always been one of the boys! In some ways I think he is rather shy of being with the ladies' (Mrs Marie Botham, Ian's mother).
3. 'People put down pint glasses to go and watch him play. They wouldn't do that for me' (Allan Border).
4. 'I wouldn't even choose Botham as the best all-rounder in the world at the moment. I'd nominate Imran Khan and then Richard Hadlee' (Ian Chappell).
5. 'The cricket writer has to be as much a sleuth, lawyer and vicar to assess Ian Botham and think of a judgment' (Tony Lewis).
6. 'I honestly think Ian would like to have a friendly punch-up with someone once a week just to relieve his pent up aggression' (Bob Willis).
7. 'If you made him Prime Minister tomorrow, he'd pick this country up in ten minutes' (Former county cricketer and umpire Bill Alley).
8. 'There is never a dull moment when he is around' (Bob Willis).
9. 'He will bowl more comfortably after all the fragments of bone and gristle have been vacuumed out of the joint – no, not that kind, silly' (Robin Marlar).
10. 'He's like a big, soft puppy, really' (County cricketer Tom Cartwright).

It Might Interest You...

SEVEN CRICKETERS WHO HAVE PLAYED WITH BOTH, THE *FATHER AND SON* IN TESTS

1. Pat Pocock (Colin and Chris Cowdrey)
2. J. Blackham (Ned and Syd Gregory)
3. Wilfred Rhodes (Fred and Maurice Tate)
4. E. Nupen (Dave and Dudley Nourse)
5. Chandu Borde (Vinoo and Ashok Mankad)
6. Zaheer Abbas (Hanif and Shoaib Mohammed)
7. Sarfraz Nawaz (Hanif and Shoaib Mohammed)

FIVE PLOYS THAT KEPT THE *BAILS* FROM FLYING

1. A bit of clay was used to secure the bails at Harrogate in 1902 in the game between Australia and Players
2. In a Sheffield Shield match in Perth, 1952-53, chewing gum was used for the same purpose
3. In a match at Leyton, 1901, rubber bails were used
4. Heavy wood lignum bails were substituted for the normal ones in Scarborough
5. Iron bails were also once put to use in matches at Scarborough

– *Next Man In* by Gerald Brodribb

TWELVE INTERESTING *SIMILARITIES* BETWEEN MOHINDER AMARNATH AND MUDASSAR NAZAR

1. Both are Punjabis
2. Both their first names start with 'M' and end with 'R'
3. The first name of each comprises eight alphabets
4. Each has an elder and a younger brother
5. The fathers of both scored maiden hundreds for their respective countries
6. The first centuries by the fathers of each came in the second ever Tests of the respective countries
7. The 101st Test century for India was scored by Mohinder Amarnath. Mudassar Nazar also scored the 101st Test century for Pakistan
8. Mohinder made his Test debut on 24.12.69 versus Australia; Mudassar made his debut on 24.12.76 against Australia

9. Both scored their 2000th Test run in the same match – Karachi, 1982
10. Mohinder holds the record for India's highest series aggregate against Pakistan (583) scored in 1982-83; Mudassar is the holder of the record for the most runs versus India by a Pakistani (761) in a series, made in 1982-83
11. Both scored their maiden Test centuries in the same week; Mohinder on 20.12.77 in Perth and Mudassar on 15.12.77 at Lahore
12. Both bat right handed and bowl right-arm gentle medium pace. Both are equally underestimated as bowlers

– *The Cricketer International*
(contributed by Vinod Sharma)

DID YOU *KNOW* THAT...

1. ....Andy Roberts is one of 16 children of a fisherman in Antigua
2. ...that Sudhir Naik contemplated taking his life after he was accused of shoplifting in England on the tour of 1974. He changed his mind, drawing inspiration from the way Richard Nixon handled the Watergate Scandal
3. ...George Headley put 'African' on his immigration papers for his 1930-31 tour of Australia
4. ...that Dennis Lillee had rubber built into the heels of his boots and rubber inserts to soften the blow when he thumped into hard wickets
5. ...Everton Weekes played bridge against actor Omar Sharif in the World Championship
6. ...that Victor Trumper's first eight hundreds in first-class cricket were: 292 not out, 253 not out, 135 not out, 104, 300 not out, 208, 165 and 230
7. ...five Indian batsmen were absent hurt in the second innings of the fourth Test against the West Indies, 1975-76
8. ...Jack Hobbs refused to accept the MCC invitation to tour Australia in 1924-25 because his wife was not allowed to accompany him. When Lord Harris heard of this, he granted Hobbs the permission, provided he paid for her
9. ...Mrs Martha Grace, mother of W.G., is the only woman to be listed in *Wisden*'s 'Births and Deaths'
10. ...Nicholas Wanostrocht ('Felix') used to keep a track of his score by writing it on his stiff shirt-front

CODE OF *ETHICS*

(Usually it is the administration which decrees the following list. But in 1980-81 the Australian cricketers surprised their Board by assuming this responsibilty. They presented the ACB a 7-point guideline)

1. Players must not assault or attempt to assault an umpire, another player, or a spectator who is not trespassing on the ground
2. Players must not abuse or dispute – as distinct from questioning – an umpire's decision, or react in a provocative or disapproving manner towards an umpire, or following an umpire's decision
3. Players must wear and use only approved clothing and equipment. A list of approved clothing and equipment will be given to players, umpires and associations before the seasons start
4. Players must not engage in conduct detrimental to the spirit of the game. Umpires would be expected to issue cautions and advise the captains of his concern before reporting any player for such behaviour
5. Players must not use 'well known' crude or abusive hand signals
6. Public acts of misconduct or unruly public behaviour while representing the ACB or a state body would be a breach of code
7. Players must abide by their contracts with the ACB and the conditions stipulated by their state body when accepting an invitation to play for their state

IN THE *RIGHT PLACE* AT THE RIGHT TIME

You need a lot of ability and a little luck to be asked to play for your country. Sometimes just the reverse!

1. George Gunn, while recuperating from an illness in Australia in 1907, was SOS'd to play for MCC in place of A.O. Jones. Gunn scored 119, 74, 65 and 122 and finished at the top of the batting averages (51.33)
2. Mike Whitney was a professional with Fleetwood club in England when the Australian side in 1981, depleted through injuries, asked him to play as an emergency choice. Whitney made his debut for Australia at Old Trafford

3. Abbas Ali Baig, a freshman at Oxford, was enjoying his summer vacation when he was summoned to replace the injured Manjrekar in the Indian team touring England in 1959. Baig went on to score a century against Middlesex at Lord's for India and 112 in his debut Test at Old Trafford.
4. Ron Headley, son of the legendary West Indian cricketer George, was drafted into the West Indies team in England, 1973. Headley was 35 years old at that time and a professional with Worcestershire.
5. George Parker was playing as a professional in the Bradford League when he was called upon to make his Test debut for South Africa versus England at Edgbaston in 1924. He took six for 152 in what was also his first first-class match!
6. Kenneth Palmer was coaching in Johannesburg when he was asked to rush to Port Elizabeth and open the England bowling in 1964-65

TEN SUCCESSFUL '*CHANGES*' IN CRICKET

1. Wes Hall, who went on to take 192 Test Wickets for the West Indies, was a wicket keeper in school
2. Leg spinner Bill O'Reilly, who took 144 wickets for his country at 22 apiece, started his career as a fast bowler
3. Lance Gibbs, who is the only slow bowler (off spinner) to take more than 300 wickets in Tests, started out as a leg spinner
4. Bob Massie, who took 16 wickets on his Test debut as a swing bowler, fancied himself as a leg spinner at the start of his career
5. Sadiq Mohammed was originally a right hander. He switched to left on the advice of his elder brother Hanif, who felt that left-handers had more scope in Pakistan
6. Wicket keeper Alan Knott, who retired with more Test dismissals than anybody, was an off-spinner in school
7. Gladstone Small started out bowling off-breaks. He represented England as a fast bowler
8. Maurice Tate bowled slow-medium off-breaks during the early part of his career. He went on to become one of the best medium-pace bowlers of all time
9. Salim Durrani was a natural right-hander as a boy. His father always wanted him to become a cricketer and a left-handed one at that. He used to tie his son's right hand to his back. 'I would have ended up being a right-handed farmer in a small

village in India had my father not forced me to change'
10. Collie Smith, who played for West Indies in the capacity of a hard-hitting batsman, was an off-spinner in school

UNUSUAL *TERMS*

1. Net system – an arrangement between the two sides whereby there are no boundaries for the match i.e. all the strokes have to be run for
2. E. T. – stands for the English Traditionalist, or an 'outdated chappie'
3. Waterdrip effect – coined by umpire David Constant. This refers to the ploy used by modern-day fielders, whereby they congratulate one another before the umpire has given his decision
4. 'Suicide corner', 'Boot hill' – short leg
5. The Dirty Dozen – the 'rebel' England cricketers who toured South Africa in 1981-82
6. Operation Chessmatch – the name given to the highly secretive build-up of the tour of South Africa by 'rebel' England cricketers while still on tour in India in 1981-82
7. Prop and Cop – Doug Insole's term for ultra-defensive batting with an odd single sneaked around the corner
8. Nightwatchbatperson – for a woman nightwatchman – as used by a journalist reporting the England vs Australia women's Test in Brisbane (Sorry girls, we don't know the year!)
9. Championshipitis – coined by R.W.V. Robins, drawing attention to a county side leading the championship table and turning over-defensive in the home-stretch, excusing it with end-of-season weariness
10. The Ian Chappell habit – turning up to look into the sun while walking out to bat. For a practical demonstration, watch Kapil Dev
11. Pickpockets — fielders at silly mid on or closer, waiting to snatch the ball off the face of the bat.

WOULD YOU BELIEVE US IF WE TOLD YOU THAT...

1. ...Kerry Packer shifted all his accounts to another bank when Ian Davis, a cricketer signed up by him, was refused permission to tour the West Indies by the first bank (Davis' employers)

2. ...Denis Compton jumped over the turnstiles when the gateman at the MCG, 1950-51, was not looking. He had been refused entry because he did not have a pass with him
3. ...in the Somerset-Oxford University match in 1901, A. P. Wickham of Somerset kept wickets for the other side too when their 'keeper was injured early in the game
4. ...a limited-overs international between India and Australia was delayed by several hours when the players' kit failed to arrive from Calcutta by road on time
5. ...South African cricketer Balaskas' initials 'X.C.' stand for Xenophon Constantine. He is of Greek descent and a chemist by profession
6. ...Bishen Bedi gave blood to a Pakistani youngster in Karachi while touring with Rohan Kanhai's International eleven in 1981
7. ...K. C. Ibrahim started the Indian season in 1947-48 with scores of 218 not out, 36 not out, 234 not out, 77 not out and 144. His average totalled 709!
8. ... amateur mountaineer Bruce French was given three days' leave in 1984-85 on the tour of India to fly to the Himalayas to inspect Mount Everest
9. ...the Sharjah Cricket Ground consumes 10,000 gallons of water each day
10. ...Zaheer Abbas and Wasim Bari were saved by a life guard after getting into difficulties while swimming near their Bridgetown hotel in February 1977

TWELVE FAMOUS AND NOT-SO-FAMOUS *WAGERS*

1. During the Australian team's voyage to England in 1882, a passenger had a £ 100 bet with G. J. Bonnor that the latter would not be able to throw a cricket ball over a distance of 115 yards on his first attempt. Bonnor collected the money with a throw of 119 yards 5 inches. Bonnor offered to throw the ball 125 yards against the increased stake of £ 200. The passenger chickened out
2. Sam Staples and Harold Larwood laid a bet on whether Larwood would be able to knock off batsman Lall Singh's turban for a packet of cigarettes. Larwood won, of course
3. Rev. James Pycroft in his book *History of Cricket* relates incidents involving both teams trying to lose, each having placed a bet on the other

4. Derek Randall bet a pint of bitter with his Nottinghamshire team-mates that he could stand still for 10 minutes. Randall conceded defeat in 30 seconds, on the grounds that he wasn't thirsty
5. During the Leeds Test in 1981, Rod Marsh and Dennis Lillee backed England to win at 500-1. They collected £ 7500 at the end of the match after Australia had collapsed in a remarkable turnaround. Surprisingly, they were not censured
6. Younis Ahmed was also guilty of the same offence; he backed rivals Leicestershire to win a John Player League match in 1983. The news leaked; Worcestershire did not take too kindly to this. Younis was sacked
7. Lord Frederick Beauclerk, a cricketer of the 18th century, admitted making around £ 600 a year from cricket. The rumour was that he earned it by backing his opponents
8. John Woodcock, Brian Johnston and Colin Cowdrey once laid a bet during MCC's 1961-62 tour of Australia, on the time Rev. David Sheppard would take to complete his sermon at the Sydney Cathedral. The sermon lasted 28 minutes. Woodcock and Cowdrey paid up
9. Henry Taberer, who played for South Africa, once threw a cricket ball 100 yards, while standing in a tub, for a wager
10. Keith Miller offered Ian Johnson 6/4 odds that Australia, 375 runs behind on the first innings at Old Trafford in 1956, would not be able to save the game. Laker, 19 for 90, won England the match and Miller his bet
11. Doug Walters was challenged to an unusual wager by a colleague in the Australian team. Walters insisted that a six could be hit off an underarm delivery. His team-mate was not impressed. They went out and an underarm delivery was bowled. Walters charged out and let the ball hit his extended left toe. The ball popped up and walters swung it out of the playing area... and collected $ 1.
12. The man who perhaps made the biggest killing in the betting shop was an unnamed Indian supporter; he backed India to win the World Cup in 1983 before the tournament began. Having put £ 1000 at 50-1, he took home winnings worth £ 50,000 on 25 June

It's Amazing But True...

IT'S *AMAZING* BUT TRUE THAT...

1. ...The only animal to be credited with a mention in *Wisden*'s 'Births and Deaths' is Peter the cat. The cat was a familiar animal at Lord's
2. ...Bruce French and Jonathan Agnew saved the lives of two college girls on the Madras beach after the girls had been drawn out by a strong current during England's tour of India, 1984-85
3. ...the most important factor for choosing the cricket ground at Sharjah was that it had a parking space for 10,000 cars
4. ...Leslie Hylton, Test cricketer for the West Indies, was hanged for the murder of his wife in 1955 at the age of 50
5. ...Nusrat Bhutto, wife of the late Pakistan leader, had to take 3 stitches following a head wound, sustained while watching the Karachi Test between England and Pakistan, 1977-78
6. ...at the end of the Sydney Ashes Test in 1974-75, the total count of the number of drink cans that had been removed from the ground came to 864,000
7. ...the purchase of 300 protectors (boxes) by Avon and Somerset police in the wake of the St Paul's riots in Bristol in 1980 created an acute shortage in sports goods shops, causing many club batsmen to bat without them
8. ...Nicholas Wanostrocht had to adopt the pseudonym 'Felix' because he feared that his association with the game would bring his career as a school teacher into disrepute
9. ...Maninder Singh is the best chess player in the Indian team.
10. ...Chetan Chauhan's most feared bowler was Javed Miandad

WERE YOU AWARE THAT....

1. ... Famous Indian singer Lata Mangeshkar gets two complimentary tickets for each international match played in India
2. ...Narottam Puna, born in Surat, India, went on to play for New Zealand in Tests
3. ...General Zia-ul-Haq's first instructor in the army was Denis Compton
4. ...An air hostess on the Melbourne-Adelaide flight made this announcement following a news item that Gatting had missed

the start of play against Victoria because he had risen late: 'Passengers are reminded that they should be as quiet as possible during this trip because Mike Gatting is trying to catch up on his sleep'

5. ...Indian film actor Pran presented gold medals to six cricketers (4 Indian and 2 Pakistanis) at the conclusion of the Delhi Test in 1979-80
6. ...Indian cricketer Yograj Singh acted in a two-reel documentary on 'Forensic Science in Crime Detection'. He played the role of a murderer committing a sexual offence
7. ...Clive Lloyd uses six grips on his bat handle
8. ...the first-ever team from England to tour Australia took 65 days to sail from Liverpool to their port of call
9. ...before he made his Test debut for India, Hanumant Singh fielded as a substitute for Mike Smith's MCC side against India at Bombay, 1963-64
10. ...Lancashire's twelfth man B. W. Reidy fielded as a substitute for opponents Nott's at Trent Bridge in 1977 and later, stood in briefly as the square leg umpire, when umpire J. van Geloven left the field

BELIEVE IT OR NOT BUT...

1. ...Derek Pringle narrowly missed an Oscar for the best ad-libbing extra in *Chariots Of Fire*
2. ...the fastest woman bowler in the world bowls at around 70 mph (according to English woman quickie Sarah Potter)
3. ...the stumping of Allan Border in the fourth Test of the 1985 Ashes series was the first time a batsman had been stumped in Tests in England in five years
4. ...Dickie Bird rates woman fast bowler Sharon Tredrea as quick as Paul Allott
5. ...there is a picturesque small ground not far from Christchurch, called 'The Valley Of Peace', because no woman has ever been permitted to set foot on it
6. ...a Nobel Prize winner actually figures in *Wisden*. Samuel Beckett, who wrote *Waiting for Godot* played for Dublin University in the Twenties
7. ...Chris Cowdrey, playing for Kent, once refused to bowl in a 3-day match in 1984 because he had left his bowling boots on the bar of a London pub the night before
8. ...Gubby Allen asked cricket writer Crawford White to be on

'match alert' during the 1947-48 Caribbean tour after the England team had been depleted due to injuries

9. ...deaf cricketers have their own World Cup
10. ...Rex Alston, veteran commentator and reporter, read his own obituary in *The Times* by John Woodcock. He was in hospital recovering from an attack of food poisoning

SEVEN *PREDICTIONS* WHICH WERE SPOT-ON

1. Everton Weekes and Balwinder Singh Sandhu were probably the only two who predicted that India would win the World Cup in 1983 even before the competition had begun!
2. When an onlooker saw the bust of W.G. Grace being removed by two workmen from the Long Room at Lord's in 1939, he turned around to the gentleman sitting next to him and said: "My God, that can mean only one thing. That means war". A few days later, World War II broke out
3. E. R. Wilson passed the following comment on the eve of the 1932-33 Ashes series in Australia: 'He (Jardine) will probably win us back the Ashes but will also lose us a Dominion'. The series turned out to be bitterly acrimonious. Jardine employed leg-theory tactics, better known as Bodyline, and won the Ashes back 4-1
4. David Frith, editor of *Wisden Cricket Monthly,* once wrote: 'I have been waiting, with trepidation, for the moment when, with 6 runs needed off the final ball and a lot of money at stake, the bowler informs the umpire of a change of action and rolls the ball along the ground'. Twenty months later, Trevor Chappell bowled the last delivery of the Australia-New Zealand one-day match to Brian McKechnie underarm
5. An American financier was quoted in *Punch* in 1901 as follows : 'First-class cricket properly organized and run as an attractive variety show would be a fine paying concern'
6. Sunil Gavaskar remarked in June 1973: 'I am more than certain that 20-odd years hence, Indian cricket will be on top of the world'. It happened sooner that he thought...exactly 10 years later, India won the third World Cup, beating twice world champions West Indies in England
7. A. C. M. Croome, a theorist of the game, predicted in the 1920s: 'The next stage in the evolution of batting will be the perfecting of back play.' The next 50 years were to prove him correct

DID YOU KNOW THAT...

1. ...The TCCB is spending £ 10,000 in trying to devise an electronic contraption to help an umpire with lbw and caught-behind decisions
2. ...when Australian actress Kate Fitzpatrick was asked what she wanted for Christmas, she replied: 'Imran Khan'
3. ...in an attempt to prevent separatist demonstrations, spectators wishing to attend the India-Australia one-day game in Srinagar, 1986-87, were asked to register their names with the local bank
4. ...Alan Knott walked to physio Bernard Thomas' room with a sample of what had been in his stomach after falling ill one evening during the Delhi Test, 1976-77
5. ...Arthur Fagg of Kent and England read his own obituary. The confusion was a result of his having the same initials as those of his father. It was Fagg sr. who had passed away.
6. ...Australian cricketer Archie Jackson married on his deathbed
7. ...Major E. G. Wynyard fell out with Ranji after the latter had eaten his grapes
8. ... R. A. Young suggested in a theoritical pamphlet that captains be allowed to pour 100 gallons of water on any part of the pitch they wished
9. ...Sunil Gavaskar, under contract with Thums Up, expressed the wish that it be served to him while batting. Campa Cola, a rival protested as they had paid a royalty for serving their products exclusively at the ground during a Test in Delhi. The batsman countered that he 'had a superstition' that he would not be able to bat well without Thums Up. Gavaskar lost the argument – and scored 46
10. ...Frank Worrell studied sociology at Manchester University, was appointed Warden of the University College of the West Indies and later became a senator in the Jamaican parliament

YOU'D NEVER BELIEVE IT BUT...

1. ...England players were banned from chewing gum after Rick Darling was hit by Bob Willis. Darling nearly died as the gum that he was chewing lodged in the back of his throat
2. ...Channel Nine actually employed actress Kate Fitzpatrick in their TV commentary team for the Brisbane Test between

Australia and West Indies in 1983-84

3. ...a spectator was knocked unconscious by a boundary hit by Wayne Larkins on the last day of a Somerset-Northants match at Taunton, 1981
4. ...Denis Compton became a father for the fifth time at the age of 66
5. ...two youths, aged 15 and 17, were charged with the rape of a 16-year-old American girl at the University Cricket Ground at Oxford, August 1984
6. ...match adjudicator Fred Trueman switched the Man of the Match award to Viv Richards because the Pakistanis did not bother to show up at the awards ceremony after a World Cup match in 1983
7. ...umpires in Tamil Nadu, a state in India, examined identity cards for the K. S. Ranga Rao Memorial Tournament before allowing players to bat. This precaution was necessitated as it was discovered that players had resorted to changing their appearance with wigs, beards and crew cuts after being eliminated in the early rounds in the tournament
8. ...a Channel Nine helicopter helped to dry the pitch after rain had held up the Queensland-Victoria Sheffield Shield match at Brisbane, 1980-81
9. ...Tony Greig suffered an epileptic attack on the field when making his Currie Cup debut in South Africa, 1970-71. Ali Bacher and Peter Pollock ran to Greig's rescue and the seizure was passed off as a sunstroke
10. ...Gerry Gomez was a Test selector when he umpired a Test in the West Indies

EIGHT UNCANNY *COINCIDENCES*

1. Born within a mile and 18 months of each other, the three Ws followed each other into the West Indian batting order. They were also among the best batsmen of their time – Weekes, Worrell and Walcott
2. Australian batsman Clem Hill hit 99, 98 and 97 in successive Test innings against England in 1901-02
3. During the Karachi Test between England and Pakistan in 1972-73, as many as 3 batsmen were dismissed on 99 – Majid Khan, Mushtaq Mohammed and Dennis Amiss
4. For all four possible results (tie, win, draw, loss) in Tests after World War II, India has recorded the highest fourth-innings

scores; 347 in the tie versus Australia, Madras, 1986; 406 for 4 to beat the West Indies at Trinidad, 1976; 429 for 8 to draw the game versus England at the Oval, 1979; and 445 when they lost to Australia, 1977-78. It might be interesting to note that Gavaskar played for India in each of these matches

5. On the same day that Ian Botham hit 99 before lunch against India at Leeds in 1979, his best friend Viv Richards also hit 99 before lunch – playing for Somerset against Middlesex at Lord's
6. The scorebook entry 'Lillee caught Willey bowled Dilley' was recorded in the match between England and Australia at Perth, 1979-80
7. Stokesley and Stockton, playing against each other in the North Yorkshire South Durham Under-17 Cup, tied, having scored 145 runs in 24 overs. In their rematch, they tied again, 118 apiece. Stokesley won at the third attempt – 111 to 54
8. During the Lord's Test between Pakistan and England in 1982, David Gower, Allan Lamb and Robin Jackman went to dinner together. They ordered duck. The following day all three were out for ducks

...AND TWO WHICH BEAT THEM ALL

9. At 3.33 pm during the day/night match between Australia and the West Indies at the SCG on 19.1.82, the scoreboard read :
   'Viv Richards 33
   F. Bacchus 3
   Wickets 3
   Last man (Gomes) 3
   G. Chappell 0 for 3
10. In the first-ever Test in 1877, Australia beat England by 45 runs. In the Centenary Test 100 years later, the result was exactly the same. The first day of the 1877 Test produced 166 runs. The first day of the Centenary Test produced 167

Memorable Lines

THE FIVE USUAL *EXCUSES* ON DROPPING A CATCH

1. 'The sun was in my eyes'
2. 'I thought *he* was going for it'
3. 'I lost the ball in the crowd'
4. 'It was beyond my reach'
5. 'Catch? What catch?'

FOUR RODNEY HOGG *INTERPRETATIONS*

1. Silly mid on…so called because you had to be stupid to stand there
2. Point…where the captain sends you from A to B
3. The field…where the captain sent you all day to ogle the crowd
4. A bouncer…has the same effect as being thrown out of a pub

THE FIVE COMMONEST *JUSTIFICATIONS* ON GETTING OUT

By Jonathan Rice

1. The bowler's chucker
2. I wanted to watch the 3.15 from Haydock
3. My bio-rhythms are all wrong
4. It's the rhubarb I had for lunch
5. I've got money on the opposition to win

– *Wisden Cricket Monthly*

FIVE *IMMORTAL* LINES BY SIR NEVILLE CARDUS

1. 'He never made a Christian stroke in all his life'. (On Ranji)
2. A cut which he flashed from Macdonald just before lunch caused us to blink; it was light reflected brightly from a day that is gone' (On Charlie Macartney).
3. 'Hobbs was the bridge over which classical cricket marched to the more complex epoch of the present'.
4. 'I imagine that he was created one day by God scooping up the nearest acre of Yorkshire soil at hand, then breathing into it saying, "Now, lad, tha's called Emmott Robinson and tha can go on with the new ball at t'pavilion end' (On Emmott Robinson).
5. 'It gets me a table at the Savoy' (On his knighthood).

TEN CLICHED *PHRASES* IN CRICKET REPORTING (in order)

1. 'glorious uncertainties of the game'
2. 'gentleman's game'
3. 'driver's seat'
4. 'tame draw'
5. 'the wicket is full of runs'
6. 'commanding position'
7. 'opened his account'
8. 'the match is evenly poised'
9. 'finding the gap'
10. 'had a few words with the umpire' (a recent addition)

SEVEN FAMOUS *PROMOTION* LINES

As part of the strategy to popularize the game amongst the masses in Australia, advertising campaigns giving the season a definite level have helped.

1. 'Series of the Century': Tests between Australia and West Indies, 1975-76 .
2. 'Superseason': Australian season, 1979-80 (England, Australia, W. Indies) .
3. 'Thunder Down Under': Australian season,1983-84 (Pakistan, Australia, W. Indies) .
4. 'Showdown For the Crown': Australian season, 1984-85 (Australia, W. Indies, Sri Lanka) .
5. 'Greatest Show on Turf': World Championship, 1985 .
6. 'Double Trouble': Australian season, 1985-86 (Australia, India, N. Zealand) .
7. 'Clashes For The Ashes': Australian season, 1986-87 (Australia, England, W. Indies) .

FIVE CLASSIC *LINES* YOU COULD ONLY EXPECT FROM ARTHUR MAILEY

1. 'Against such weak batting, I could have taken 10 for 47 – only that it wouldn't have sounded so good' (after he had taken 10/66 versus Gloucestershire in 1921).
2. 'Few chances were given but I think a chap in a tweed coat dropped Ryder near the shilling stand' (after taking 4 for 362 against Victoria in 1926-27).
3. 'He must have practised his run up in his sentry box' (on ex-guardsman Alan Oakman's run-up off only 3-4 steps).

4. 'I bowled tripe. Now I sell it' (over his meat shop).
5. 'None for some' (on his grave).

FOUR LINES IN APPRECIATION OF THE WRITER-KNIGHT *NEVILLE CARDUS*

1. 'We shall not see his like again and when he stopped writing brightness fell from the air'. (Arthur Gibson).
2. 'The lasting achievement of Neville Cardus is that in company with Bernard Darwin, he made writing about sport into a popular art'. (Michael Kennedy).
3. 'The father of literate sports writing'. (John Arlott).
4. 'His ghost walks there still on that sacred turf together with the great names he knew so well'. (Gordon Ross).

...AND A DISSENTING VOICE

'What Cardus knew about the game could be written on the back of a post-card' – a distinguished cricket writer who preferred to remain anonymous.

***YABBA*'S SEVEN FAMOUS ONE-LINERS**

(Legendary Australian barracker who sold rabbits for a living, Yabba illuminated play in Sydney during the early part of this century with his sparkling wit)

1. 'It's no use umpire; you'll have to wait until lunch time like the rest of us' (gawking at the umpire's upraised hand).
2. 'Don't worry, son, it would have bowled me' (after Tibby Cotter had bowled a batsman).
3. 'Please, can I bat with a knitting needle' (if runs were easy to get).
4. 'Whoa, he's bolted!' (when J. W. Hearne broke a runless spell).
5. 'Mind your stays, old man!' (to Douglas Jardine).
6. 'Throw him a piano; let's see if he can play that!'
7. 'Your length's lousy but you bowl a good width' (at one Victorian medium pace bowler).

CRICKETERS WHO CARRIED THE GAME TO THEIR *GRAVE*

Five lines on tombstones.

1. 'Bowled at last': On the grave of R. G. Barlow, Lancashire and England

2. 'None for some': On Arthur Mailey's grave
3. 'I bow'd, I struck, I caught, I stopp'd
   Sure life's a game of cricket;
   I block'd with care, with caution popp'd,
   Yet Death has hit my wicket.'
   – Epitaph of The Salisbury Cricketer
4. 'For his skill as a cricketer and his work as a Man': Fuller Pilch, one of the finest cricketers of the early 19th century
5. 'To the memory of John Willes Esq., of Bellingham in this parish. Born 1777, died 1852, at Staunton, near Gloucester. He was a patron of many sports and the first to introduce round-arm bowling in cricket. This memorial is erected by the few friends who remember him as a genuine sportsman, staunch friend, kind neighbour and genial companion.'

THE DYING *WORDS* OF SIX CRICKETERS

1. 'Keep going': Hedley Verity during the Second World War
2. 'Neuralgia, I think; I have a pain here': W. Murdoch, suffering an apoplectic fit while watching a Test in 1911
3. 'Bury me 22 yards from Arthur (Shrewsbury), so I can send him down a ball now and then': Alfred Shaw
4. 'Forget me like this. Remember me like I used to be when they couldn't beat me': George Brown
5. 'If I could only sleep': Ranji
6. 'Blue, you can have the fish supper on your own': Tibby Cotter after having been shot in the head during World War I at Beersheba, South Palestine

HIT ON THE...OOPS, WHAT DO YOU CALL IT?

Thirteen substitutes used in describing the abdomen in cricket reporting.

1. 'The ball struck Barnes between wind and water' (Neville Cardus).
2. 'Dexter has been hit in the breadbasket, perhaps slightly lower' (E. W. Swanton).
3. 'Below the belt' (Peter Johnson).
4. 'Pit of the stomach' (Mike Stevenson).
5. 'In the box' (Derek Hodgson).
6. 'The private parts' (Paul Fitzpatrick).
7. 'Suffered a severe blow on the crotch' (A *Guardian* sub-

editor's version).

8. 'Struck amidships' (John Thicknesse).
9. 'The nether regions' (Lawrie Mumford).
10. 'In the groin' (Brian Bearshaw).
11. 'Pubic area or scrotal sack' (A physiotherapist).
12. 'Male hammer' (Mike Brearley).
13. 'Wood having retired...' (The *Express*).

SIX OF THE MOST MOVING LINES IN CRICKET *LITERATURE*

1. 'He was clean bowled on the occasion I have in mind for none, but nobody other than a giant of the game could have made a duck so immaculately. He played cricket as some proud Roman might have played it' (Sir Neville Cardus on Archie MacLaren).
2. 'Cricket has achieved a unique place in the English scene because its champions were admired for themselves. They were men of dignity who stood in the eyes of their countrymen for a code of conduct' (E. W. Swanton).
3. 'The cricket player is not an actor on a stage, merely a personality to be lost in the creation of a poet's brain or a playwright's mind; he is himself the poet and the playwright' (A. E. Knight).
4. 'The essence of the champion is either inherent in the individual or it isn't and he prefers to work out a destiny along his own lines' (Jack Fingleton).
5. 'What do they know of cricket who only cricket know?' (C. L. R. James).
6. 'The noblest fires, whether of batting or bowling, can be fed only by the concurrent culture of every power we have' (A. E. Knight).

– *Selected* by Raju Mukherjee

WHAT THEY SAID WHEN INDIA *WON* THE WORLD CUP, 1983

1. 'I didn't know there were so many Indians in London, mate, until they won this bleedin' cricket match' (A London fruit seller).
2. 'Not today, this is India's day' (Sir Gary Sobers, when asked for an autograph).
3. 'Simply unbelievable' (Bishen Bedi).

4. 'My slogan is: "Indian can do it" '. (Mrs Indira Gandhi)
5. 'Simply thousands of miles away you could almost smell the joyful whiff of November 5 cordite, mixed in the sultry scents of jasmine, frangipani, cowdung smoke and curry' (Frank Keating of *The Guardian*).
6. 'A feat which will rank among the finest achievements of the country' (Editorial in *The Telegraph,* a Calcutta daily).
7. 'I have had to eat some of my own words, but what a delight it has been to do so' (Isif Iqbal).
8. 'The shock will do us all good' (Matthew Engel of *The Guardian*).
9. 'We are still to get down to earth' (Roger Binny).
10. 'We are being treated like gods' (Mohinder Amarnath).
11. 'Luck played a great part ' (Kapil Dev).
12. 'The greatest day since Independence' (An Indian).

FIVE FAMOUS *UNDERSTATEMENTS*

1. Johnny Tyldesly once wrote in the *Daily Mail:* 'On a perfect Worcester wicket we had the good luck to win the toss. Mr MacLaren was at his best, and Mr Spooner scored all round the wicket in his finest style. I also managed to get a few'. Maclaren had scored 86, Spooner 46 and Tyldesly 186 not out!
2. 'It would be wrong to paint a black picture. We have been playing a very well organized and talented side', said David Gower during the tour of West Indies in 1985-86. England lost 0-5
3. 'It's just a piece of wood...' – Viv Richards on his achievements with the bat
4. 'I think I was a very good player before the War. Afterwards, I was more stereotyped', felt Jack Hobbs. The Surrey and England batsman scored more first-class centuries than any one and retired with 61,237 runs in the game
5. 'The better team won,' said Australian captain Jack Ryder after his side had been defeated in what must rate as one of the most one-sided matches in Test history. England won by 675 runs. It was Bradman's first Test

TEN IMMORTAL *CARDUS* LINES

1. 'He was himself, morning, noon and night, and inimitable.' (On George Gunn).

2. 'A snick by a Jack Hobbs is a sort of disturbance of cosmic orderliness'.
3. 'If all that we know today of batsmanship as a science were somehow taken from our consciousness, the grammer and alphabet could be deduced from the cricket of Hutton, and codified again. He is all the text books in an omnibus edition.'
4. 'He was always the gentleman. He might well have kept wicket in the gloves in which he was married'. (On Bert Oldfield).
5. 'Some cricketers – especially batsmen – are born; some have old age thrust upon them, while in the act of batting.'
6. 'When he came up to the wicket to release the ball, he called to mind a great wave of the sea about to break.' (On Tom Richardson).
7. 'His was the batsmanship of good manners.' (On Ernest Tyldesly).
8. 'Please, God, let Victor Trumper score a century today for Australia vs England out of a total of 137 all out.'
9. 'Trent Bridge...where it was always afternoon and 304 for two'.
10. 'To be stumped by Oldfield off Grimmett is like an amputation done under an anaesthetic.'

(*Researched* by Dr Surapriya Mukherjee)

WHAT CRICKETERS HAVE SAID ABOUT *MOTIVATION*

1. 'I'll die for a cap and kill for my captain' (Australian wicket keeper Tim Zoehrer).
2. 'I hate the batsmen. They are the enemy. I prey on them' (Wayne Daniel).
3. 'When I gripped the ball I loved the game and hated the batsman' (Harold Larwood).
4. 'I want to hit you, baby. I want to hit you over the heart' (Peter Heine to Trevor Bailey).
5. 'I want blokes who are prepared to go out there and die on the field' (Tony Greig).
6. 'I try to get them before they get me.' (Dilip Vengsarkar when playing fast bowlers).
7. 'Come on lads. Let's get a thirst on for tonight' (Godfrey Evans often used this line to inspire team-mates during the last session of an exacting day).

8. 'A cricketer should be ready to bleed for Middlesex' (Sir Pelham Warner).
9. 'The sight of the glossy ball made me want to use it' (Kapil Dev).
10. 'The sound of the ball hitting the batsman's skull was music to my ears' (Jeff Thomson).

SIX *QUEEN-PLAYER* EXCHANGES

It is customary for England's royalty to visit Lord's during a Test match. Exchanges between the player and Her Majesty have always been pleasant, sometimes hilarious.

1. 'I see it is a family affair,' Queen Elizabeth told Sunil Gavaskar when he had introduced G. R. Vishwanath to her as his brother-in-law.
2. 'I have heard a lot about you.' To a West Indian fast bowler, who replied : 'I have heard a lot about you too.'
3. When Dennis Lillee asked Queen Elizabeth for her autograph during the Centenary Test in 1977, she replied with a smile: 'Oh no, there are so many people around'.
4. 'I am very well and how are you, Your Majesty?' (A West Indian fast bowler.)
5. 'G'day Queen'. (Dennis Lillee, 1975.)
6. 'Sir!' (An official touring with the Indian team.)

TEN MORE IMMORTAL *QUOTES* ON CRICKET

1. 'It's better than being down t'pit.' (Geoff Boycott)
2. 'As is customary when great issues hang in the balance, men set themselves to a quiet but determined enjoyment. They turn to cricket as to an old friend, who gives you a seat, a glass of beer and something to talk about.' (R. C. Robertson-Glasgow) .
3. 'What do they know of cricket who only cricket know?' (C. L. R. James) .
4. 'Cricket? It civilizes people and creates good gentlemen. I want everyone to play cricket in Zimbabwe. I want ours to be a nation of gentlemen.' (Robert Mugabe) .
5. 'I want to play cricket. It doesn't seem to matter whether you win or lose'. (Rock star Meatloaf) .
6. '...a game more British than Asian'. (A group in Pakistan demanding that cricket be banned. They felt that attendances

fell at mosques when India-Pakistan matches were telecast 'live' in 1982-83).

7. 'Cricket is a stalwart Goliath striding across the British Empire. MCC is his devoted wife, anxious only to further his best interest'. (Sir Home Gordon).
8. '...a game of eunuchs'. (Theologian Dr Israr Ahmed)
9. 'Basically an individual's sport disguised as a team game'. (Geoff Boycott).
10. 'Cricket for peace is my mission'. (General Zia ul Haq).

TEN NOTABLE *TELEGRAMS*

1. 'SATISFACTORY. A TRIER': To Bill O'Reilly from his school students after he had taken his hundredth Test wicket
2. 'CONGRATULATION SELF AND WHOLE TEAM, PARTICULARLY TO MARTIN SNEDDEN, WHO BOWLED THE LAST BALL OVERARM': To Geoff Howarth from the then New Zealand Prime Minister Robert Muldoon, after New Zealand's 2-run victory over England in a WSC match, 1982-83
3. 'CONGRATULATIONS. MAGNIFICENT BOWLING. GOOD LUCK ALL MATCHES ARCHIE JACKSON': To Harold Larwood from a dying Archie Jackson, Australian batsman, in hospital
4. 'BRAVO': To Harld Larwood from the MCC
5. 'WELL BOWLED, NOTTS': To Harold Larwood from the MCC
6. 'YOUR TASK IS HARDER THAN MINE WAS': To Len Hutton in Australia, 1954-55, from Douglas Jardine
7. 'KEEP CORPSE ON ICE TILL INNINGS DECLARED': Sent by Dr. E. M. Grace to his clinic in Bristol after he had received a request for his presence at an inquest. Dr. E. M. Grace was a coroner by profession
8. 'THAT'S THE ONLY WAY TO SHOW THE BASTARDS GOOD WISHES BRIAN BARBARA AND THE KIDS': To Geoff Boycott from footballer Brian Clough, after the Yorkshire opener had scored a century on the opening day of the county championship season
9. 'YOU HAVE DONE FOR AUSTRALIAN CRICKET WHAT THE BOSTON STRANGLER DID FOR DOOR-TO-DOOR SALESMEN': To Geoff Boycott from Australian

Mr Jack Burney, after the England batsman had scored a painstakingly slow fifty in the second Ashes Test, 1978-79.

10. 'SINCERE CONGRATULATIONS TO YOU ALL, EDWARD P.': To Percy Chapman from the Prince of Wales, after Chapman's side had retained the Ashes in Australia, 1928-29

TWELVE LINES WORTH *REMEMBERING*

1. 'Joe Guy, all ease and elegance; fit to play before the Queen in Her Majesty's parlour'.
2. 'An Oval sausage roll was a poor thing compared to a Yankee stadium hotdog'. (Paul Gallico)
3. 'My God, Jacker, look what they've sent me. Do they think I am playing the blind eleven?' (Captain Archie MacLaren to F. S. Jackson after seeing the England team selected to play Australia in 1901-02)
4. 'Drinking the best tea in the world on an empty cricket ground – that,I think, is the final pleasure left to man' (C. P. Snow)
5. 'There are so many great players out there. So many kings...we come in cycles' (Viv Richards)
6. 'Knott ravaged by Anno Domini is as unthinkable as Peter Pan with side-whiskers' (Paul Weaver)
7. 'Please, Wilfred, give me some peace' (Victor Trumper after being tormented and teased by Wilfred Rhodes in a Test)
8. 'If ability is any guide, the alphabet is the wrong way round' (David Foot on Zaheer Abbas)
9. 'Ten for 49 would not have sounded good enough'. (Arthur Mailey, after having 10 for 66 in a match versus Glocestershire in 1921. An observer pointed out that Mailey had given away a few runs which could have been saved; Mailey, ever the wit, had a ready reply)
10. 'I avoid the billing of "Test match" out of concern for prosecution under the Trade Descriptions Act. A test it obviously is. A match it is most certainly not' (Ian Woolridge referring to the Kingston Test between England and the West Indies, 1973-74)
11. When bowler John Warr of England was asked whether his figures for the 1950-51 tour of Australia were "73 overs, 281 runs and one wicket," he replied: 'That's right. I remember exactly because Hymn number 281 asks 'Art thou weary, Art

thou languid, Art thou sore distressed?'

12. I felt like a boy who had killed a dove'. (Arthur Mailey on clean bowling Victor Trumper in a Sydney club match)

FAMOUS *LINES* THAT DID THE TRICK

1. 'Don't give up, let's fight it out together' (Kapil Dev to his team-mates before going out to defend a meagre total of 183 in the World Cup final against the West Indies in 1983. India bowled the West Indies out for 140 and won an unforgettable encounter).
2. 'Don't worry skipper, if I can see 'em I'll hit 'em' (Lancashire's David Hughes when faced with an intimidating 24 runs to get in the last over of a Gillette Cup match in 1971 against Gloucestershire. Hughes scored 26 not out and won the match for his side).
3. *'Tu sau kar de, bas aur mainu kuch nahi chaida'* (You just get a century. I don't want anything else) – Lala Amarnath to his son Mohinder at Lahore in 1982. The younger Amarnath got the hundred all right.
4. 'Mean it makes no difference if you bat lower. The score will still be zero' (Viv Richards to Sunil Gavaskar after the latter came out to bat in Madras, 1983-84, on a hat trick. Gavaskar went on to score an unbeaten 236).
5. 'Before the Australian team toured India in 1984, they were lectured by psychologist Dick Telford on motivation, professionalism and attitude. Dr Telford, who is the senior adviser to marathoner Rob de Castella, made an impact; the Australians went on to beat the Indians in India in a series of limited-overs games.
6. 'Girls don't play cricket' (As a child while playing cricket in the street, Rachel Heyhoe Flint, her brother and his friends landed in trouble. A policeman walked up and took the boys' names down. When she insisted that her name should be taken down as well, this was the policeman's furious reply. The girl went on to become one of the leading women cricketers of all time).
7. 'Frank, England hath need of thee' (Len Hutton tossed the ball to Frank Tyson with these words during the 1954-5 Ashes series. Tyson, who used lines from Shakespeare and Wordsworth to inspire himself, appeared to have been appropriately charged. He went on to take 28 wickets in the

series at around 21 runs apiece).

8. 'I bumped into Geoff Boycott at Brisbane and he gave me some good advice. He said that I must bowl fast in Australia when the ball is hard and new, because it soon gets soft and the batsmen then flourish when the shine has worn off. He said that I definitely had the capacity to bowl fast and I set out to prove him right' (Imran Khan, psychologically fortified, picked up 12 for 165 in the third Test at Sydney in 1976-77. Pakistan won its first Test on Australian soil).'
9. 'Remember, Wes, if you bowl a no-ball, you'll never be able to go back to Barbados' (That line of Frank Worrell, bowler Wes Hall later admitted, got him together. With scores tied between West Indies and Australia at Brisbane in 1960, Hall made sure his boot landed a foot behind the crease for the next ball. Joe Solomon relieved his anxiety by running out Ian Meckiff and making history).

Miscellany

THE FIVE BOYHOOD *HEROES* OF RANJAN MADUGALLE

1. Doug Walters
2. Roy Dias
3. Michael Holding
4. Sunil Gavaskar
5. Ajit de Silva

THREE *HEROES* DAVID GOWER DREAMT OF EMULATING

1. John Edrich
2. Gary Sobers
3. Graeme Pollock

FIVE CRICKETERS WHO COULD HAVE BEEN SUCCESSFUL *DECATHLETES*

By Dennis Waight, the West Indian team's physiotherapist

1. Martin Crowe
2. Ian Botham
3. Viv Richards

4. Imran Khan (before the stress fracture of his shin in 1983)
5. Gordon Greenidge

FIVE WAYS IN WHICH ROD MARSH PREPARED FOR THE SEASON AHEAD

1. Got cracking at least 4 months before the first game.
2. Reached the peak of his fitness 2 months before the season got underway.
3. Ran a series of short sprints at every training session.
4. Practised catching at a close range for at least 15 minutes every training session without gloves.
5. Stood about 3 metres away from a team-mate and threw the ball wider and wider until they were diving yards and holding on to most of the catches.

THE MOST HOT-TEMPERED CRICKETERS ACCORDING TO DILIP VENGSARKAR

1. S. Venkataraghavan ('We generally tried to steer clear of his temper').
2. Viv Richards ('Sometimes niggling things upset him').
3. Imran Khan ('He blows up when he finds a fielder not giving his best').
4. Bishen Bedi ('Boy, could he get wild...')
5. I can't think of any other to rank in this company.

THE MOST EXPENSIVE ITEMS OF *CRICKETANA* SOLD IN ENGLAND

1. A set of *Wisden*s for about £ 15,000 (sold in piecemeal lots).
2. A W G Grace linen handkerchief which fetched £ 850.
3. A suitcase full of Percy Fender's photographs, letters, diaries and menus for £ 600.
4. 'Spy' caricatures (originals) of Spofforth and Bonnor at over £ 2,000 each.
5. A painting too unspectacular to recall but which fetched about £ 7,000.

– David Frith (*from memory*)

THE FIRST *BLACK* TO...

... represent England was Roland Butcher.
... be elected to honorary life membership of the MCC was

'Snuffy' Browne.

... play for Australia was Samuel Morris (and the only one to date).

... lead the West Indies was George Headley.

... play for South Africa was Omar Henry.

... to be made a Peer and knighted was Learie Constantine.

... to be given a memorial service in Westminster Abbey was Sir Frank Worrell.

THREE CRICKETERS WHO WERE HOAXED

1. Peter Smith arrived at The Oval to play against West Indies for England in 1933, only to learn that the invitation telegram was a hoax. He did not represent his country until 13 years later.
2. Krish Srikkanth flew to Bombay in 1984 with the intention of joining the Indian team in Pakistan on receiving a telephone call. It was only somebody posing as selector Hanumant Singh on the telephone.
3. West Indian Basil Williams received a cable on the last day of the Bombay Test, 1978-79, that his mother had expired in the Caribbean. When he reached Hyderabad he spoke to her on the telephone!

SWAROOP KISHEN'S FIVE MOST *GENTLEMANLY* CRICKETERS

1. Lance Gibbs
2. B. Chandrasekhar
3. Kim Hughes
4. M. Amarnath
5. G. Vishwanath

FIVE *CHANGES* THAT ASIF IQBAL EXPECTS TO SEE IN CRICKET IN THE NEXT 50 YEARS

1. Cricket going in a big way to America which will totally revolutionize the game
2. Test matches at night to accommodate the office-goer
3. Off-shore Test matches i.e. West Indies playing Australia in New Zealand
4. An annual limited-overs tournament involving all Test playing countries

5. The money generated in the game could increase ten fold. More people will watch the game on TV, which again will result in a lot more revenue from advertisements. I can envisage a situation where very few people will turn up to watch matches at the ground. It could become like what baseball is in America today

TEN MAJOR *INNOVATIONS* AND THE PEOPLE BEHIND THEM

1. Round-arm bowling – J. Willes' sister, 1807
2. Over-arm bowling – E. Willsher, 1862
3. Standing up to the stumps – J. Blackham, 1877
4. The googly – B.J.T. Bosanquet, 1901
5. Umbrella field – Keith Carmody, 1945
6. Pads – Robert Robinson, end 18th century
7. Batting Gloves – Nicholas 'Felix' Wanostrocht, 1835
8. Wicketkeeping gloves – Manufactured by Duke and Son, 1848
9. Off break – A farmer called Lambert
10. The helmet – first used by Graham Yallop in a Test match

THE TRADITIONAL CONCEPT OF TOURING ACCORDING TO PHIL EDMONDS

1. The first tour : New and exciting, and you are learning
2. The second tour : New to the extent that it is a different place, but by the end of it, you are beginning to wonder
3. The third tour : About halfway through, you think – shit! What am I doing in this place for four months when I could be home with the wife and the kids?

Phil Edmonds : A Singular Man by Simon Barnes

FIVE REASONS WHY BEING A *MANAGER* IS NOT A JOKE

By Raj Singh Dungarpur

1. My appetite is so great that I end up eating more food in the dressing room than any player – including Ravi Shastri
2. I am beginning to get very conscious of myself because Sunil Gavaskar, Srikkanth and Shivlal Yadav can imitate me so well
3. I am very frustrated. I read so much about the Kapil Dev-Sunil

Gavaskar feud but have not seen the two get into a single argument on the four tours that I have managed the Indian team

4. I get very lonely because I am the only one in the side without a Walkman
5. ...because V. Prabhudesai will not be around any more to assist me. We made an excellent pair of heavyweight managers

HAPPINESS IS...

'Being the middle of Norman Cowans' bat – it never gets used' (Stephen Smith).
'Feilding at slip with Graeme Fowler batting' (Christopher Norris).
'To find out after all that, Sir Jack scored those 3 centuries and Sir Donald those 4 runs' (Mahinda Wijesinghe).
'When a county cricketer speaks to you in the year before or after his benefit year' (John Criggen).
'Having the West Indian team agreeing to tour South Africa and being banned for life–before the next series against England' (Anthony George).
'Seeing Ian Botham performing in Swan Lake' (Christopher Norris).

– *Wisden Cricket Monthly*,

FOR WINNING THE *PRUDENTIAL CUP* IN 1983, THE INDIANS RECEIVED...

...£ 2,500 from Swraj Paul, an Indian industrialist in London.
...Rs 125,000 from the chief minister of Maharashtra.
...Rs 100,000 from the Mayor of Ahmedabad.
...Rs 350,000 from the Indian Board.
...Rs 20,00,000 by way of proceeds from a cultural show in New Delhi.
...£20,000 as prize money and £ 600 to Man of the Match Mohinder Amarnath.
...Rs 50,000 by way of a donation from Charanjit Singh, MP.
...Flats from the Delhi and Districts Cricket Association to the Delhi players in the team.
...free bags of rice for a year from a North Indian businessman.
...complimentary tickets from Air India for players' wives and children for the return flight from London to Bombay.

...free supply of beer for a year from a brewery, which later introduced a new brand to commemorate the event: Trophy.
...The replica of the pickaxe used by mountaineers Ahluwalia and Kohli on their Everest climb of 1965.

FIVE *SOUVENIRS* I'D NEVER PART WITH

By Raj Singh Dungarpur

1. A book signed by Sir Neville Cardus which he presented to me. He wrote on the fly leaf : 'With love for Indian cricket'.
2. Six bottles of champagne which were consumed after matches that India won – at Wankhede Stadium vs England in 1981 and 1984; vs Pakistan in 1979-80; the 1983 World Cup win and the victories at Lord's and Leeds in 1986 over England.
3. Vinoo Mankad's bat.
4. An ash tray stolen from the dressing room at Melbourne after India's win over Australia in 1980-81.
5. The ball with which Subhash Gupte, the Indian leg spinner, bowled his last delivery in first-class cricket before he migrated to the West Indies.

WE *DARE* YOU TO...

...call Greg Matthews a queer.
...sit through 5 days of a Madras Test in a 3-piece suit.
...give Joel Garner a piggy-back ride.
...ring Viv Richards for an interview at 2.30 am.
...tell Kapil Dev that he has a Haryanvi accent.
...convince Geoff Boycott that his defence is suspect.
...ask Syed Kirmani who styles his hair.
...give Imran Khan a complex about his looks – inferiority, that is!
...tell Ian Botham that he ought to go back to Sunday school.

THE SEVEN *INTERRUPTIONS* IN GEOFF BOYCOTT'S CAREER

1. July 1968; back injury during the Edgbaston Test; missed rest of the season
2. September 1969; struck by John Snow; a broken bone in his hand kept him out of the season
3. February 1971; struck by Mckenzie in the Sydney Test; missed the remainder of the tour
4. July 1972; struck by Willis at Leeds on his right hand; ten

stitches on his middle finger; out for three months, missed 3 Tests

5. 1974-77 : self exile
6. January 1982; sent back to England after the Calcutta Test; ostensibly the return was on medical grounds but the world knew that Boycott had been disciplined for preferring golf to fielding during the Calcutta Test; missed the rest of the series.
7. 1982-1985 : banned for taking part in a 'rebel' tour of South Africa

REGRETS OF FIVE CRICKETERS CRICKET WRITERS

1. Basil D'Oliveira – 'I can honestly say I have only one regret in life, and that is I didn't come to England sooner'.
2. Dilip Vengsarkar – 'I wish I had worked harder on my fitness'.
3. Viv Richards – 'Trusting people too much and being let down by them'.
4. Robin Marlar – 'To me it seems a matter of regret that Clive Lloyd has been granted British citizenship; spending the rest of his life in racially divided Guyana might have been suitable penance for helping to destroy much that was precious in cricket'.
5. Sunil Gavaskar – 'The only thing that will bother me when I hang up my boots is that I have not scored a century in Sri Lanka'.

FOUR THINGS ROBIN MARLAR WAS *WORRIED* ABOUT ACCORDING TO JOHN BENAUD (1979-80)

1. Australian cricket's administrators, players, TV commentators
2. Dennis Lillee's bald spot and aluminium bat
3. Ian Chappell's vocabulary
4. The effect all that might have on the Lord's Centenary Test

...AND WAS NOT WORRIED ABOUT

1. Dennis Lillee's bowling
2. Ian Chappell's batting
3. The effect they might have on the same Test
4. His own bald spot

(Robin Marlar is the cricket writer of the *Sunday Times*. Benaud, a former Australian Test cricketer, is a prominent journalist)

— *Australian Cricket*

SEVEN *PREDICTIONS* THAT MISFIRED

1. 'I think one day he will develop into a really great one-day batsman' (Jim Burke said this of Ian Davis. The latter went on to play 3 one-day internationals for Australia, scoring 12 runs at an average of 6.00).
2. Ian Colquhon, who played for New Zealand against England in 1955, fell out of bed as he dreamt that he dropped Len Hutton. He went on to catch Hutton in each innings of the match.
3. 'Jeff Thomson looks like a flash in the pan'. (Keith Miller)
4. 'Our aim is to win 6-0' (Graham Yallop before the 1978-79 Ashes series, before losing 1-5).
5. 'We will make them grovel' (Tony Greig's confidence was misplaced. The West Indies went on to beat England 3-0 in the 1976 series).
6. '...Pakistan will smash India to pulp' (Captain Sunil Gavaskar didn't mind being proved wrong on this occasion. His side went on to beat Pakistan 2-0 in the 1979-80 series).
7. 'He will always be in the category of the brilliant and unsound ones...he does not correct mistakes or look as if he were trying to' (Percy Fender on Don Bradman in 1930. In the very next game Bradman hit 252 not out against Fender's team).

TEN UNUSUAL *AWARDS* OR PRESENTATIONS

1. Ian Botham received *Playboy*'s Victoria Club Champagne Century Award in 1979-80 which comprised 100 bottles of bubbly
2. Derek Randall got 174 chops from a butcher in England after scoring 174 in the Centenary Test against Australia in 1977
3. Australian policemen at Melbourne in 1977-78 presented Indian spinner B. S. Chandrasekhar with two large pies. They had promised him a pizza each time he took 5 wickets in an innings
4. Percy Chapman received a gold cricket ball after a game versus Bendigo, the once famous gold mining town, on MCC's 1928-29 tour of Australia
5. Colin Cowdrey must have been in high spirits after scoring 105 versus South Africa at Nottingham in 1965. A South African organization presented 100 bottles of wine, spirits and liqueurs to Cowdrey after his century

6. After scoring 118, India's first Test century versus England at Bombay in 1933-34, Lala Amarnath was presented with a car and £ 800. Women spectators showered the young batsmen with the jewellery they had on their person
7. In the MCC-Victoria County match in 1962, a batsman received a pair of socks for every four that he hit and a case of fruit for each six. MCC ended up with two cases of fruit and 22 pairs of socks
8. Fred Trueman gave his 300th Test victim, Neil Hawke, a bottle of champagne 20 years after getting him out. Hawke has kept the bottle unopened.
9. Peter Willey received 2016 pints of beer from a brewery in Northampton as a reward for his contribution in the 1978-79 Ashes series
10. After Arthur Morris had been dismissed for the fourth time by Alec Bedser, the latter presented him a book titled *Better Cricket* written by Lindsay Hassett and Ian Johnson. Bedser said: 'I hope this will help you!' Morris scored 206 in his next Test innings

FIFTEEN CRICKETING *ROBBERIES*

1. Melbourne's largest bat retailer – 'Bat and Ball' – was robbed of 148 bats in 1983. The owner was perplexed as there was no sign of forced entry
2. Mushtaq Mohammed was relieved of $ 1500 worth of travellers' cheques during Pakistan's 1976-77 tour of Australia
3. While Nottinghamshire were playing Sri Lanka in 1984, £ 600, jewellery and credit cards were stolen from the dressing room of the Notts players
4. The Indian cricketers lost their clothes during the tour of England in 1982. A thief broke into the team bus while the players were engaged in a match in London
5. Thieves stole cricket equipment worth £ 200 from the Middlesex dressing room during their Benson and Hedges Cup match against Glamorgan in 1983 at Uxbridge. The Middlesex players were playing cards and squash at the time
6. Viv Richards lost a cap and a gold watch while Richard Gabriel had his bat stolen from the West Indian dressing room in Sydney during their day/night WSC match versus Pakistan in 1983-84

7. John Lever was robbed of £ 400 worth travellers cheques during the Sixth Ashes Test in 1978-79
8. Geoff Boycott had his batting gloves stolen before MCC's fixture against Northern NSW, 1978-79
9. On the eve of the Centenary Test in 1980 at The Oval, David Bairstow's hotel room was burgled while he slept. The culprit made away with Mrs Bairstow's fur coat and £ 120 in cash
10. Brian Rose had £ 100 refunded to him by Pakistan cricket officials after having been pickpocketed at the National Stadium in Karachi in 1977-78
11. Malcolm Marshall's Afro-styling hair comb was pinched by Hampshire colleague, Chris Smith, for three days. Marshall threatened to report it to the cricket committee – and even retire. Essex meanwhile lost eight wickets to him and Hampshire won the match
12. Cricket mementoes were robbed from Colin Cowdrey's home some years back. A public appeal for their return went unheeded
13. Dickie Bird's familiar golf cap was pinched by an intrepid hand during an intrusion by spectators before the last ball of the Lord's World Cup final in 1975. A few days later, while he was on a bus in London, he recognised it on the head of a West Indian bus conductor. 'Where did you get that cap from?' enquired Bird. 'Haven't you heard of Dickie Bird, the Test umpire', countered the bus conductor. 'He's my friend; he gave it to me.'
14. Ian Botham had his bat – 'Boomer' – with which he had made 1500 Test runs, swiped from the Sydney dressing room in 1986-87. Jack Richards also lost a bat while Bruce French was relieved of two bats and a pair of batting gloves. A public appeal restored Botham's bat in a packet marked 'urgent'; the thieves showed little sympathy for the others
15. Denis Compton, 67, was surrounded by four 'muggers' near High Wycombe. They demanded money. Compton said: 'Sorry, I haven't any on me. But I have something for you in the car'. He pulled out a cricket bat, signed by the 1985 England and Australian teams. 'I may not be able to take you all, but I'll certainly take the first one of you, because I must tell you that I know how to use this.' The would-be assailants fled

TEN EMBARRASSING HOWLERS

1. During the 1971-72 series between Rest of the World and Australia, Hylton Ackerman, a member of the former side, asked an aging man at the Adelaide airport to hold his bat while he went to the toilet. Ackerman later enquired whether the old gent had played any cricket in his time. Somebody later pointed out to him that he had been talking to Sir Donald Bradman
2. The Australians are not the most tactful of cricketers. But Dennis Lillee had quite a few of his colleagues around him struggling to keep a straight face while he was being introduced to Queen Elizabeth in 1975. He greeted her with a cheery 'G'day Queen'
3. Colin Cowdrey absentmindedly drove down a one-way street in Canterbury after his son Chris had taken a wicket with his fourth ball in Test cricket on the tour of India in 1984-85. The policeman who hauled him up was sympathetic and let him go
4. After he had been given out leg before at Perth in 1979-80, Allan Border walked into the dressing room furious at the decision. He threw his bat across the room, shrugged his gloves and sighed heavily. England's team manager Alec Bedser, assistant manager Ken Barrington, David Bairstow and John Lever were most surprised; Border had entered the wrong dressing room!
5. During the afternoon of the last day of the Brisbane Test between West Indies and Australia in 1960-61, Keith Miller and Alan McGilvray decided they would be better off with an early flight to Sydney. They left the ground and did just that. They learnt with horror on alighting that the match had ended in a tie!
6. A correspondent of a weekend newspaper, covering his first international cricket game, struck a bet with another journalist that the Madras Test between India and Australia would end in a draw. After the match had been tied, he turned round to collect his Rs 10. When his colleague in the press box objected saying that neither had won, the debutant journalist replied: 'What do you mean "a tie"? It's the same thing, isn't it ?'
7. During a tour by Pakistan of the Commonwealth, on the pockets of the blazers of the touring cricketers was

embroidered : 'Parkistan'.

8. Harold Larwood wrote in his autobiography : 'He (Pataudi sr.) was anxious to follow in the footsteps of two other members of his family line by scoring a century in his last Test against Australia'. Larwood was referring to Ranji and Duleep who were in no way related to the Nawab of Pataudi.
9. 'That blackcurrant jam tastes like fish to me,' said Derek Randall on tasting caviar in India, 1976-77.
10. The *Star*, an English newspaper, carried the following line in 1950 : 'Bedser finally clean bowled Weekes with a ball he should have left well alone.'

TEN CRICKETERS WHO *CRIED* (AND WERE SEEN DOING SO!)

1. Geoff Boycott, after a slice of orange and a cherry on a cocktail stick was handed to him at Scarborough in 1963. He burst into tears saying, 'They think I am not a man because I won't drink beer.'
2. Bishen Singh Bedi, during the 1967 tour of England after the manager had chastised him
3. Charlie Griffith, after hitting Nari Contractor on the head in the match between Barbados and India, 1962. Contractor underwent a lifesaving operation. Griffith prayed and stayed at the hospital while Contractor battled for his life.
4. Peter Lever, after hitting Ewen Chatfield on his left temple in the Auckland Test between England and New Zealand in 1974-75
5. Don Bradman during his last Test innings at The Oval, 1948. After having been applauded all the way to the wicket, Bradman was moved to tears. His innings lasted two balls; he said he could hardly see anything due to blurred vision
6. Fred Tate at the conclusion of the Old Trafford Test against Australia in 1902. 'I've a little lad at home who'll make up for that,' said the tearful Tate, looking back on his dismal performance in the game. Twenty-two years later, his son Maurice played for England
7. Australian captain Kim Hughes at a press conference after his side's defeat against the West Indies in Brisbane, 1984-85
8. Peter Taylor,after he had bowled Australia to victory in his first Test. He took eight wickets and scored a useful 42. Taylor broke down as he embraced his parents and three sisters on

returning to the pavilion
9 and 10.Graham Dilley and Graham Gooch in his dressing room in Bridgetown, 1980-81. Assistant Manager Ken Barrington had died during the Test.

Money

SIX PRONOUNCEMENTS ON THE *MONEY* GAME

1. 'Apart from cricket, I would most like to be remembered for amassing wealth' (Dirk Wellham).
2. 'I don't come cheap'(Geoff Boycott asking Bob Woolmer for payment in exchange for technical advice on batting).
3. 'Money has always interested me; not just the making of it, but the way people use money' (Greg Chappell).
5. 'I might have fame – but no money' (Viv Richards).
6. 'Cricket is spoilt when money puts its ugly nose in. To think of playing cricket for hard cash!' (Mary Russell Mitford, 1823).

THE £ 100,000 *MAN* OF CRICKET

That's Greg Chappell for you. And this is why!

1. Is one of the 3 directors of Living Insurance, Queensland Pvt Ltd
2. Is involved in the Greg Chappell Cricket Centre
3. Is one of 5 partners in two Adelaide hotels – The Legtrap and Holdfast
4. Is tied up for contracting arrangements with Mt Isa Mines
5. Is involved in a travel and property development agency
6. Is a model for advertisements issued by a Brisbane building society
7. Is a newspaper columnist
8. Endorses Gray Nicolls cricket bats
9. Endorses cricket boots and shoes
10. Is a retired Test cricketer, having played top cricket for a decade and a half

WHAT THEY DID (OR ALMOST DID) FOR *MONEY*

1. In 1986 at The Oval, Lohmann, Abel, Hayward, Richardson and Gunn refused to play unless they were paid £ 20. All except Lohmann and Gunn finally gave in
2. Dennis Lillee considered posing in the nude for what was believed to be a staggering amount. He said his wife would agree if it could add another room to the house or help put the kids through college
3. Mike Procter put all his money into his sports goods business. His business collapsed and he lost all his assets, including his house and Rolls Royce and ended up in debt to the tune of £ 700,000. Following this disaster, Procter worked for four days for former Test cricketer Geoff Griffin as a liquor store manager. Procter gave it up saying: 'Let's just say that I am just surviving'
4. Tony Greig posed without his clothes for cricket equipment manufacturers, St Peter's. 'It's good to know that I have St Peter's protecting me', was the ad-line. Greig wore only gloves, pads, abdomen guard and a thigh guard with a bat in hand
5. Terry Jenner was arrested in Adelaide and charged with falsification of accounts. Two charges of embezzlement were also levelled at him
6. To protest against the BCCP's refusal to grant him a wage hike, Sarfraz Nawaz flew back home in the middle of a series against England in 1977-78
7. Glenn Turner demanded that he be re-imbursed certain airfares by the New Zealand Board. When the Board refused to compensate him, he refused to play for the country for a considerable period of time
8. Clive Rice of South Africa posed in the nude (with the bat placed in a strategic position) for the centrespread of a women's magazine. It earned him a rebuke from the Board of his country
9. Jeff Thomson : 'I'd catch any fish that brings in a dollar'

Names

SIX CRICKETERS BETTER KNOWN BY THEIR *INITIALS*

1. W. G. Grace (England)
2. C. K. Nayudu (India)
3. C. B. Fry (England)
4. M. L. Jaisimha (India)
5. J. T. Brown (England)
6. F. T. Mann (England)

TEST CRICKETERS WITH *NAMES* OF ANIMALS/BIRDS/ INSECTS

1. A. LAMB (England)
2. A. DOLPHIN (England)
3. R. ROBINS (England)
4. N. HAWKE (England)
5. R. HOGG (Australia)
6. M. C. BIRD (England)
7. J. AND M. CROWE (N. Zealand)
8. A. E. AND A. L. OCHSE (South Africa)
9. C. ROACH (W. Indies)

TEN *ABORIGINES* WHO TOURED ENGLAND IN 1868

Aborigines playing cricket?! Well, *Wisden* can't have it wrong either. A team of aborigines actually undertook a long voyage to England in 1868 with a none-too formidable reputation and some of the most curious names to break the monotony of a cricketing index.

1. Dick-a-Dick
2. Mosquito
3. Jim Crow
4. Tiger
5. Red Cap
6. Sundown
7. Tuppenny
8. King Cole
9. Bullocky
10. Johnny Mullagh

ELEVEN *INDIAN* CRICKETERS YOU THOUGHT YOU KNEW!

1. Vijay Thackersey (Vijay Merchant)
2. Salim A. A. Khan (Salim Durrani)
3. V. Srinivasaraghavan (S. Venkataraghavan)
4. M. Sharma (Madan Lal)
5. J. H. Kenia (K Jayantilal)
6. N. J. Makhija (Naoomal Jeoomal)
7. V. Gundappa (G. R. Vishwanath)
8. V. Palwankar (P. Vithal)
9. K. D. Nikhanj (Kapil Dev)
10. R. G. Sipahmalani (G. S. Ramchand)
11. B. Palwankar (P. Baloo)

SEVEN CRICKETERS WHO *PLAYED* FOR THE WRONG TEAM

1. Bob Holland (Australia)
2. Bruce French (England)
3. Ted Lester (Yorkshire)
4. APE Knott (Kent)
5. John Hampshire (Yorkshire, Derbyshire, Tasmania)
6. Hon C. J. Coventry (Worcestershire)
7. Martin Kent (Queensland)

NAMES OF SEVENTEEN TEST CRICKETERS THAT CAN BE USED AS *ADJECTIVES*

1. Ray BRIGHT (Australia)
2. Rick, Len and Joe DARLING (Australia)
3. Chris OLD (England)
4. John SHARP (England)
5. John Cornish WHITE (England)
6. Harding, Jack, Richard YOUNG (England)
7. Alan, David, Freddie, Jack, Bill and Lennox BROWN (England, Australia, Africa)
8. Jim SLIGHT (Australia)
9. Charlie and Billy FRANK (South Africa)
10. Bob CRISP (South Africa)
11. Ron GAUNT (Australia)
12. Eddie FULLER (South Africa)
13. Chris BROAD (England)
14. Cyril MERRY (West Indies)
15. Roger BLUNT (New Zealand)
16. Wilf SLACK (England)
17. Colin BLAND (South Africa)

THINGS YOU DIDN'T KNOW HAD *NAMES*

1. Bill Woodfull's bat – 'Big Bertha', because nothing ever got past it
2. The bowling machine at Lord's – 'Chris Old', because it kept breaking down
3. Dennis Lillee's aluminium bat – 'Combat', which was the brand name
4. Ian Botham's bat – 'Boomer'
5. The duck that made its appearance on Australian TV screens during WSC in the early Eighties – 'Daddles'
6. Stumps joined at their base to keep them from uprooting and ideal for indoor cricket – 'Wilkins Wicket'
7. The weather vane at Lord's – 'Father Time'
8. The scarecrow at Lord's – 'Old Jem '

THE FIVE COMMONEST *SURNAMES* IN TEST CRICKET

1. 'Smith': 22 (2 from the West Indies, 3 from New Zealand, 2 from Australia, 3 from South Africa and 12 from England)
2. 'Ali': 12 (2 from the West Indies, 4 from India, 6 from Pakistan)
3. 'Ahmed': 9 (1 from India, 8 from Pakistan)
4. 'Khan': 8 (1 from India, 7 from Pakistan)
5. 'Mohammed': 8 (all from Pakistan, including Gul Mohammed who also played for India)

DID YOU KNOW THE *MIDDLE NAMES* OF THESE TEN CRICKETERS?

1. Everton Weekes (West Indies) – de Courcy
2. Leslie Ames (England) – Ethelbert
3. Gladstone Small (England) – Cleophas
4. Sylvester Clarke (West Indies) – Theophilus
5. Alan Kippax (Australia) – Falconer
6. Andy Roberts (West Indies) – Montgomery
7. John Snow (England) – Augustine
8. Ken Hutchings (England) – Lotherington
9. Hon. Frederick Calthorpe (England) – Somerset
10. Glenn Turner (New Zealand) – Maitland

FIFTEEN CRICKETERS WITH UNUSUAL *INITIALS*

1. 'LEG' – Leslie Ethelbert George Ames (England)
2. 'APE' – Alan Philip Eric Knott (England)
3. 'CARD' – Christopher Anthony Russell Duckworth (South Africa)
4. 'ROB' – Roland Orlando Butcher (England)
5. 'MCC' – Michael Colin Cowdrey (England)
6. 'SCG' – Stewart Cathie Griffith (England)
7. 'SAD' – Salim Aziz Durrani (India)
8. 'BBC' – Bransby Beauchamp Cooper (Australia)
9. 'BAR' – Barry Anderson Richards (South Africa)
10. 'DIG' – David Ivon Gower (England)
11. 'FEW' – Frank Edward Woolley (England)
12. 'DAM' – David Anthony Murray (West Indies)
13. 'SHE' – Sidney Hand Emery (Australia)
14. 'AIR' – Asif Iqbal Rizvi (Pakistan)
15. 'DRAG' – Donald Reaburn Algernon Gehrs (Australia)

THE LONGEST *SURNAMES* IN TEST CRICKET

(Hyphenated surnames have not been considered)

1. L. Sivaramakrishnan, India (16 alphabets)
2. S. Venkataraghavan, India (15 alphabets)
3. Kuruppuarachchi, Sri Lanka (15 alphabets)
4. J. Yajurvinder Singh, India (15 alphabets)
5. K. S. Indrasinhji, India (14 alphabets)
6. S. Christopherson, England (14 alphabets).

NAMES OF TWELVE TEST CRICKETERS WHICH CAN BE USED AS *VERBS*

1. 'Tavare has gone to (Peter) SLEEP at the crease'.
2. 'I just ('Hammy') LOVE Imran Khan'.
3. 'Ask the captain to (Brian) CLOSE the innings'.
4. 'Don't (Kenneth) BURN your fingers'.
5. 'I am going to (Bill) HUNT down the fella who hit a six off my bowling'.
6. 'Pleasc ask the groundsman to (Doug) RING the bell five minutes before play.
7. 'If God could ('Jackie') GRANT me just one wish...'
8. 'A leg spinner usually (Izek) BUYS his wicket'.
9. 'I wonder if more India-Pakistan Tests will (Frank) FOSTER good relations between the two countries'.
10. 'They had to (Herbie) WADE through the ground to catch the team bus back to the hotel that evening'.
11. '(Geoff) BOYCOTT the English opener'.
12. '(C.B.) FRY me an egg'.

THE MAKING OF A *NAME*

There have been many instances when famous cricketers, or their sons, have been named with someone or something in mind.

1. Former Sri Lankan wicket keeper Ranjit Fernando named his son after Eknath Solkar
2. Everton Weekes' father was a supporter of the Everton soccer club
3. Colin Cowdrey's father made sure his son's initials were MCC.
4. Bishen Bedi named his son Gavasinder, after team-mate Gavaskar had scored 774 runs in his first series
5. Rohan Jaivishwa, Gavaskar's son's name, was a consequence

of the Indian batsman's admiration for Rohan Kanhai, ML Jaisimha and GR Vishwanath

6. Herbert Sutcliffe christened his son 'William Herbert Hobbs' as a token of his admiration for his England batting partner Jack
7. Keith Ross Miller's parents named him after two pilots of World War I, Keith and Ross
8. County cricketer Neil Harvey Fairbrother's mother was an admirer of the Australian post-War batsman
9. West Indian cricketer Furlonge was given the forename 'Hammond' by keen cricket parents

AND...

Born on the night of India's historic World Cup win, Prudential Singh, a baby girl, left her parents with little choice.

THIRTY-THREE CRICKETERS BETTER KNOWN BY THEIR *MIDDLE NAMES*

Dennis BRIAN Close
William ERIC Hollies
William GILBERT Parkhouse
Arthur LINDSAY Hassett
Kevin DOUGLAS Walters
Derrick JOHN McGlew
Isaac VIVIAN Richards
Peter JEFFREY Dujon
John MICHAEL Brearley
Michael COLIN Cowdrey
Alfred JOHN Evans
Charles FREDERICK Root
Robert JOHN Inverarity
William RUSSELL Endean
Cuthbert GORDON Greenidge
Balfour PATRICK Patterson
Thomas PETER Smith
Norman FRANK Bruce
Graham ANTHONY Lock
Robert NEIL Harvey
William ALBERT Oldfield
Kenneth COLIN Bland
George STEPHEN Camacho
Bernard LANCE Cairns
John CHRISTOPHER Balderstone
Arthur PERCY Chapman
George HUBERT Doggart
Thomas GODFREY Evans
Charles AUBREY Smith
Andrew PAUL Sheahan
Robert GRAEME Pollock
Robert KARL Nunes
John GREG Thomas

***NAMES* YOU'D NEVER THINK CRICKETERS WOULD HAVE**

1. XENOPHON Constantine Balaskas (South Africa)
2. SEPTIMUS Kinneir (England)

3. SEW Shivnaraine (West Indies)
4. UTON Dowe (West Indies)
5. EIULF Peter Nupen (South Africa)
6. MORDECAL Sherwin (England)
7. IZAK Buys (South Africa)
8. ELQUEMEDO Willett (West Indies)
9. SRINIVASARAGHAVAN Venkataraghavan (India)
10. MOTGANHALLI Lakshminarsu Jaisimha (India)
11. COMMANDUR Rajagopalachari Rangachari (India)
12. COIMBATARAO Doraikannu Gopinath (India)
13. PHILIPPE Henri Edmonds (England)
14. WALDEMAR Frederick Eric Marx (South Africa)
15. GUNDIBAIL Rama Sunderam (India)

Nicknames

THE NICKNAMES OF *RICHARD ELLISON*

1. 'Brains'
2. 'Muss'
3. 'Snooker'
4. 'Plank'
5. 'Chopper'

FIVE CRICKETERS NICKNAMED *TIGER*

1. Bill O'Reilly
2. M.A.K. Pataudi
3. E.J. Smith
4. H.R. Lance
5. Abdul Qadir

SEVEN *INITIALS* FOR NICKNAMES

1. 'A.B.' – Allan Border (Australia)
2. 'W.G.' – Dr W.G. Grace (England)
3. 'G.C.' – Greg Chappell (Australia)
4. 'T.C.' – Trevor Chappell (Australia)
5. 'M.J.' – Majid Jahangir Khan (Pakistan)
6. 'K.T.' – Sonny Ramadhin (West Indies)
7. 'C.K.' – C.K. Nayudu (India)

FOUR NICKNAMES FOR *PHIL EDMONDS*

1. 'Maggie' : Christened when Margaret Thatcher was Leader of the Opposition
2. 'Henri' : His middle name
3. 'Goat : Reason unprintable
4. 'Rommel'

TEN *NICKNAMES* – AND WHO COINED THEM

1. 'Side-step Queen' – Given to Ian Botham by Mike Brearley
2. 'Rent-a-waggon' – Given to Venkataraghavan by Brian Johnston
3. 'The Boil' – Given to Trevor Bailey by Brian Johnston
4. 'FOT' – Given to Dennis Lillee by Tony Lock. The initials stand for 'flamin' old tart'
5. 'Fiery'–Coined for Boycott by David Gower
6. 'ARL' – Coined for Tony Lewis by Brian Johnston. Note Lewis' initials
7. 'Cootamundra Kid' – What Bradman thought he would have been called had he been a boxer
8. 'Rambo' – Given to Raman Lamba by Sunil Gavaskar
9. 'George' – Arthur Mailey generally called everybody 'George'. When he called Bradman that, the latter turned round and called him 'George' too!
10. 'One and only' – Legendary Sydney barracker Yabba for himself

TEN NICKNAMES INSPIRED BY *PERFORMANCES* ON THE FIELD

1. 'Rowdy' Chris Tavare – after his batting
2. 'Slasher' Ken Mackay – because he was exactly the opposite!
3. 'Croucher' Gilbert Jessop – after his stance
4. 'Johnny Won't Hit Today' Johnny Douglas – because he seldom revealed his ability to hit
5. 'Electric Heels' Learie Constantine – because of his running in the outfield
6. 'Ticker' Mitchell – because he had the irritating habit of chattering on the field
7. 'Tanglefoot' Max Walker – because he criss-crossed his feet in the delivery stride
8. 'Don Quixote' Nitschke – b ecause of his penchant at using the

long handle against the best of bowlers and hitting them over their heads

9. 'Toey' Hugh Tayfield – because he pushed his toe into the ground before bowling or receiving a ball
10 'Wormkiller' Bill Woodfull – because of his dour and impenetrable batting

INGENIOUS *NICKNAMES*

1. Chris Old – 'Chilly'
2. Steve Waugh – 'Drobe'
3. Graham Dilley – 'Picca'
4. Shaun Graf – 'Porno'
5. Allan Lamb – 'Lego'
6. Peter Sleep – 'Sounda'
7. Jonathan Agnew – 'Spiro'.
8. David Steele – 'Crime' ...both never pay!
9. Bruce Taylor – 'Haystack'...he was so lucky that if he fell off a tree he would land ina haystack.
10. Asif Din – 'Gunga'
11. Geoff Marsh – 'Swampy'
12. Ray Bright – 'Candles'
13. Tony Piggott – 'Lester'
14. Ian Davis – 'Wizard'...his initials are 'ID'

SIXTEEN CRICKETERS WITH 'ANIMAL' NICKNAMES

1. Ian Botham (England) – 'Guy the Gorilla'
2. A.L. Thompson (Australia) – 'Froggy'
3. A.N. Hornby (England) – 'Monkey'
4. Graeme Pollock (South Africa) – 'Little dog'
5. Harry Alexander (Australia) – 'Bull'
6. Bob Willis (England) – 'Goose'
7. Hunter Hendry (Australia) – 'Stork'
8. Clarrie Grimmett (Australia) – 'The Old Fox'
9. Joel Garner (West Indies) – 'Big Bird'
10. Clive Lloyd (West Indies) – 'Supercat'
11. Bruce French (England) – 'Frog'
12. Chris Cowdrey (England) – 'Cow'
13. Nick Cook (England) – 'Beast'
14. Derek Randall (England) – 'Arkle', after the champion greyhound

15. Geoff Arnold (England) – 'orse!'
16. Arun Lal (India) – 'Piggy'

APPEARANCES WHICH INSPIRED NICKNAMES

1. Philip de Freitas – 'Half chocolate'
2. Viv Richards – Smokin' Joe…his colleagues felt that he bore a resemblance to the boxer Joe Frazier
3. Warwick Armstrong – 'Big Ship'
4. Dr H.V. Hordern – 'Ranji' (because of his dark complexion)
5. Graham Gooch — 'Zapata' …. the moustache !
6. David Gower – 'Lulu'…because of his hair.
7. Peter Willey – 'Clint Eastwood'
8. Sylvester Clarke – 'Big Sly'
9. Bruce Reid – 'Lizard'
10. Roger Binny – 'Jackie' …because his posterior is shaped like a couple of jack-fruits
11. Richard Hadlee – 'Paddles' …because of the splayed feet.

NICKNAMES AND HOW THEY CAME ABOUT

1. 'Round the corner' – C.A. Smith's nickname because of his circuitous bowling run-up
2. 'Starlight' – because F.L. Mooney 'stumped like a rattlesnake and was very energetic socializing and dancing'
3. 'Nymph' – umpire David Constant was called this after Margaret Kennedy produced a play called 'A Constant Nymph'
4. 'Rowdy' – because Ashley Mallett was among the quieter elements in the dressing room
5. 'Rhubarb' – because when you intoned the name 'Venkataraghavan' the buzz was quite like an artificial stage-mumble
6. 'Dattubhai' – when Dilip Doshi was selected for the Indian team in 1979, he kept referring to the selector from his zone: "Dattubhai (Phadkar) said this…" and "Dattubhai said that." So Doshi became 'Dattubhai'
7. 'Colonel' – After Dilip Vengsarkar had hit half-a-dozen sixes in the Irani Trophy match in 1976 and gained selection into the Indian team, critics started comparing him with Col. C.K. Nayudu. The nickname stuck – much to Vengsarkar's displeasure

8. 'Bacchus' – Rod Marsh's nickname had nothing to do with his appetite for drink. In fact, it was inspired by a small town in Australia which has the name 'Bacchus-Marsh'
9. 'Niszi' – Imran Khan earned this nickname after his matchwinning pace in the Sydney Test in 1976-77. 'Niszi' is a fierce Pathan tribe near his country's North-West border
10. 'Dial-a-moan' : Ray Illingworth's nickname...do we have to explain this one too?

On the Ground

SIX RECORDED INSTANCES OF ALL *THREE STUMPS* BEING UPROOTED

1. Jean Dean bowled by E. Napper, Brighton, 1839
2. C. Lawrence bowled by N. Felix, Edinburgh, 1849
3. H. W. Fellowes bowled by G. Kelston, Canterbury, 1864
4. G. Freeman bowled by C. Filgate, Lord's, 1870
5. W. Ashdown bowled by J. Parsons, Tunbridge Wells, 1926
6. Kapil Dev bowled by Sarfraz Nawaz, Hyderabad, 1982-83

– *Next Man in* by Gerald Brodribb

FOUR NOT-SO-PLEASANT *EXCHANGES* ON THE FIELD

1. 'If I don't pull you, short-arse, how am I going to score any runs?' (Ian Chappell to Joel Garner).
2. 'I've run you out, cunt'. (Ian Botham to Geoff Boycott in New Zealand, 1977-78).
3. 'I'll come down there and shove this bat down your throat'. (Viv Richards to Imran Khan).
4. 'Get off my fucking back, Brearley, or I'll fix you'. (Phil Edmonds).

FIVE MATTHEWS *BANNERS* IN NEW ZEALAND, 1985-86

1. 'What do Greg Matthews and Rock Hudson have in common?'
2. 'Greg Matthews – Aussie closet epilectic'.
3. 'Matthews for the next shuttle mission'.
4. 'It was Matthews who ate the baby'.
5. 'I hate Greg Matthews'.

THE FIVE *COMMONEST* EXCHANGES BETWEEN BATSMEN IN THE MIDDLE

1. 'I'll take care of this bloke. You handle the spinner'.
2. 'Let's open out now'.
3. 'You are doing just fine. Keep going'.
4. 'Just concentrate'.
5. 'Check out that one in the blue skirt'.

EIGHT BATSMEN WHO WERE *RECALLED* AFTER BEING GIVEN OUT

1. Iqbal Qasim by Mike Brearley at Lahore, 1977, England vs Pakistan
2. Bob Christiani by Keith Miller at Melbourne, 1951, West Indies vs Australia
3. A.B. Reid by Keith Miller at Newlands, 1949, W. Provinces vs Australia
4. Budhi Kunderan by Gary Sobers at Bombay, 1967, India vs West Indies
5. Keith Stackpole by Gary Sobers at Bombay, 1968, India vs West Indies
6. Glenn Turner by Gary Sobers at Bridgetown, 1972, N. Zealand vs West Indies. Turner, then on 40, went on to score 259
7. Derek Randall by Rod Marsh at Melbourne, 1977, England vs Australia
8. Bob Taylor by G. Vishwanath at Bombay, 1980, England vs India. Following his recall, Taylor, with Botham, went on to post an important partnership, which was instrumental in England's winning the match

UNUSUAL REASONS FOR A *BREAK IN PLAY*

1. The Nottinghamshire-India match at Trent Bridge in 1974 was interrupted by descending parachutists intending to land in a nearby river
2. The extreme heat forced the umpires to suspend the Surrey-Lancashire match at The Oval in 1868 for an hour
3. An earthquake of sorts held up play for five minutes during a one-day international between India and West Indies in Trinidad, 1983
4. It was not possible to continue play late during the 1963

England-New Zealand Test at Christchurch. This was mainly on account of the sun's rays being reflected off an aluminium roof of a stand

5. The second day of the Golden Jubilee Test between India and England at Bombay in 1980 was declared as one of rest because it coincided with a solar eclipse

FOUR LEVELS OF *UMPIRING* INTIMIDATION

By Dr John Sumner of Royal Melbourne Institute of Technology.

1. By appeals ('Now the whole team goes up; eleven Nureyevs leaping in ecstacy')
2. Batsmen staying their ground ('If a batsman walks these days he is considered weak in the head')
3. Physical or verbal abuse at the umpire
4. Umpires coerced into 'seeing' decisions to suit the home nation

SIX INCIDENTS OF *STREAKING* AT CRICKET MATCHES

1. On 4 August 1975, a new chapter was opened in the history of the game when a young man streaked across Lord's and jumped over both sets of stumps. The intruder's punishment was a fine of £ 20 and a whack from Greg Chappell's bat on you-know-where
2. The first instance of a woman streaker at a first-class match was at Perth during W. Australia's game versus S. Australia in 1975-76. Three female streakers shed their inhibitions and ran onto the WACA. They were charged with 'disorderly conduct'
3. Miss Ashley Summers appeared topless during the Lord's Test between India and England in 1986. She displayed a banner advocating the recall of Ian Botham. While Paul Downton and Mike Gatting had a good laugh, Phil Edmonds blindfolded himself, Srikkanth looked away and Gavaskar asked the young lady to get off the pitch. Miss Summers' boyfriend broke up with her. She later said, 'If he forgives me, I promise to be a good girl and keep my clothes on'
4. A nude spectator (sex not known!) ran onto the playing area during a WSC fixture between Australia and West Indies in 1979-80 at Brisbane
5. A young man did the same in an Auckland Test between

Australia and New Zealand. He was fined £ 40 for disorderly conduct. Greg Chappell hit the offender several times on his buttocks

6. A strongly-built man with a pair of red shorts (in his hand) ran onto the ground during a WSC match between New Zealand and India in Australia, 1985-86

TEN *HOWLERS* ON THE CRICKET FIELD

1. Krish Srikkanth was refused permission to open the innings against Leicestershire in 1986 on the grounds that he could only bat after five wickets had fallen or after an hour of the Indian innings. The umpires later apologized as they were not aware that the county rules did not apply to a match between a county side and a touring team
2. During the Yorkshire-Derbyshire match at Chesterfield in 1946, it was after two overs had been bowled that someone realized that the pitch was 24 yards long instead of the stipulated 22
3. While Worcestershire was playing Derbyshire in a county fixture in 1974, the new ball was requisitioned by Worcs' captain after 85 overs had been bowled in Derbyshire's second innings. During the lunch interval the skipper of the batting side informed the umpires that a new ball could only be asked for after 100 overs of an innings. The new ball, 11 deliveries old, was put aside and play was resumed with the old one
4. During a limited-overs match between England and Australia in 1979-80, Geoff Boycott took strike following a drinks interval. The scorers revealed that it was Randall who should have done so
5. Two bowlers are credited with having bowled successive overs in a Test innings. One was Warwick Armstrong who did so during the Manchester Test against England in 1921. The other one who escaped the attention of the umpires was A.M. Moir of New Zealand against England at Wellington in 1950-51
6. Krish Srikkanth was given out by the umpire at the striker's end and the one at square leg in the Kandy Test vs Sri Lanka in 1985
7. The umpires in the Leeds Test between India and England in 1986 allowed 12 Indians on the field during play. The error dawned upon them after an over, and substitute Raman Lamba

had to leave the field.

8. The umpires in a India-England Test in 1986 unwittingly allowed more than two men on the leg side behind the square leg umpire
9. When Imran Khan repeatedly overstepped the crease while bowling in the India-Pakistan series of 1978 in Pakistan, the umpires refused to signal a no-ball. The logic used by them was that 'Imran's boots are bigger'
10. During the Test between England and New Zealand at Trent Bridge in 1986, the latter side's winning score was given as 77 for two. Martin Crowe had hit a four off the last ball, which incidentally happened to be declared a chucker. Since New Zealand needed only a run before the ball had been bowled, the match was won as soon as the no-ball had been recorded. The scores were later changed from 77/2 to 74/2 and Crowe's 48 not out was changed to 44 not out

FIVE *HENRY BLOFELD* BANNERS AT THE SYDNEY CRICKET GROUND, 1982-83

Henry Blofeld is one of the better known radio commentators. He also writes on cricket for *The Guardian* and blows apart the theory that you need to be a cricketer to be popular.

1. 'Henry Blofly is to cricket as Tony Greig is to limbo dancing'
2. 'Our Henry can even outdrink Keith Miller'
3. 'The Bespectacled Henry Blofly Stand'
4. 'Henry Blofly asks if Irving Rosenwater has scored with Wendy Wimbush'
5. 'Henry Blofly doesn't even pay for the sheets'

ACCIDENT-PRONE RICK DARLING'S TEN *INJURIES*

1. Traces of cartilage fragments in the left cheek after having been struck on the head by a bouncer during the Bombay Test, 1979-80
2. In 1975, 'A cartridge jammed in the gun I was using. It blew up in my face. I was very lucky. The left eye could have been severely damaged. Worst of all were the powderburns on my face.'
3. Misjudged a catch during a game at Hyderabad, 1979-80. Received seven stitches over a gashed left eye
4. Playing for South Australia vs the West Indies in 1979-80 ,

Darling escaped serious injury when a ball from Michael Holding crashed into the visor of his helmet

5. Was hit below the heart by Bob Willis in January 1979 and declared 'clinically dead' for a few seconds. Darling was resuscitated by John Emburey
6. During a charity match in 1979-80, Darling ran to cut off a ball, missed and landed in the pickets. He sustained three stitches in the right palm
7. In 1978 he broke a thumb while intercepting a hard drive.
8. Broke his arm playing football at the age of 10
9. Cracked his skull playing 'A' Grade football for Waikerie at the age of 17. Spent four days in hospital
10. Received a serious eye injury via a delivery from John Maguire. The ball passed between the peak and the visor of his helmet. So profuse was the flow of blood that the ball had to be changed! Darling underwent plastic surgery. His right pupil is permanently enlarged.

– *Australian Cricket*

FOUR INSTANCES OF MATCHES INTERRUPTED OR RUINED BY ACTS OF *VANDALISM*

1. Anti-apartheid demonstrators,protesting the second Aussie 'rebel' tour of South Africa in 1986-87, poured 200 litres of motor oil over the pitch at Newlands
2. Spectators dragged furniture from the pavilion at Hove in the Eighties and started a bonfire on the field. The pitch area was unaffected
3. The Leeds Test between England and Australia in 1975 had to be abandoned when the pitch was dug up by vandals
4. Vandals cut the name 'Margaret' into the pitch during Kent's match with Sussex at Hove in 1975

'WHAT WE TALK ABOUT AT THE FALL OF EACH WICKET' ACCORDING TO DAVID GOWER

1. Females
2. Food
3. Drink
4. Television
5. Often, cricket hardly merits a mention in the conversation

– *With Time to Spare* by David Gower and Alan Lee

FIVE NEAR-FATAL *INJURIES* ON THE FIELD

1. H.B. Cameron was unconscious for several days after being struck by a delivery from Harold Larwood, Lord's, 1929
2. Nari Contractor was admitted to the Intensive Care Unit of a Barbados Hospital in 1961-62 after being struck on the head by Charlie Griffith on the Caribbean tour of 1961-62
3. Ewen Chatfield, playing his first Test, was clinically dead for a few seconds after being hit on the temple by a bouncer from Peter Lever. Chatfield had swallowed his tongue and was saved by physio Bernard Thomas who cleared his wind pipe
4. Rick Darling was hit on the heart by a ball from Bob Willis during the Adelaide Test, 1978-79. The gum that he was chewing got stuck at the back of his throat. Darling was revived by England's John Emburey who gave him a 'precordial thump' and got him breathing again
5. Frank Tyson was rendered unconscious after being knocked out by a bouncer from Ray Lindwall in 1954-55 at Sydney. Tyson came back to bowl England to victory by 38 runs

THE TEN MOST READABLE *BANNERS* SEEN ON CRICKET GROUNDS

1. 'Geoff Borecott'
2. 'THE PETER TOOHEY STAND – Such a brilliant batsman, they've named a brewery after him.'
3. 'Bird eats Rice for breakfast.'
4. 'England needs Botham on grass.'
5. 'O-mar, he's making eyes at me.' (during a Pakistan – New Zealand Test 1984-85)
6. 'Gavaskar – idol or idle?' (after Gavaskar refused to play in the Calcutta Test against Pakistan in 1986-87)
7. 'Bus drivers vs tram conductors...' (during the India vs Pakistan World Championship final in 1985)
8. 'Bring back Bradman'. (when things were going unfavourably for Australia in 1985)
9. 'Dowe shall not bowl'. (following Uton Dowe's wild bowling, West Indies versus Australia, Kingston, 1972-73)
10. 'First it was convicts, then it was rabbits, then it was Botham'. (during the 1978-79 Ashes series in Australia)

Opinions

THE CRICKETER I WOULD LOVE TO SPEND AN *EVENING* WITH

The following survey was conducted in a Calcutta college for girls between the ages 18 and 21

1. Sunil Gavaskar (33 percent of the girls)
2. Imran Khan (15 percent)
3. Ravi Shastri (12 percent)
4. Kapil Dev (12 percent)
5. Tiger Pataudi (4 percent)
6. Rest (26 percent)

I'D *HATE* BEING A CRICKETER LIKE...

The following survey was conducted in a school in Calcutta for boys between the ages 15 and 18.

1. Ravi Shastri and Mohinder Amarnath (24 per cent each)
2. Ian Botham (10 per cent)
3. Dilip Doshi (20 per cent)
4. Sunil Gavaskar (12 per cent)
   Tilak Raj, Malcolm Nash, Gary Sobers and Abdul Qadir (10 per cent)

FIVE REASONS WHY ENGLISH CRICKET HAS *SLUMPED*

According to Johnny Wardle, former England left-arm bowler

1. Too many overseas internationals in county cricket
2. Introduction of heavy loam in search of quicker pitches results in the uneven bounce of wickets
3. The covering of pitches at the expense of spinners
4. Proliferation of limited-overs cricket – even at the League level
5. Outdated coaching methods – youngsters ought to be taught to attack the bowling and play the ball on the rise

FIVE *VERDICTS* AGAINST THE GENTLEMEN OF THE FOURTH ESTATE

1. '...Brylcreemed £ 30 suited Fleet Street hacks' (Ian Botham)
2. 'My ghost is writing rubbish' (An England player on the tour of West Indies, 1985-86)
3. 'There are absolutely no depths to which they will not stoop'

(Frances Edmonds)

4. 'Henry Blofeld is frequently long on opinions and short on facts' (Geoff Boycott)
5. '...the *Express* not content with dragging up a story more dead than dated, has spiced it up with all kinds of innuendos' (Bob Willis, 1983-84)

THE TOUGHEST *JOB* IN THE GAME

Dickie Bird on umpiring

1. 'You cannot win as an umpire.'
2. 'You have got to learn to live with criticism.'
3. 'All umpires are fair and honest men.'
4. 'You can't let your mind wander to the party in the evening'. You do that even once and something happens.'
5. 'It's difficult for us because people don't smile and seem to enjoy Test matches anymore.'

THE ONE CRICKETER I WOULDN'T MIND SPENDING AN *EVENING* WITH BY SHABANA AZMI

The contributor is one of India's leading actresses. 'You couldn't have chosen a worse person to speak about cricketers and cricket', she confessed with a smile.

1. Sunil Gavaskar ('He is an intelligent person with whom you can talk on just about everything. I mean he is that sort of person with whom you don't have to say anything "heavy" about cricket. I am sure he can converse on any topic. I can see some parallels between him and me. There is a feeling of kinship with him, even though I know nothing about cricket and he may not have seen any of my films. He is the one cricketer I would like to spend time with.')

SIX FRANK STATEMENTS ABOUT THE CRICKET ENTREPRENEUR KERRY PACKER

1. 'My idiot son' (Sir Frank Packer on his son Kerry).
2. 'If Packer can be brought to see that its prostitution to TV will be the death of the game as it has evolved over the centuries, cricket may ride this crisis, as it has others in the past. If not...' (E. W. Swanton).
3. 'The man in the stocking mask' (Michael Davie).

4. 'Packer has been good for cricketers, not cricket' (Bishen Bedi).
5. 'I would think Packer has had as much influence over cricket as Bradman himself' (Jack Fingleton).
6. 'He is not interested in the well-being of cricket. If he had been, he would have put money into schools cricket, university cricket' (Bishen Bedi).

SIX *DESCRIPTIONS* OF HAROLD LARWOOD BY THE AUSTRALIAN PRESS DURING THE BODYLINE SERIES

1. 'Larwood the wrecker'
2. 'Lightning Larwood'
3. 'Larwood the killer'
4. 'The silent killer'
5. 'Hoodoo Larwood'
6. 'Murder on tiptoe'

PASSING JUDGEMENT ON *SELECTORS*

Normally it is the selector who issues a statement on the cricketers that he has selected – or not. The instances when the reverse has taken place, has made headlines.

1. 'Gin-soaked dodderers' (Ian Botham, 1986)
2. 'A bunch of jokers' (Sunil Gavaskar, 1974)
3. 'A bunch of idiots' (Wayne Phillips, 1986)
4. 'The typical England selector is brought out of a loft. Someone takes the dust-sheet off him, gives him a pink gin and sends him in there. He can't go out of a 30-mile radius of London because he is usually too pissed to get back' (Ian Botham, 1986)

FIVE CONFLICTING VIEWS ON *NEUTRAL* UMPIRING

1. Sir Don Bradman: 'This neutral umpires' business is an emotional concept which is not practicable. The argument must be bound up in the inference that home umpires are biased'.
2. Michael Melford: 'Though I see no virtue in neutral umpires being appointed just for the sake of their neutrality, I would support a Test panel of the best umpires in the world, if these could be so built up'.
3. Dickie Bird: 'Umpires all over the world are fair and honest men. The question of neutral umpiring does not arise'.
4. Ravi Shastri: 'I don't think neutral umpiring is feasible. Is there any guarantee that people will not say that the neutral

umpires were bribed?'

5. Imran Khan: 'Neutral umpires, backed up by electronic aids would help...it would be a move towards professionalism'.

TEN VIEWS ON THE *GAME*

1. 'Cricket is the only game that has inspired a continuous flow of books which, without pomposity, can be described as literature'. (Neville Cardus).
2. 'God, but it's England, someone cried, and there's a cricket field.' (This line, scrawled on a piece of paper, was found in the pocket of an RAF pilot killed in air combat during World War II).
3. 'How many people in other jobs can get up on a Monday morning and honestly say they are looking forward to going to work'. (Ian Botham).
4. 'No game holds up such a clear mirror to character as cricket'. (E. W. Swanton).
5. 'The fiercest and fastest living thing on 44 legs'. (J. L. Manning).
6. 'Cricket would be a better game if the papers didn't publish the averages'. (Jack Hobbs).
7. 'Cricket flutters her eyelashes and we all come running'. (Tony Lewis).
8. 'In cricket, top class cricket, style, technique and character are the first and the only long-staying essentials'. (Neville Cardus)
9. '...like a religion in the West Indies'. (Subhas Gupte).
10. 'The greatest things which have been invented are cricket and soul music'. (Wayne Daniel).

FIVE MORE *IMPRESSIONS* OF SOUTH AFRICA

1. 'Most of us came to South Africa not knowing what to expect. Believe me, most of us are so impressed it ain't funny. There's no way a guy can come up to you – a black guy – and say to you: "We are glad you are here".' (Colin Croft).
2. 'I really feel that you have to visit South Africa first and see how complex the apartheid question is before making the kind of declamatory statements I indulged in from the comfort of my left-wing inexperienced stance'. (Bob Willis).
3. 'I believe South Africa's cricketers should be brought back to the international sphere because of the tremendous progress

which has been made in integrated cricket throughout the country'. (Richie Benaud).

4. 'Our cricket is now completely non-racial, and I think that the ICC should at least acknowledge that.' (Ali Bacher).
5. 'There's so much money in South Africa now, the top players of the world will be attracted here, make no mistake about that', (New Zealand cricketer John Reid, settled in South Africa).

WHAT THEY *SAID* WHEN KERRY PACKER AND THE AUSTRALIAN BOARD MADE THEIR PEACE IN 1979...

1. 'The rebirth of the game'. (Peter Laker).
2. 'Packer has won'. (John Arlott).
3. 'I think the cricket world is now a better place for what happened'. (Ian Chappell)
4. 'Cricket is headed for the biggest boom in its life, particularly in Australia'. (Greg Chappell).
5. 'This will lead to the best summer of Australian cricket ever'. (Rod Marsh)
6. 'Packer hasn't won. Nor has cricket. The result is a draw, and an uninspiring one at that'. (*Daily Mail* editorial).
7. 'The real victory is Packer's'. (Peter Laker).
8. 'There is never any winner in this sort of thing. Let us say simply that the winner is the game of cricket'. (ACB chairman Bob Parish).

THE *QUOTES* THAT WENT BACK TO ENGLAND WHEN WEST INDIAN FAST BOWLERS TERRIFIED THE ENGLISH BATSMEN IN 1985-86. ENGLAND LOST 0-5

1. 'I have never felt it more likely that we should see someone killed'. (John Woodcock).
2. 'If we had shown the kind of attitude and guts in the war that our cricketers have in the West Indies, Hitler would have walked over us'. (Brian Close).
3. 'If you get six head balls an over, that's showbiz'. (Phil Edmonds after an assault by Patrick Patterson).
4. 'I was sorry and depressed to witness what bowlers will do to get a wicket'. (Len Hutton).
5. 'The real wonder is that of the 273 balls fired at England on Friday, they managed to survive all but ten of them'. (Scyld Berry).

6. 'Every batsman who stayed more than an over was hit'. (Robin Marlar).
7. 'Make no difference if you are blind or not, man, no one sees Patrick' – a Jamaican youth on Patrick Patterson.

THE OUTSPOKEN *PHIL EDMONDS* ON OTHERS...

1. 'I think Bob Willis is mad'.
2. 'This threatened split between the "white" and "black" cricketing nations will never happen. It's all these naive cricket writers talking rubbish again'.
3. 'I am convinced that sport as a vehicle for advertising is a growing market'.
4. 'I am slightly paranoid about Brearley'.

...AND *ON HIMSELF*

1. 'I am so naive – I don't think that if I tell someone to ... off, they'll take it to heart and hold it against me all the time'.
2. 'I think I should be in charge of Middlesex'.
3. 'Some of the things that I hear about myself are just amazing'.
4. 'I suppose I must be one of the upsetting types'.
5. 'Yes, I'd have gone to South Africa. I'd have made sure the money was right though'.

POINTING FINGERS AT THE *UMPIRING*

Ten accusations/confessions

1. 'After years of playing cricket in Australia, I have come to the conclusion that there is no such thing as a good Australian umpire' (Gordon Greenidge).
2. 'Pakistani umpires favour the visitors more than they do the home team' (Zaheer Abbas).
3. 'Cricket umpiring – that's the filthiest phrase in the Australian sporting dictionary' (Tony Greig).
4. 'You felt we had to get 14 of their wickets and they only had to get 10 of ours' (Ian Botham on the Australian supervision, 1982-83).
5. 'No team can win against India in India. Their umpiring is diabolical' (Pakistan commentator, Iftekhar Ahmed, while on the Indian tour, 1979-80).
6. 'We saved the match despite the best efforts of the Pakistan umpires to prevent us from doing so' (Sunil Gavaskar after

the Lahore Test, 1984-85).

7. 'It became a waste of time appealing since all we could get were catches *far* from the bat' (Michael Holding in New Zealand, 1979-80).
8. 'Crooked umps and Pommie beer, what a mixture!' (An Aussie journalist in England, 1977).
9. 'It's common knowledge on the international circuit that Indian umpires are the worst in the world. They are congenitally blind, indolent, temperamentally unsound and philosophically incapable of reaching a decision unfavourable to the home team. They are as bent as the fiddler's elbow' (A correspondent of *The Australian* 1986-87).
10. 'The Sri Lankan umpiring that we encountered during the series in 1986 was frankly the worst I have experienced in my entire career' (Imran Khan).

FIVE REACTIONS TO *SPORTS ILLUSTRATED'S* CLAIM THAT IAN BOTHAM IS THE 'BEST PLAYER OF THE CENTURY' AND THE 'BEST ENGLISH CRICKETER SINCE THE DAYS OF W. G. GRACE'

1. It must have been written by an American. It's just nonsensical. (Ian Chappell)
2. 'It's the greatest lot of tommytrot I have ever heard'. (Bill O'Reilly)
3. 'I don't think you could rank him with the all-time greats'. (Alan McGilvray)
4. 'I don't know how anyone can compare anyone with W. G. Grace. After all, who saw Grace?' (Alan McGilvray)
5. 'It's an example of the razzmatazz public relations image being put forward these days – portraying Botham as the greatest entertainer of cricket'. (Frank Tyson)

People

DIPAK PATEL'S IDENTITY CRISIS

1. He is of Indian origin.
2. ...was born in Nairobi, Kenya.
3. ...has lived in England since 1967, playing for Worcestershire.

4. ...worked for six years in New Zealand, married a citizen of that country and finally played Tests for them in 1987.

SWAROOP KISHEN'S FIVE LOUDEST *APPEALERS*

(This Indian umpire has been referred to as the 'Oliver Hardy of Indian cricket' but, as cricketers will testify, is no laughing matter)

1. Keith Boyce
2. Greg Matthews
3. Richard Ellison
4. Norbert Phillip
5. Abdul Qadir

SEVEN THINGS YOU DIDN'T KNOW ABOUT *KERRY PACKER*

1. He is addicted to milk shakes
2. ...does not touch alcohol
3. ...smokes 70 cigarettes a day
4. ...stays at 8-star hotels
5. ...uses a private aeroplane when timetables for scheduled flights are inconvenient
6. ...once hired a Daimler for a two-mile journey
7. ...has a liking for ice cream and puddings and anything sweet

FIVE NON-SPORTING *PERSONALITIES* VIV RICHARDS WOULD LOVE TO BE FOR A DAY

1. Martin Luther King jr
2. Bob Marley
3. Steven Biko
4. Dr Franken
5. Lech Walesa

THE FIVE MOST VOCIFEROUS *APPEALERS* ACCORDING TO DICKIE BIRD

1. Robin Jackman
2. Paul Allott
3. Norbert Phillip
4. Neal Radford ('Phoo! He appeals more than anybody')
5. Arnold Sidebottom ('Ooh!')

THE *AMBITIONS* OF TEN CRICKETERS

1. Colin Croft and Raman Lamba – 'To become an airline pilot'.
3. Martin Crowe – 'For me and my brother to score Test hundreds on the same day in front of our parents'.
4. Faoud Bacchus – 'Becoming the Prime Minister of Canada'.
5. Graham Cowdrey – 'To see the Van Morrison 100 times in

concert'.

6. Ian Botham – 'To enjoy life'.
7. Sunil Gavaskar – 'To become a good human being'.
8. Iqbal Qasim – 'To become a successful banker'.
9. Derek Randall – 'Always wanted to play football for Nottingham Forest and lead the choir as a kid'.

SIX TEST CRICKETERS WHO ALSO REPRESENTED THEIR COUNTRY IN *ANOTHER SPORT*

1. Iftikhar Ali Pataudi (Hockey for India)
2. Everton Weekes (Bridge)
3. Viv Richards (Football)
4. M.J.Gopalan (Hockey)
5. C. Ramaswami (Lawn tennis)
6. Johnny Douglas (Boxing)

And one lady who beats them all...
Shireen Kiash (hockey, basketball and cricket for India)

SIX *REJECTS* WHO TURNED FAMOUS...

1. Bob Massie was spurned by Northants in 1970. He took 16 wickets on his Test debut
2. Arthur Wellard held the record for hitting the most sixes in a season (72) and more than 500 in his entire career. Kent rejected him, telling him that he would better utilize his abilities better as policeman
3. Jack Hobbs, later to score more first-class hundreds than any other batsman, was turned down by Essex. He qualified for Surrey
4. Harold Gimblett was given a regret note when he turned up for a Somerset trial in 1935. However, an emergency in their match against Essex at Frome resulted in young Gimblett being conscripted in a hurry; he hit the fastest century of the season and later went on to play for England on three occasions
5. Sydney Barnes enjoyed moderate success with Warwickshire but was allowed to drift into the Lancashire League. MacLaren spotted him and took him to Australia. He went on to play 27 Tests, taking 189 wickets at 16 apiece. He continued playing League cricket into his late sixties
6. Glenn Turner was recommended by Billy Ibadulla to a county while still in his teens. The county was not interested in him as they had a full complement of overseas cricketers!

TEN *CRICKET-CRAZY* PEOPLE

1. Boris Karloff's widow left the Ken Barrington Memorial Trust a sizable bequest in her will
2. Sunil Gavaskar had spent 2½ days on his honeymoon when he got an urgent call from Bombay that he was required to play in a club final. His wife – annoyed, no doubt – and he packed up and flew back
3. Len Braund had both his legs amputated during the Second World War. Nevertheless he continued to attend matches at Lord's in his bath chair
4. A. M. Matheson of New Zealand drove 100 miles over rough country roads every Friday night to play four hours of club cricket in Auckland
5. Abdul Rehman Bukhatir, Sharjah-based tycoon, flies to London and stays at the Dorchester only to watch cricket on television
6. Former Australian Prime Minister Sir Robert Menzies once arranged a Commonwealth conference in London to coincide with a Test at Lord's
7. Mick Jagger is so devoted to the game that he ensures that a video recording of England's performance reaches him within 72 hours, irrespective of wherever on earth his concert might be
8. Australian opener Geoff Marsh goes to sleep with a cricket bat in his arms
9. Fred Spofforth rode 400 miles on horseback to play a minor match in 1881 in Australia – and returned with a haul of 20 wickets, all bowled!
10. But the man to beat them all is J. Paul Getty jr. Amongst his innumerable acts of generosity towards the cause of cricket, he donated £ 5000 to assist Halifax League club, Sowerby Bridge, whose pavilion burnt down a few years back. He also offered to build a pavilion for the club which played on the land he purchased at Ipstone, Buicks. He gave £ 10,000 towards Leicestershire's indoor sports centre at Grace Road. A cheque of £ 1.5 million was handed over by him for the proposed Mound Stand at Lord's, the total expenses of which are estimated at £ 4.3 million

Places

FOURTEEN ENGLISH TEST CRICKETERS WHO WERE BORN IN *INDIA*

1. Robin Jackman (Simla)
2. Ranji (Sarodar)
3. Bob Woolmer (Kanpur)
4. Major E. G. Wynyard (Saharanpur)
5. Neville Tufnell (Simla)
6. Dick Young (Bombay)
7. Errol Holmes (Calcutta)
8. Duleep (Sarodar)
9. Iftikhar Pataudi (Pataudi)
10. Douglas Jardine (Bombay)
11. N. Mitchell-Innes (Calcutta)
12. George Emmett (Agra)
13. Colin Cowdrey (Nilgiri Hills)
14. John Jameson (Bombay)

THE FIVE HIGHLIGHTS/LOWLIGHTS OF AUSTRALIA'S TOUR OF INDIA, 1979-80, ACCORDING TO KIM HUGHES

1. 'Beautiful Srinagar.'
2. 'The unforgettable Taj Mahal.'
3. 'Our hotel in Nagpur served cockroaches in our soup.'
4. '...and crickets with our steak.'
5. 'The wicket in Cuttack's Barabati Stadium.'

— *Sportsweek*

HOW *POPULAR* IS CRICKET IN AUSTRALIA?

The Department of Home Affairs, Australia, conducted a survey to assess 'how many' played 'what' in that country.

1. 498,219 men and women cricketers
2. 480,747 lawn bowls players
3. 463,000 Australian Rules footballers
4. 454,694 soccer players
5. 370,807 golfers
6. 273,000 netball players
7. 214,600 lawn tennis players
8. 158 (?) people were into aerobatics

THE FRUSTRATIONS OF PLAYING CRICKET IN *PAKISTAN*

1. 'In Pakistan a touring cricketer has to be content with seeing the fairer sex in faraway exclusive stands reserved for them'. (Bishen Bedi).

2. 'Concerted wailing outside my window woke me before six. It took me a while to locate the source of the racket but it turned out to be the calling of the faithful to morning prayers at the mosque'. (Bob Willis).
3. 'It was American humourist Tom Lehrer, I think, who once said: "If you want a long holiday, spend the night in Adelaide". I don't know about Adelaide, but it certainly applies to Pakistan'. (Rod Marsh).
4. 'It's a place to send your mother-in-law to, all expenses paid'. (Ian Botham).
5. 'They don't play cricket in Pakistan, only politics'. (A West Indian cricketer touring Pakistan in 1986).

O *CALCUTTA!*

One city you just cannot be indifferent about. Six views on what it is like to play cricket in Calcutta.

1. 'When the ball hits your pad, it is deafening – the Indian cricketers appeal, 85,000 spectators inside the ground appeal and so do the 85,000 outside, the ones with the duplicated tickets'. (Tony Lewis).
2. 'I would rather play before a Calcutta crowd than at Lord's where the applause is strictly limited to 3 or 4 claps'. (Sunil Gavaskar).
3. 'You haven't seen Test cricket till you've been there'. (Tony Greig).
4. 'Eden Gardens, and not Lord's, should be the cricket capital of the world'. (Abdul Hafeez Kardar).
5. 'You feel like a film star when you walk out there'. (Tony Greig).
6. 'I will never play at Eden Gardens again'. (Sunil Gavaskar after he had been booed during the Test against England in 1984-85).

UNUSUAL *PLACES* WHERE CRICKET WAS PLAYED

1. A match was once played over a two-million gallon oil tank in Adelaide in 1940. The playing area was over 100 feet wide and illuminated by electric bulbs
2. A match at the Goodwin Sands had to be abandoned after the stumps slowly disappered into the quicksand
3. Cricket was played at the South Pole in 1969. New Zealand

Test cricketer John Reid hit hard and the ball was not found again. The players used the South Pole – a striped pole with a glass ball atop – as the stump. Every shot hit by the batsmen, irrespective of the direction, eventually veered northwards.

4. Scientists, diplomats, lawyers and environmentalists from 13 countries split up into two sides for a match on Bowden Neve Snowfield during the Antarctic Treaty Conference in 1985. The match was won by Gondwanaland Casuals (129) who got the better of Beardmore Casuals (102). The 'pitch' was rolled by Hercules Transport Aircraft. There was only one regret: the beer froze!
5. Sunil Gavaskar and Mohinder Amarnath played cricket with the inmates of the juvenile section of Tihar Jail, India's maximum security prison, after play had been washed out on the second day of the Delhi Test between Australia and India in 1986. While Gavaskar almost hit the ball out of the ward, Amarnath managed to keep the humour of the inmates up by getting out a few times
6. Cricket was played by the members of Alfred Shaw's team at Icefiord at Spitzbergen in the light of the midnight sun.
7. Schoolboys were seen playing cricket with a tennis ball between two Up and Down railway tracks four metres wide in a suburb of Bombay. The participants did not bother to stop for passing trains
8. A game was once played on ice at Harewood in Yorkshire in 1838
9. Cricket was played in moonlight at Windsor Park in 1878-79. The runs scored by both teams added up to 32
10. Allied prisoners of war played cricket in Chieti, Libya, in 1942 with sentries, armed with tommy guns, keeping constant vigil – '...the greatest and most memorable match in which I ever took part,' wrote England cricketer Bill Bowes

THE MAGIC OF THE *EAST*

A tour of India is always a memorable experience – happy or otherwise. Ten views of tourists

1. 'They're (pitches and girls) both very grassy there, maan'. (Alvin Kallicharran).
2. One of the most fascinating countries of all to visit in terms of both, the present and the past'. (Henry Blofeld).

3. 'One week you could be as fit as a fiddle; the next you might want to crawl away and die'. (Raman Subba Row on the 1953 tour of India).
4. 'The heat, travelling and constant social functions, always very pleasant, could be held responsible for anyone failing to do himself justice'. (Hubert Preston, 1933-34).
5. 'Not many years hence...although the game grew up thousands of miles away, India is destined to become the capital of cricket'. Scyld Berry).
6. '30 December: Dinner and then to bed. Read Gill's letter again'. (An extract from Bob Woolmer's personal diary, 1976-77).
7. 'I'll never forget lying in my bath when there was a knock at the door and I called out "Come in", and there was this rather embarrassed lad with an autograph book and camera in hand. I signed his book and suggested that he came back later for his photograph' (Derek Underwood).
8. 'Anything or anybody associated with cricket was as high as third in the order of national precedence in India; behind film stars, government ministers and no others'. (Robin Marlar).
9. 'We were treated as the nearest thing to royalty; garlanded everywhere and besieged by wide-eyed young fans in the streets of every city...the Indians' enthusiasm for the game and hero-worshipping of its players was something that will live with me for ever' (Derek Randall).
10. 'We were in a country where, even at the hotel, everyone was coloured' (Keith Stackpole).

Professions

THE TEN *PROFESSIONS* OF ARTHUR MAILEY

1. Trouser presser
2. Cartoonist
3. Painter
4. Plumber
5. Paper Seller
6. Bottle Collector
7. Glassblower
8. Journalist
9. Dancing teacher
10. Labourer with the Sydney Water and Sewerage Board

THE FIVE *PROFESSIONS* OF JACK FINGLETON

1. Bottle-washer
2. Messenger
3. Bookmaker's apprentice
4. Newspaperman
5. Cricketer

THE SIX *PROFESSIONS* OF HAROLD LARWOOD

1. Worked at a grocery at the age of 13
2. Worked as a pit boy
3. Was a caddie at the local golf club at 14
4. Was admitted to the Notts staff to clean dressing rooms and boots at 32 shillings a week
5. When he was 41, he bought a sweet and tobacco shop
6. Storekeeper and nightwatchman in Australia

THE FIFTEEN *PROFESSIONS* OF ARCHIE MACLAREN

1. Journalist
2. Radio broadcaster
3. Hotel owner
4. Bloodstock agent
5. Banker
6. Cotton merchant
7. Marketed cricket equipment
8. Sold whisky
9. Sold cars
10. Hollywood actor
11. Edited a cricket magazine
12. Managed cricket teams
13. Acted as secretary to Ranji
14. Acted as assistant secretary to the Lancashire County Club
15. We haven't forgotten...Maclaren played cricket for Lancashire and England, but only as an amateur

TWENTY-FIVE CRICKETERS IN THE WRONG *PROFESSION*

1. Roland and Basil BUTCHER (England, West Indies)
2. Harold BUTLER (England)
3. Keith and Geoff MILLER (Australia, England)
4. Ken and Ron ARCHER (Australia)
5. Ghulam GUARD (India)
6. Milford PAGE (New Zealand)
7. Ronald DRAPER (South Africa)
8. John and Barrie SHEPHERD (West Indies, Australia)
9. Rex SELLERS (Australia)
10. Bill STORER (England)

11. Bob and Wilf BARBER (England)
12. Charles PRINCE (South Africa)
13. A. E. Barry and Don KNIGHT (England)
14. J. H. and Collis KING (England, West Indies)
15. Cecil and Geoff COOK (England)
16. George and Roland POPE (England, Australia)

AND THREE IN THE RIGHT ONE

1. Arthur FIELDER (England)
2. Peter and Max WALKER (England, Australia)

CRICKETERS IN DIFFERENT *PROFESSIONS:* BEFORE/AFTER/DURING THEIR CAREERS

Dean Jones – clerk in the Victorian Department of Community Services
Michael Holding – computer programmer
Rodney Hogg – milkman
Graham Yallop – manufacturer of slip cradles
Godfrey Evans – adviser of bookmakers on Test grounds
Ewen Chatfield – qualified laboratory technician
Lance Cairns – undertaker
Sandeep Patil – editor, owns a share in a hotel in Lonavla
Hedley Howarth — Oyster catcher and fisherman
Doug Walters and Trevor Chappell – co-owners of a travel agency
Roy Fredericks – Guyana Sports Minister
Herbie Collins – bookmaker
Chandu Sarwate – dactyloscopist (fingerprint expert)
Norman Gifford – estimator in industrial decorating
Graham Gooch – toolmaker
Joel Garner – telephone operator
Graeme Fowler – swimming instructor
Bruce French – warehouseman, window cleaner and bricklayer's labourer
Ian Gould – barman
Derek Aslett – postman, orderly, window cleaner
Bill Athey – barman, building labourer, sports shop assitant
Phil Bainbridge – winemaking and beermaking
Chris Broad – floorlaying and lorry loading

Nick Cook – general fund-raising projects
Graham Dilley – diamond setter (sacked from his first job after taking time off to play for Kent Second Eleven)
Sidath Wettimuny – jeweller
Norman Cowans – glassblower, squash and real tennis professional
Bill Lawry – plumber
Javed Miandad – vice president, Habib Bank, Pakistan
Paul Allott – cricket coach for Manchester Education Committee
Geoff Boycott – civil servant with Yorkshire Electricity Board
Roland Butcher – football coach
Allan Lamb – timber company representative
Wayne Larkins, J. J. Kotze and Geoff Marsh – farmers
Younis Ahmed – owns and runs a travel agency
Chris Old – bank clerk
Viv Richards – waiter, apprentice attached to a mechanic, assistant groundsman
Derek Underwood – director of a law company
Peter Willey – groundsman and labourer at a shoe factory
Clive Lloyd – civil servant in the Guyana Ministry for Health
Douglas Jardine – solicitor
K. Srikkanth – engineer
Dilip Doshi – ball bearings business
Wilf Slack – digital electronics test engineer
Tiger Pataudi – editor
Jack Hobbs – business in sports goods
Ian Redpath – antique dealer
Monty Noble and Dr H. V. Hordern – dentists
J. Inverarity – deputy headmaster
Paul Sheahan, Bill O'Reilly and Bill Woodfull – teachers
Craig Serjeant – pharmacist
Geoff Lawson – qualified optometrist
E. L. A'Buckett – barrister
Fred Titmus – ran a post office in Hertfordshire
Ray Lindwall – florist
Walter Livesey – butler to Lionel Tennyson
X. Balaskas – chemist
Hanson Carter – undertaker (he sometimes came to matches in a hearse)
Conrad Hunte – fulltime worker with the Moral Re-armament Movement

Dr. Ali Bacher – doctor
H. V. Baumgartner – Customs officer
Bob Crisp – ran a duck farm
Faoud Bacchus – insurance agent
Paul Gibb – bus driver
Jeff Thomson – bank clerk, dock labourer, engineering company representative
Jim Laker and Godfrey Evans – Partners in insurance brokerage
Clarrie Grimmett – calligraphist
Mike Brearley – psychoanalyst

Statistics

THREE BATSMEN OUT *'HIT WICKET'* WHEN THEIR CAPS FELL ONTO THE STUMPS

1. Joe Solomon while facing Richie Benaud at Melbourne, 1960-61
2. Dilip Vengsarkar while facing Jeff Thomson at Brisbane, 1977-78
3. Ashok Mankad while facing Chris Old at Edgbaston, 1974

BATSMEN WHO HAVE SCORED TWO SEPARATE *HUNDREDS* IN A MATCH ON MOST OCCASIONS

1. Zaheer Abbas (8 times)
2. Walter Hammond (7 times)
3. Jack Hobbs (6 times)
4. Glenn Turner (6 times)
5. C. B. Fry (5 times)

THE FIVE *LOWEST* TOTALS IN FIRST-CLASS CRICKET

1. 12… Oxford University vs MCC, Oxford, 1877
2. 12… Northamptonshire vs Gloucestershire, Gloucester, 1907
3. 13… Auckland vs Centerbury, Auckland, 1877–78
4. 13… Nottinghamsire vs Yorkshire, Nottingham, 1901
5. 14… Surrey vs Essex, Chelmsford, 1983

THE FIVE *HIGHEST* TOTALS IN FIRST-CLASS CRICKET

1. 1107… Victoria vs N.S.W., Melbourne, 1926-27
2. 1059… Victoria vs Tasmania, Melbourne, 1922-23
3. 951/7d… Sind vs Baluchistan, Karachi, 1973-74

4. 918... N.S.W. vs S. Australia, Sydney, 1900-01
5. 912/8d... Holkar vs Mysore, Indore, 1945-46

THE FIVE *HIGHEST* TEST TOTALS

1. 903/7d... England vs Australia, The Oval, 1938
2. 849... England vs West Indies, Kingston, 1929-30
3. 790/3d... West Indies vs Pakistan, Kingston, 1957-58
4. 758/8d... Australia vs West Indies, Kingston, 1954-55
5. 729/6d... Australia vs England, Lord's, 1930

THE FOUR INSTANCES OF *'HANDLING THE BALL'* IN TESTS

1. W. R. Endean vs England, Cape Town, 1956-57
2. Andrew Hilditch vs Pakistan, Perth, 1979-80
3. Mohsin Khan vs Australia, Karachi, 1981-82
4. Desmond Haynes vs India, Bombay, 1983-84

THE FIVE *FASTEST* TEST DOUBLE CENTURIES

1. 214 mts... Don Bradman, Australia vs England, Leeds, 1930
2. 223 mts... Stan McCabe, Australia vs England, Nottingham, 1938
3. 226 mts... Victor Trumper, Australia vs S. Africa, Adelaide, 1910-11
4. 234 mts... Don Bradman, Australia vs England, Lord's, 1930
5. 240 mts... Walter Hammond, England vs N. Zealand, Auckland, 1932-33

THE FIVE *FASTEST* TEST FIFTIES

1. 28 mts... J. T. Brown, England vs Australia, Melbourne, 1894-95
2. 29 mts... Salim Durrani, India vs England, Kanpur, 1963-64
3. 30 mts... E.A.V. Williams, West Indies vs England, Bridgetown, 1947-48
4. 30 mts... Bruce Taylor, New Zealand vs W. Indies, Auckland, 1968-69
5. 33 mts... C. A. Roach, West Indies Vs England, Oval, 1933

FOUR INSTANCES OF BATSMEN BEING *'MANKADED'* IN TESTS

When Bill Brown, the non striker, was run out while backing up too far by Vinoo Mankad, an entirely new term was coined

1. Bill Brown, 18 by Vinoo Mankad, Australia vs India, Sydney, 1947-48
2. D. Randall, 13 by E. Chatfield, England vs N. Zealand, Christchurch, 1977-78
3. S. Bakht, 0 by Alan Hurst, Pakistan vs Australia, Perth, 1978-79
4. Ian Redpath, 9 by Charlie Griffith, Australia vs W. Indies, Adelaide, 1968-69

MOST *RUNS* SCORED OFF A SIX-BALL OVER

1. Gary Sobers off Malcolm Nash, for Notts versus Glamorgan at Swansea, 1968 — 36
2. Ravi Shastri off Tilak Raj, for Bombay versus Baroda at Bombay, 1984-85 — 36
3. E. B. Alletson off E. H. Killick for Notts versus Sussex at Hove in 1911 — 34
4. Frank Hayes off Malcolm Nash for Lancashire versus Glamorgan at Swansea, 1977 — 34

CRICKETER WHO HAVE MADE THE MOST CONSECUTIVE COUNTY CHAMPIONSHIP *APPEARANCES*

1. 423: K. Suttle of Sussex
2. 412: J. Binks of Yorkshire
3. 399: J. Vine of Sussex
4. 344: E. H. Killick of Sussex
5. 326: C. N. Woolley of Northants

TV FIGURES OF *AUDIENCES* WHEN THE WSC OPENED OFFICIALLY ON 2.12.77

Sydney	*Melbourne*
WSC 46.5%	WSC 41.6%
Davis Cup 26.3%	Davis Cup 30.3%
Test match 6.5%	Test match 12.7%

CRICKETERS WHO HAVE MADE THE MOST TEST *APPEARANCES* AFTER 40

1. Bob Taylor (England) – 30
2. Jack Hobbs (England) – 27
3. Pasty Hendren (England) – 23

4. Tom Graveney (England) – 19
5. Clarrie Grimmett (Australia) – 16

THE FIVE FASTEST TEST *HUNDREDS*

1. 70 mts... Jack Gregory, Australia vs S. Africa, Johannesburg, 1921-22
2. 75 mts... Gilbert Jessop, England vs. Australia, Oval, 1902
3. 78 mts... Richie Benaud, Australia vs W. Indies, Kingston, 1954-55
4. 80 mts... J. H. Sinclair, S. Africa vs Australia, Cape Town, 1902-03
5. 86 mts... Bruce Taylor, New Zealand vs W. Indies, Auckland, 1968-69

THREE BATSMEN WHO BENEFITED (BY 5 RUNS) FROM THE BALL *HITTING* THE HELMET BEHIND THE 'KEEPER

1. David Gower, 1980, England vs Australia at Lord's
2. Phil Carrick, 1980, Lancashire vs Yorkshire at Old Trafford
3. Martin Crowe, 1983-84, New Zealand vs England at Wellington

FIVE YOUNGEST FIRST-CLASS CRICKETERS

1. Alimuddin (Pakistan), 12 years old (!), represented Rajputana in 1942-43
2. Qasim Feroze, 12 years 363 days, played for Bahawalpur in 1971
3. C. C. Dacre, 14 years 5 months, played for Auckland in 1914
4. W. H. Ashdown, 15 years 6 months, played for G. Weigall's XI versus Oxford in 1914
5. B. H. Pairaudeau, 15 years 11 months, played for British Guiana in 1947

THE SIX *LOWEST* TEST TOTALS

1. 26... New Zealand vs England, Auckland, 1954-55
2. 30... South Africa vs England, Port Elizabeth, 1895-96
3. 30... South Africa vs England, Birmingham, 1924
4. 35... South Africa vs England, Cape Town, 1898-99
5. 36... Australia vs England, Birmingham, 1902
6. 36... South Africa vs Australia, Melbourne, 1931-32

THE FIVE *OLDEST* MEN TO PLAY FIRST-CLASS CRICKET

1. Raja Maharaj Singh, 72, led Bombay Governor's XI vs a Commonwealth side in November 1950 in Bombay
2. C. K. Nayudu was 62 when he made his last first-class appearance in 1958
3. Lord Harris was 60 years and 5 months in his final first-class match
4. WG Grace was 59 years 10 months ...
5. Rev. A. E. Greenpiece was 59 years 6 months ...

THE *LONGEST* FIRST-CLASS CAREERS

1. W. G. Grace, 43 years (1865-1908)
2. A. D. Nourse sr., 40 years (1896-1935)
3. G. Hirst, 37 years (1892-1929)
4. C. E. de Trafford, 36 years (1884-1920)
5. W. G. Quaife, 35 years (1893-1928), E. Smith of Yorkshire (1888-1923)
6. J. Gunn (1897-1932), J. T. Hearne (1888-1923)

FIVE *YOUNGEST* TEST CRICKETERS

1. Mushtaq Mohammed (Pakistan), 15 years 124 days, versus West Indies in Lahore in 1959
2. Aftab Baloch (Pakistan), 16 years 191 days, versus New Zealand at Dacca in 1969
3. Nasim ul Ghani (Pakistan), 16 years 248 days, versus West Indies at Barbados in 1957-58
4. Khalid Hassan (Pakistan), 16 years 252 days, versus England at Trent Bridge in 1954
5. L. Sivaramakrishnan (Ind), 17 years 118 days, versus West Indies at Antigua in 1983

CRICKETERS WHO HIT THE MOST *SIXES* IN AN INDIVIDUAL INNINGS IN FIRST-CLASS CRICKET

15 – John Reid (296) for Wellington vs N. Districts at Wellington, 1962-63

13 – Majid Khan (147 n.o.) for Pakistan vs Glamorgan at Swansea, 1967

13 – Gordon Greenidge (273 n.o.) for D. H. Robins' XI vs Pakistan at Eastbourne, 1974

13 – Gordon Greenidge (259) for Hampshire vs Sussex at

Southampton, 1975
13 – Geoff Humpage (254) for Warwickshire vs Lancs at Southport, 1982
13 – Ravi Shastri (200 n.o.) for Bombay versus Baroda at Bombay, 1984-85

MOST *RUNS* SCORED IN A DAY OF TEST CRICKET BY ONE SIDE

1. ... England vs South Africa, Lord's, 1924 — 503
2. ... Australia vs South Africa, Sydney, 1910-11 — 494
3. ... Australia vs England, The Oval, 1934 — 475
4. ... England vs India, The Oval, 1936 — 471
5. ... Australia vs England, Leeds, 1930 — 458

THE EIGHT *TALLEST* CRICKETERS EVER

1. A. T. C. Allom, Surrey, 6 ft 10 ½ in
2. P. Dunkels, Warwickshire, 6 ft 10 in
3. Bruce Reid, Australia, 6 ft 8½ in
4. Joel Garner, West Indies, 6 ft 8 in
5. N. A. Paul, Warwickshire, 6 ft 7½ in
6. J. Larter, Northants, 6 ft 7½ in
7. Tony Greig, Sussex and England, 6 ft 7½ in
8. J. Graham, Kent, 6 ft. 7½ in

HOW FAR CAN A *BAIL* FLY?

The four longest recorded distances

1. 67 yds 6 ins by R. D. Burrows while bowling W. Huddleston, Worcestershire vs Lancashire, Manchester, 1911
2. 66 yds 0 ins by Harold Larwood while bowling G. W. Martin, MCC vs Tasmania, Lounceston, 1928-29
3. 64 yds 6 ins by R. D. Burrows while bowling A. Maclaren, Worcestershire vs Lancashire, Manchester, 1901
4. 63 yds 6 in by A. Mold while bowling G. Lohmann, Lancashire vs Surrey. Oval, 1896

THE FIVE *FASTEST* DOUBLE CENTURIES IN FIRST-CLASS CRICKET

1. 113 minutes... Ravi Shastri (200 n.o.) for Bombay vs Baroda at Bombay, 1984-85
2. 120 minutes... Gilberi Jessop (286) for Gloucestershire vs

Sussex at Hove, 1903

3. 120 minutes... Clive Lloyd (201 n.o.) for West Indies vs Glamorgan at Swansea, 1976
4. 130 minutes... Gilbert Jessop (234) for Gloucestershire vs Somerset at Bristol, 1905
5. 131 minutes... Victor Trumper (293) for Australia vs Canterbury at Christchurch, 1913-14

THE FOUR *FASTEST* TRIPLE CENTURIES IN FIRST-CLASS CRICKET

1. 181 minutes... Denis Compton (300) for MCC vs N. E. Transvaal at Benoni, 1948-49
2. 205 minutes... Frank Woolley (305 n.o.) for MCC vs Tasmania at Hobart, 1911-12
3. 205 minutes... C. G. Macartney (345) for Australia vs Notts at Nottingham, 1921
4. 213 minutes... Don Bradman (369) for S. Australia vs Tasmania at Adelaide, 1935-36

THE SIX *FASTEST* FIFTIES IN FIRST-CLASS CRICKET

1. 8 minutes ... C. Inman (57) for Leicestershire vs Notts at Nottingham, 1965
2. 11 minutes... C.I.J. Smith (66) for Middlesex vs Gloucestershire at Bristol, 1938
3. 14 minutes... S. J. Pegler (50) for South Africa vs Tasmania at Launceston, 1910-11
4. 14 minutes... F. T. Mann (53) for Middlesex vs Notts at Lord's, 1921
5. 14 minutes... H. B. Cameron (56) for Transvaal vs Orange Free State at Johannesburg, 1934-35
6. 14 minutes... C.I.J. Smith (52) for Middlesex vs Kent at Maidstone, 1935

THE FIVE FASTEST *HUNDREDS IN FIRST-CLASS CRICKET*

1. 35 minutes... Percy Fender (113 n.o.) for Surrey vs Northants at Northampton, 1920
2. 35 minutes... Steve O'Shaughnessy (105) for Lancashire vs Leicestershire at Manchester, 1983
3. 37 minutes... Chris Old (107) for Yorkshire versus at Birmingham 1977

4. 40 minutes... Gilbert Jessop (101) for Gloucestershire vs Yorkshire at Harrogate, 1897
5. 41 minutes... Nigel Popplewell (143) for Somerset vs Gloucestershire at Bath in 1983

THREE BATSMEN TAILENDER BOB WILLIS *LET DOWN* IN THEIR LATE NINETIES

1. Geoff Boycott (99 not out) vs Australia, Perth 1979-80
2. David Gower (98 not out) vs Australia, Sydney, 1979-80
3. Geoff Miller (98 not out) vs Australia, Lahore, 1977-78

THE HIGHEST SCORES IN EACH MONTH OF THE YEAR

1. January: 499 by Hanif Mohammed, Karachi vs Bahawalpur, Karachi, 1959
2. February: 429 by Bill Ponsford, Victoria vs Tasmania, Melbourne 1923
3. March: 329 by Don Bradman, S. Australia vs Tasmania, Adelaide, 1936
4. April: 336 not out by Walter Hammond, England vs N. Zealand, Auckland, 1933
5. May: 405 not out by Graeme Hick, Worcestershire vs Somerset, Taunton, 1988
6. June: 345 by C. Macartney, Australia vs Notts, Trent Bridge, 1921
7. July: 424 by A. C. MacLaren, Lancashire vs Somerset, Taunton, 1895
8. August: 364 by Len Hutton, England vs Australia, The Oval, 1938
9. September: 270 not out by Len Hutton, Yorkshire vs Hampshire, Bournemouth, 1947
10. October: 359 by Bobby Simpson, NSW vs Queensland, Brisbane, 1963
11. November: 383 by C.W. Gregory, NSW vs Queensland, Brisbane, 1906
12. December: 443 not out by B.B. Nimbalkar, Maharashtra vs Kathiawar, 1948

– *Wisden Cricket Montly*

THE FIVE *OLDEST* MEN TO PLAY TEST CRICKET

1. 52 years 165 days ... Wilfred Rhodes, England vs W.Indies, Kingston, 1929-30

2. 50 years 327 days ... H. Ironmonger, Australia vs England, Sydney, 1932-33
3. 50 years 320 days ... W. G. Grace, England vs Australia, Nottingham, 1899
4. 50 years 303 days ... George Gunn, England vs W. Indies at Kingston, 1929-30
5. 49 years 139 days ... J. Southerton, England vs Australia, Melbourne, 1876-77

(Ages as on the last day they played Test cricket)

FOUR FREAK BOWLING *ANALYSES*

1. 32-27-5-0: Indian off-spinner Bapu Nadkarni bowled 23 maidens in succession and established a world record during a Test between India and England in Madras, 1964
2. 0-0-4-0: How is that possible you may ask? Very simple. Against Lancashire at Old Trafford in 1955, Derbyshire's John Kelly bowled just one delivery – a no ball. It was hit for four
3. 1-1-0-0: Now, what's so unusual about that? The fact is that in an unofficial Test against New Zealand, J. H. Human bowled 6 wides, each of which was hit for four. The scoring sheet however reflected a flattering proficiency
4. 0-0-1-0: David Gower bowled just one ball to Martin Crowe in the England-New Zealand Test at Trent Bridge in 1986. Since the ball was deemed to be a 'throw', a no-ball was called. That single won the Test for New Zealand

THE APPROXIMATE *BOWLING SPEEDS* OF EIGHT BOWLERS

1. Bishen Bedi (38.50 mph)
2. Chris Old (74.30 mph)
3. Bob Willis (74.30 mph)
4. Dennis Lillee (84.72 mph)
5. Garth le Roux (86.58 mph)
6. Imran Khan (86.77 mph)
7. Michael Holding (87.76 mph)
8. Jeff Thomson (91.86 mph)

– *The Art Of Fast Bowling* by Dennis Lillee

SIX OF THE MOST OUTSTANDING *ANALYSES* IN FIRST-CLASS CRICKET

1. Hedley Verity, 19.4-16-10-10 : Yorkshire vs Notts at Leeds, 1932
2. G. Elliott, 19-17-2-9 : Victoria vs Tasmania at Launceston,

1857-58

3. Ahad Khan, 6.3-4-7-9 : Railways vs Dera Ismail Khat at Lahore, 1964-65
4. Jim Laker, 14-12-2-8 : England vs The Rest at Bradford, 1960
5. Derek Shackleton, 11.1-7-4-8 : Hampshire vs Somerset at Weston-Super-Mare, 1955
6. E. Peate, 16-11-5-8 : Yorkshire vs Surrey at Holbeck, 1883

THE FIVE MOST *EXPENSIVE* BOWLING ANALYSES IN TESTS

1. 87-11-298-1: By L.O.B. Fleetwood Smith for Australia vs England, The Oval, 1938
2. 80.2-13-266-5: By O.C. Scott for West Indies vs England, Kingston, 1929-30
3. 54-5-259-0: By Khan Mohammed for Pakistan vs West Indies, Kingston, 1957-58
4. 85.7-20-247-2: By Fazal Mahmood for Pakistan vs West Indies, Kingston, 1957-58
5. 82-17-228-5: By Vinoo Mankad for India vs West Indies, Kingston, 1952-53

THE FIVE *SLOWEST* TEST INNINGS

1. Colin Croft, 2 not out in 80 mts, W. Indies vs Australia, Brisbane, 1979-80
2. J. T. Murray, 3 not out in 100 mts, England vs Australia, Sydney, 1962-63
3. Tiger Pataudi, 5 in 102 mts, India vs England, Bombay 1972-73
4. Trevor Bailey, 8 in 120 minutes, England vs S. Africa, Leeds, 1955
5. W. Newham, 9 in 120 mts, England vs Australia, Sydney, 1887-88

THE MAXIMUM *BOUNDARIES* IN AN INDIVIDUAL INNINGS IN FIRST-CLASS CRICKET

1. 68 ... Peter Perrin (343 n.o.) for Essex vs Derbyshire at Chesterfield, 1904
2. 65 ... A. C. Maclaren (424) for Lancashire vs Somerset at Taunton, 1895
3. 64 ... Hanif Mohammed (499) for Karachi vs Bahawalpur at

Karachi, 1958-59
4. 57 ... John Edrich (310) for England vs N. Zealand at Leeds, 1965
5. 55 ... C. W. Gregory (383) for N.S.W. vs Queensland at Brisbane, 1906-07

THE FIVE NEAREST *MISSES*

1. According to records maintained by G. Neville Weston, W. G. Grace scored over a period of 57 years, 99840 runs...only 160 short of the six-figure mark.
2. Don Bradman, in a Test career stretching from late 1928 to 1948, aggregated 6996 in Tests. He was bowled for 0 in his last Test innings, leaving him stranded with an average of 99.94.
3. Jack Hobbs, who scored more first-class hundreds than anybody, retired with 197 centuries.
4. Hanif Mohammed was out at 499 while batting for Karachi vs Bahawalpur in 1958-59.
5. Jim Laker fell one short of taking all 20 Australian wickets at Old Trafford in 1956. 'The surprising thing is not that I took 19, but Tony Lock got only one,' he said. Laker's 19 wickets cost him 90 runs.

The Australians

FIVE REASONS WHY THE AUSSIES DIDN'T LIKE HIM, ACCORDING TO *MIKE BREARLEY*

1. I talked too much
2. I talked too glibly
3. I talked with the wrong accent
4. I ignored them
5. I wore my sweater over my bum for a start

– *Art of Captaincy*

THE JINGOISTIC AUSSIES

(*The Age,* a Melbourne newspaper, issued the following guidelines during the WSC tournament, 1982-83)

1. Never applaud a boundary by an English or New Zealand batsman

2. Try to be in the toilet or snack bar when they reach a century
3. Cheer loudly when an Australian player cuts off a boundary, hiss when an opposing fielder does likewise
4. When Australia is fielding, vociferously support all appeals for lbw and catches. Boo the umpire if they are rejected
5. Reverse procedure when Australia bats
6. Jeer all opposing batsmen entering the arena, specially opposition captains Bob Willis and Geoff Howarth
7. Constantly refer to English all-rounder Ian Botham's physical condition
8. Destroy all foreign flags (Warning: Don't confuse Australian and New Zealand flags, which are similar. Interfering with the former is an act of vandalism, with the latter an act of patriotism)

THE *AUSTRALIAN*

Ten views on this distinctive nationality.

1. 'The Australian is a naughty animal. When it is attacked it defends itself'. (Sir Neville Cardus).
2. 'He is dedicated to the proposition that literature begins and ends with the *Man with the Golden Gun,* that Eileen Joyce playing the Warsaw Concerto is too highbrow to contemplate, and that Rolph Harris is to the fine arts what Killer Devosky is to Aussie Rules Football'. (Ian Woolridge).
3. 'Australia plays like an accident waiting somewhere to happen'. (Terry Brindle).
4. 'Australians can, and do, quite readily and often in my experience, throw off all their 180 years of civilized nationhood; they gaily revive every prejudice they ever knew, whether to do with accent, class consciousness or even the original convict complex, and sally forth into battle with a dedication which would not disgrace the most committed of the world's political agitators' (Ted Dexter).
5. 'They are capital winners out nere; but I am afraid I cannot apply the same adjective to them as losers'. (Lord Harris).
6. 'In my opinion, Melbournians are like piranha fish when it comes to sport. They will devour everything that will satisfy their appetite for competition'. (John Snow).
7. 'They need to have a few subtleties of the game spelt out to them'. (Geoff Boycott).

8. 'Put one of those bulky green hats on a farm hand or a bank clerk and you have a motivated man to play above himself.' (Ian Woolridge).
9. 'We have a few beers and talk about life with Sanyo…and cricket and sex, drugs, rock 'n roll and everything'. (Greg Matthews).
10. 'It's unfortunate we Australians inherited the English mentality rather than the American'. (Kerry Packer).

The Best of….

GRAHAM GOOCH ADMIRES…

…Mike Procter for his enthusiasm
…Barry Richards for his ability
…Bob Taylor – 'a model sportsman'

ROY DIAS' FIVE GREATEST SRI LANKAN CRICKETERS

1. Michael Tissera
2. Anura Tennekoon
3. Sidath Wettimuny
4. Arjuna Ranatunga
5. Ajit de Silva

THE FIVE *STRONGEST* CRICKETERS ACCORDING TO DENNIS WAIGHT

1. Joel Garner
2. Peter Willey
3. Jeff Thomson
4. Ian Botham
5. Viv Richards

SIR GARFIELD SOBERS' TEN BEST BATSMEN

(In order of preference)

1. Vivian Richards
2. Ian Chappell
3. Barry Richards
4. Sunil Gavaskar
5. Greg Chappell
6. Zaheer Abbas
7. Clive Lloyd
8. Alvin Kallicharran
9. Gordon Greenidge
10. Derek Randall

– Australian Cricket

THE *MAGNIFICENT* SEVEN

Cricket writer Tony Becca selects his finest batsmen to play for the West Indies

1. George Headley
2. Gary Sobers
3. Vivian Richards
4. Everton Weekes
5. Rohan Kanhai
6. Frank Worrell
7. Clyde Walcott

MY BEST *FRIEND*

1. Wasim Bari – My peon, Muhammed Ilyas
2. Ian Botham – Viv Richards
3. Viv Richards – Beckett, an old school friend
4. Zaheer Abbas – My wife
5. Majid Khan – Myself

THE FIVE OUTSTANDING *INNINGS* SEEN BY E.W. SWANTON

1. J. Hobbs and H. Sutcliffe's partnership at The Oval against Australia in 1926
2. Bradman's 254 against England at Lord's in 1930
3. Ted Dexter's 70 vs West Indies at Lord's in 1963
4. Graeme Pollock's 125 against England at Trent Bridge in 1965
5. Bob Barber's 185 vs Australia at Sydney in 1965-66

COLIN COWDREY'S THREE MOST SKILFUL *BOWLERS*

1. Ray Lindwall
2. Fred Trueman
3. Alec Bedser

...THREE FASTEST BOWLERS

1. Frank Tyson
2. Wes Hall
3. Brian Statham

...THREE *MOST AWKWARD BOWLERS* TO FACE

1. Roy Gilchrist
2. C. Griffith
3. Ian Meckiff

THE LORD'S TAVERNERS' 50 *GREATEST* POST-WAR CRICKETERS

Selected by Trevor Bailey, Richie Benaud, Jim Laker and Colin Cowdrey

Sir Don Bradman
Mike Procter
Lance Gibbs
Frank Worrell
Derek Underwood
Graeme Pollock
Vinoo Mankad
Alan Knott
Denis Compton
Alec Bedser
Rodney Marsh
Joel Garner
Zaheer Abbas
Fred Trueman
Viv Richards
Hanif Mohammed
Clyde Walcott
Andy Roberts
Wesley Hall
Bert Sutcliffe
Kapil Dev
Brian Statham
Rohan Kanhai
Barry Richards
Glenn Turner
Sunil Gavaskar
Ray Lindwall
Keith Miller
Richard Hadlee
Len Hutton
Ian Chappell
Dennis Lillee
Arthur Morris
Neil Harvey
Imran Khan
Alan Davidson
Bishen Bedi
Ted Dexter
Godfrey Evans
Ken Barrington
Everton Weekes
Wally Grout
Ian Botham
Greg Chappell
Peter May
Hugh Tayfield
Sir Garfield Sobers
Geoff Boycott
Clive Lloyd
Graham McKenzie

(The selectors in all their modesty have chosen to overlook themselves. Each of them would have walked into this company and held their own, we are sure)

RAY ILLINGWORTH'S *FAVOURITE FIVE*

1. Peter May – 'The best killer of a bowler I've seen'
2. Gary Sobers – 'The best of all time, Sobers was certainly the finest batter I've ever bowled against and the sheer range and improvizational qualities of his strokeplay made it quite impossible to set a field for him'

3. Ted Dexter – 'The hardest driver of the ball I've ever played against'
4. Ray Lindwall – 'I admired him for his control'
5. Fred Trueman – 'He was so strong…'

– *Cricket Conversations* by Peter Walker

THE 14 BEST *ALL-ROUNDERS* THAT JIM LAKER SAW

(In order of preference)

1. Ian Botham
2. Gary Sobers
3. Trevor Goddard
4. Vinoo Mankad
5. Imran Khan
6. Keith Miller
7. Kapil Dev
8. Tony Greig
9. Richard Hadlee
10. Richie Benaud
11. Alan Davidson
12. Ray Illingworth
13. Trevor Bailey
14. Ray Lindwall

DENIS COMPTON'S *FAVOURITES*

Best Australian captain : Don Bradman
Best England captain : Freddie Brown
Fastest bowler faced : Frank Tyson
Most consistent quality bowler : Ray Lindwall
Most awkward bowler faced: Keith Miller
Best English batsman : Len Hutton
Best Australian batsman : Don Bradman
Best English spinner : Jim Laker
Best Australian spinner : Bill O'Reilly
Best innings seen : Stan McCabe's 232 vs England, Trent Bridge, 1938

THE THREE *BEST BATSMEN* I BOWLED TO ACCORDING TO RAY LINDWALL

1. Len Hutton
2. Denis Compton
3. Peter May

THE BEST…ACCORDING TO…

1. 'Clarrie Grimmett, my friend 'Grum', was the greatest spin bowler I ever saw' (Bill O'Reilly).
2. 'I have always thought Tom Graveney to be the finest specialist batsman I have ever played with or against' (Basil

D'Oliveira).

3. 'Without hesitation I rate Learie Constantine as the greatest fieldsman ever seen' (Don Bradman).
4. 'My ideal cricketer? Very difficult. I'd have to name about three. Denis Compton is one because he summed up the youth of cricket, a great improviser who always played like a boy. But if I was asked which player I would have walked fifty miles to watch bat, it wouldn't be an Englishman. It would be Ranjitsinhji. I would add just one other player, Victor Trumper, who was the most gracious batsman you ever saw' (Neville Cardus).
5. 'The fastest bowler I ever faced' (Colin Cowdrey on Wes Hall).

The Unusual World of Cricket

UNUSUAL REASONS FOR *MISSING* MATCHES

1. Graham Gooch once missed Essex's game vs Glamorgan at Southend in 1984 as he was engaged in court proceedings in a libel suit against *The Sun*. Gooch's absence was worth it; he was awarded £1,000 as damages
2. Australia's Kim Hughes missed two limited-overs games in early 1982 due to the death of his father-in-law
3. In 1979 Viv Richards was forced to skip four matches for Somerset after he had been beaten up with an iron bar by a man in Antigua. Richards suffered a broken finger
4. Glenn Turner of New Zealand refused to play for his country in the Australasian Gillette Cup; he disagreed with the principle of New Zealand taking part in a domestic tournament of Australia
5. Fred Spofforth refused to play in the first-ever Test because his favourite wicketkeeper Bill Murdoch had not been included in the side

TEN STRANGE REASONS FOR REPORTING *UNFIT* FOR PLAY

1. Dilip Sardesai had no luck on India's 1967 tour of England. He fell down the steps at Lord's and had to miss the first Test. He broke his finger in the second and had to take the flight home

2. Australian wicketkeeper Gil Langley was once forced to miss a Test match because he sprained his arm while sleeping on it the previous night
3. Derek Pringle missed a Test against Pakistan in 1982 when he sprained his back while stretching himself after finishing a letter on the eve of the game
4. New Zealand cricketer H.M. McGirr slipped while taking in the milk at home at the age of 67. He had scored 70 in a club fixture the previous day. This injury finally forced him to give up the game
5. While jogging with Greg Thomas in Antigua during the 1985-86 tour of the West Indies, Bruce French was bitten by a dog on his right knee
6. Majid Khan suffered a slipped disc when he fell backwards in the dressing room while waiting to bat against Australia in 1981-82. He was paralysed for several minutes
7. Ian Botham received five stitches on the third finger of his left hand after a champagne glass broke in his hand in June 1984.
8. Five Sri Lankans suffered food poisoning after a Chinese meal during their match against Notts in 1984
9. Leicestershire batsman Barry Duddleston was forced to sit out several games after accidentally shooting himself in the leg
10. Lancashire and England batsman David Lloyd was badly burnt when he spilt boiling water on himself in the tea room at Edgbaston in 1980

UNUSUAL BIRTHPLACES OF FOURTEEN CRICKETERS

1. F.J. Cook (South Africa) – Java
2. Donald Carr (England) – Germany
3. Freddie Brown (England) – Peru
4. Ashok Gandotra (India) – Brazil
5. Neal Radford (England) – Zambia
6. Ted Dexter (England) – Italy
7. Dave Whatmore (Australia) – Sri Lanka
8. Paul Terry (England) – W. Germany
9. J. Traicos (S. Africa) – Egypt
10. P. Edmonds (England) – Zambia
11. G. Headley (W. Indies) – Panama
12. Lall Singh (India) – Malaysia
13. Walter Hammond (England) – Malta
14. Dipak Patel (N. Zealand) – Kenya

FREAK SCOREBOOK *ENTRIES*

1. 'Boardman...not arrived yet 0' (Surrey vs Notts, Trent Bridge, 1878)
2. 'F. Buckle...not sent for in time 0'
   ...absent (unwell) 0, (Surrey vs Middlesex, 1869)
3. 'Abdul Aziz...retired hurt 0'
   ...absent (dead) 0, (Karachi vs Services XI, 1958-59)
4. 'J. Southerton...retired, thinking he was out 0' (At The Oval, 1878)
5. 'Khalid Aziz c Brearley b Hobbs'
   'Khalid Aziz c Brearley b Hobbs' (MCC vs North Zone, Pakistan, 1967. There were two Khalid Azizs in the latter side)
6. 'J. Williams...retired hurt' (Dorset Rangers vs Carcavelos, Portugal, 1981)
7. 'Jaideep...retired' (Rajasthan vs Vidarbha, Jaipur, 1986-87. The batsman mistook the umpire's signal for 'over' as 'out' and did not return)

UNUSUAL *INJURIES* CRICKETERS HAVE SUSTAINED

1. Ian Redpath tore his achilles tendon when he leapt in the air to appeal against Clive Lloyd in the WSC match between Australia and the West Indies at Geelong, 1977-78
2. The crucifix around Wes Hall's neck flew off and hit his eye while he was in the act of delivering the ball
3. Jeff Moss, while fielding for Victoria against Queensland at Brisbane in 1976-77, jammed his right foot into a boundary gutter when trying to stop a stroke from Greg Chappell. The batsmen ran four as Moss lay helpless
4. Jeff Thomson collided with Alan Turner in the Adelaide Test against Pakistan in 1976-77 and tore his right shoulder muscle. Thomson missed the rest of the series and the Centenary Test in Melbourne
5. Mike Hendrick snapped a hamstring while running in to bowl the first over of the third Test in Melbourne against Australia in 1974-75
6. Don Bradman twisted an ankle when he stepped into the bowlers' rough while bowling at The Oval vs England in 1938. It was the match in which Hutton scored 364 and England piled up 903 for seven declared

EIGHT UNUSUAL *DISMISSALS*

1. Three of the first four Middlesex batsmen were out 'hit wicket' to 'Tich' Freeman of Kent at Lord's in 1921
2. Denis Compton kicked the ball onto the stumps and ran out Vijay Merchant during the Oval Test between India and England in 1946
3. Talat Ali was dismissed in all his five Test innings in the 1978-79 series by Richard Hadlee. The batsman later claimed that on one of the occasions, he was deceived by the New Zealand fast bowler's grunt as he delivered the ball. Ali thought that it was a 'no ball' called by the umpire
4. H.E. Roberts of Sussex once bowled a delivery which hit a bird and deflected onto the stumps. The Alton C.C. batsman Bernard Bentick was given out
5. Playing for Lancashire against Derbyshire in 1899, A. Ward was declared out hit wicket when a delivery broke his bat, the shoulder falling onto the stumps
6. Representing England against Australia at Leeds in 1921, Andy Ducat had a chipped splinter of his bat fly onto the stumps. The ball deflected to Jack Gregory at slip. Ducat was declared out 'caught Gregory bowled McDonald'
7. James Ironmonger was once given out bowled in a match between Surrey and Notts. A delivery from Neville Knox flew past a bail. The fielders were convinced that the ball had not touched the bail. The only explanation was that the wind from Knox's express delivery had caused the bail to shift
8. Martin Donnelly was bowled by R. Young in a match at Lord's in 1948. The ball hit Donnelly on his foot, lobbed over the stumps, and spun back to hit it from behind

TEN UNUSUAL *CONTESTS* INVOLVING CRICKETERS

1. Bill O'Reilly, 70, bowled just one delivery to Sir Don Bradman, 68, to mark the opening of the Bradman Oval in Bowral. The batsman missed it.
2. Arthur Mailey bowled a single ball to Tommy Andrews many years after they had both retired from the game in Sydney in the Fifties. It got Mailey a wicket. 'I should have always bowled with my coat on,' said the veteran leg spinner.
4. A cricket match was played at Bromley in 1735 with all the players on horseback

5. In 1972, Jeff Thomson attempted to get into the *Guinness Book of Records* by beating the world egg-throwing record. He failed because he couldn't work out a method by which eggs thrown over a long distance would remain intact when they landed in his hand
7. For the last 47 years, every Christmas, The Yule Logs and Noel Bennet XI have played each other at Brighton
5. In a trotting race, Botham rode. So Sensitive to victory by 3 yards over Dennis Lillee on Beau Lincoln. The contest, run on Adelaide's Globe Derby Raceway in January 1983, made Botham richer by $ 500. He donated it to a charity for crippled children
7. Len Hutton took on the legendary Walter Lindrum to a frame of snooker during his 1954-55 tour of Australia. Hutton broke, but did not get another shot afterwards
8. The Raghuramaiyah Trophy is contested annually by both the Houses of the Indian Parliament – the Rajya Sabha and the Lok Sabha
9. Dr M.E. Pavri in 1889 single-handedly took on an eleven from Matheran. He scored 52 not out and bowled them out for 38. Leg byes and byes were not permitted while the other side batted
10. As the Australian captain Joe Darling was having a poor run of luck with the coin – he was to lose all the five tosses of the 1905 series — he suggested that the toss of one of the Tests be decided by a wrestling bout with F.S. Jackson, the England captain. He stripped down to only a towel round his waist at the start of one of the games, but Jackson was not equally enthusiastic

TEN UNUSUAL REASONS FOR BEING *SUSPENDED*

1. Bobby Peel...was banned by Lord Hawke in 1897 because he arrived at the ground drunk and urinated on the pitch
2. Banned Pakistan batsman Younis Ahmed...was sacked by Worcestershire for having placed a £ 100 bet on his team to lose a John Player League match against Leicestershire in 1983. He had also been suspended in 1981 for a game after he had kicked down the stumps in a championship match at Chesterfield and questioned a ' wide' decision of the umpire while bowling to Greenidge of Hampshire

3. John Benaud...was forced to miss two matches in 1969-70 following his insistence on wearing ripple-heeled boots against the directive of the State Association.
4. David Thomas of Surrey...was suspended for one match for twice running in and not delivering the ball. He had also kicked the stumps over during a John Player League match against Nottinghamshire in 1984
5. Neil Taylor of Kent...dropped for a game against Essex because he played golf against standing instructions before the John Player League fixture against Notts in 1984
6. Geoff Boycott...was dropped for Yorkshire's match against Derbyshire because he did not report his recovery from a hamstring injury early enough. He went and scored a century for the second eleven instead
7. Phil Edmonds was out for one match because he was 15 minutes late for the Nat West Trophy final in 1984.
8. Two students at Brighton College were dropped for 'gross disobedience' after they chose to study for their 'A' level examinations rather than play for their headmaster's cricket team in a commemoration day match against the Old Boys in 1976
9. Derbyshire Cooperation busmen were dismissed for playing cricket during working hours in 1976. Their colleagues went on strike for several hours as a token of protest against the decision
10. Umpire Pearce was suspended when the MCC were playing a game at Bendigo on their 1928-29 tour of Australia. Douglas Jardine hit a ball in the direction of Pearce, the square leg umpire. It came in the air so temptingly to him that he could not resist catching it. The Cricket Association failed to be amused by the umpire's version that he was carried away by the 'picnic spirit'. Pearce was disallowed from umpiring again

AND TWO PUBLICATIONS THAT WERE *SUSPENDED*...

1. The sale of *South African Cricketer* was prohibited on the grounds of Cape Town and Johnnesburg after the touring Australian 'rebel' team of 1985-86 had complained about an article in one of the issues
2. The Victorian Supreme Court stopped publication of excerpts from *Lambs To The Slaughter* by Graham Yallop till a court hearing in 1979

World Series Cricket

Having been denied television rights for a series in 1976-77, Kerry Packer launched his breakaway movement, parallel to Test cricket. He signed the leading cricketers of the world and effected the biggest change in cricket in a short period of two years. Initially outlawed by the game's establishment, Packer subsequently made his peace. The rights he coveted were granted and his 'circus' disbanded.

FIVE *REACTIONS* TO THE FIRST PACKER SUPERTEST, VFL PARK, 1977-78.

The traditionalists were not too impressed by what they saw

1. 'All that happened was that rarely a single dinkum Australian paid it more than abstract attention' (Ian Woolridge).
2. 'It will only be some time before the intangible aspects of these series develop' (Greg Chappell).
3. 'I came with open mind to see these Packer cricket matches and have failed to be interested in the cricket' (Tony Lewis)
4. 'Is it really worth it?' (John Woodcock).
5. 'Mr Packer's main fault (is) he wants to monopolize sport and one of the earliest things I learnt in the sporting sphere is that any game is greater than the individual' (Jack Fingleton).

THE SIXTEEN *INNOVATIONS* OF WORLD SERIES CRICKET

1. The drinks buggy manned by girls (during WSC's first season)
2. Variety entertainment programmes during breaks in play
3. Night cricket
4. Coloured clothing
5. White balls (one for each end)
6. Black sightscreens
7. Microphones placed under the stumps
8. The fielding circle for limited-overs matches
9. Pitch analyses conducted by dials and meters before the day's play
10. Television interviews of the two captains in the middle after the toss
11. Daddles – the duck on the screen that accompanies the poor batsman, who has failed to score, back to the pavilion.

12. Free parking outside the Sydney Cricket Ground
13. Free transport to the Waverley Ground in Melbourne
14. Advance ticket sales
15. Active marketing for caps, t-shirts etc. with 'sexy' slogans on them
16. Advertisements in newspapers explaining what lay in store that season

THE GOOD THINGS TO COME OUT OF *WSC* ACCORDING TO RICHIE BENAUD

1. 'The fielding circle devised by Tony Greig.'
2. '...payments to players – both Test and county – have risen a great deal.'
3. 'Night cricket is one of the most exciting things I have seen.'
4. '...the Australian adminstrators have come to terms with the fact that they have been given a chance to live with the times and to provide a balanced diet of cricket to the paying public.'
5. 'The television coverage of cricket matches has advanced by light years.'
6. 'International one-day competition played on a 3-team basis.'

– *On Reflection* by Richie Benaud

EIGHT CHARACTERISTIC *KERRY PACKER* LINES

1. 'It's taken cricket authorities a hundred years to recognize the plight of cricketers'
2. 'Well, damn. I don't know why we don't put on our own cricket matches'. (To a colleague after his offer for TV rights for the series against Pakistan had been refused in 1976-77)
3. 'The ultimate purgatory for me would be to go to the Opera House and hear Joan Sutherland sing...ugh'
4. 'Power is the most over-rated thing in life. I have been in a position to see it wielded. It doesn't keep you warm at nights'.
5. 'The cricket they are putting on is a joke'. (On Test matches, 1977)
6. 'It's just becoming so difficult to find anyone to have a chat with'
7. 'I am only in this because of my conflict with the Australian Cricket Board. Had I got those (TV) rights I was prepared to withdraw from the scene and leave the running of cricket to the Board. I will now take no steps to help anyone. Every man

for himself and the devil takes the hindmost'.

8. 'They talk about not being able to pay the cricketers enough. They could have had my money to do it.' (If he had been given the TV contract)

IN DEFENCE/CONTEMPT

Not since 1932-33 were cricket players, writers and enthusiasts so seized about a particular point of debate as the breakaway 'circus'. The varying emotions have surprised, even amused, the indifferent. 'Funny' they said. 'After all we thought it was only a game...'

1. 'It's too good to ignore' (Zaheer Abbas).
2. 'I've always been a loyalist. It was a very good offer, well above anything I get over here, but I knew I could give only one answer' (Dickie Bird).
3. 'There's no way I'll be trying to wriggle out of my contract' (Dennis Lillee).
4. 'I've worked far too hard to reach the top of my sport and I did not agree to be banned from representative play' (Jeff Thomson on why he withdrew from the Packer contract).
5. 'The cricketers who signed up with Packer are mercenaries – soldiers who will fight any war as long as they are paid' (Abdul Hafeez Kardar).
6. 'The contract seems harsh and authoritarian. It appears to give the promoter virtually unlimited powers over the players who have signed' (A legal expert consulted by *The Mail,* England).
7. 'The players who have signed, wanted the penny and the bun' (Geoff Boycott).
8. '(The administrators needed) a jolly good shake-up' (Tony Greig).
9. 'I preached compromise more keenly than most, and I spent days trying to think of new formulae to get the sides together' (Tony Greig).
10. 'I've heard the only way to get out of a Packer contract is by becoming pregnant' (Raymond Steele).

TEN JUDGEMENTS

Condemning WSC was considered 'in' from 1977 to 1979. If you did the reverse people doubted your knowledge of the game, branded you a heretic and wrote you off as insensitive and insane.

1. 'What satisfaction can great cricketers like Alan Knott and Underwood get from playing limited-overs cricket on football fields under floodlights with a hefty ration of 'Blood and Bouncers'? (Brian Johnston).
2. 'Crowds will eventually come – if the Martians land in New York, 90% of the population would rather stay at home and watch it on television than actually go along and have a look.' (Sam Chisholm, general manager of Packer's TV networks)
3. 'I understand *Wisden* will stop giving batting and bowling averages and just publish bank balances' (A Roy Ullyett cartoon).
4. 'I have no doubt that if Packer's revolution is successful, the ultimate loser will be the game of cricket' (Henry Blofeld)
5. 'Soon there'll be 10 Mr Packers on the scene' (Ghulam Ahmed).
6. 'WSC is essentially parasitic in nature' (Michael Kemster, QC).
7. 'It cannot continue without acute financial and human damage to cricket' (John Arlott).
8. 'It gave me the chance to prove myself among Test players again' (Barry Richards).
9. 'Packer's WSC is like Charlemagne's Holy Roman Empire, which was neither holy, Roman, nor when closely scrutinized, an empire' ('Mullagh').
10. 'We have attracted a different audience. The kids come to watch in their thousands – that must be good – and we have whole families who come for outings. If we've brought these people into contact with cricket we must have done a service' (Kerry Packer).

Writers and Broadcasters

FOUR INSTANCES OF A *SLIP OF THE TONGUE IN THE BOX*

1. 'And Brian Toss has won the close...' (Henry Blofeld on Radio 2).
2. 'Boycott; somewhat a creature of habit, likes exactly the sort of book he himself prefers' (Don Mosey).

3. During the India-Australia Test at Calcutta in 1979-80, veteran Indian player Lala Amarnath directed the choicest expletives at a fellow commentator on television under the impression that the microphone had been switched off. The following day he apologized.
4. Ian Chappell was suspended from his TV sports programme for making a blasphemous remark during the live coverage of a West Indies-Australia match at Adelaide in 1981-82. He later said on television : 'I make a sincere apology. I didn't realize that the microphones were open and that the comment was going to air'.

FOUR *TRIBUTES* TO JOHN ARLOTT

John Arlott, cricket commentator for the BBC, is one of cricket's great institutions.

1. 'The voice of the village green and rustic England and leisurely days in the sun' (E.W. Swanton).
2. 'He has continued to be a source of happiness to a great many' (Alan Gibson).
3. '...the authoritative air of the High Priest, John Arlott, whose very imitable description of Colin Cowdrey rocking massively onto the back foot and playing the ball in the shadow of his enormous pad could never be forgotten' (Mike Howell, a blind radio commentary addict).
4. 'In a way, John will be everlastingly accessible. To read his words is to bring back immediately the sound of voice' (David Rayvern Allen).

...AND ONE CRITICISM

'You've got an interesting mind but a vulgar voice'. (The head of Outside Broadcasting to a young Arlott who had gone for an audition)

RICHIE BENAUD'S FIVE *PET PHRASES* ON TELEVISON

1. 'In the air...but safe!'
2. 'In the air...and gone!'
3. 'Down!' (when a catch is dropped)
4. 'Bowled him!'
5. 'Good shot for three...'

FIVE *HOWLERS* BY BROADCASTER BRIAN JOHNSTON – OR WERE THEY DELIBERATE?

1. 'And the news here is that Warr's declared'.
2. 'Gul's all right now. The doctor examined his head this morning – and found nothing in it!' (After Pakistan batsman Aftab Gul had been hurt).
3. 'Now Compton is up around the corner, legs wide apart, waiting for a tickle. And he's got it'.
4. 'The batsman's Holding, the bowler's Willey'.
5. 'Illingworth is relieving himself at the pavilion end'.

DEAR SIR, CAN YOU TELL ME WHAT MAKES A CRICKET *COMMENTATOR?*

Brian Johnston's recipe for success is one that every commentator–budding or established – will do well to keep before him when broadcasting – or trying to.

1. Have light and shade in your voice so that during quiet periods you can talk normally and not too fast. Then when there is sudden action or excitement you can increase your tempo and raise your voice, though of course, without shouting
2. Always think of yourself as speaking to *one* person, not to millions. You are that person's friend and guide. Tell him or her what you yourself would like to hear if you were not at that match
3. Try not to talk above applause, especially when a batsman is returning to the pavilion after a big score
4. Try not to describe in too much detail how a batsman is out. Leave that to the expert
5. Remember you are a commentator and not a critic. So don't criticize an umpire's decision. Whatever you may think about it, he is in better position to judge than you
6. At the end of each over give the bowler's analysis, the total and the scores of the two batsmen. Then shut up, so that the summarizer can come straight in
7. Give the score as often and as unobtrusively as possible without interrupting the action because tens of thousands are switching on every minute
8. As he has no camera to help him, the radio commentator must paint the picture himself–with words
9. A brief description of the main features and characteristics of

the players bring the game to life – 'he has red, curly hair, wears size 14 boots, scratches his nose before every ball...'
10. But whatever the style of commentary one final word of warning – NEVER MISS A BALL. If you do, it's sure to be the one that takes a wicket

– *It's a Funny Game* by Brian Johnston

NINE THINGS ONLY *JOHN ARLOTT* COULD HAVE SAID

1. 'Here comes Fred Trueman, deep-chested hair flopping. He delivers the ball and Neil Harvey with a roll of the wrists plays it down to third man.'
2. 'He (G. Vishwanath) has a very crouching stance – almost as if someone has pulled the stool from *beneath* him'.
3. 'A constable is using his helmet to cover the confusion'. (when a streaker was escorted out of Lord's in 1972 by a policeman)
4. 'Mann's inhumanity to Mann. (a description of 'Tufty' Mann bowling to George Mann)
5. 'As the train withdraws from Warwick Road, so does Boycott, caught Marsh bowled Lillee, no score'.
6. 'If you can see the Pennines it is about to rain; if you can't see the Pennines, it's raining'.
7. 'There was a time, when Johnny (Douglas) said he would attempt to score in one hour approximately four more than the number of trains that pass through the Warwick Road station in a day. The trains won by nine'.
8. 'After Trevor Bailey, it'll be Christopher Martin-Jenkins'. (John Arlott's last words on the BBC ever, Centenary Test, 1980)
9. 'I can't do it any longer. I am not as I was. Haven't thought of something new to say for ages'. (circa 1980)

RICHIE BENAUD'S TEN COMMANDMENTS FOR *TV COMMENTATORS*

1. Keep one eye on the monitor, one eye on the field of play, and your third eye on your tongue and your fellow commentator
2. Never talk over your fellow commentator – just as your fellow commentator should never talk over you.
3. Remember, silence is the greatest weapon you have in your armoury. Listen to your director with an ear as keen as a ferret's – just as your director will listen avidly to the

commentary, thus ensuring your magic phrases are pertinent to the viewer's picture

5. Think constantly over voice-over cassettes, animations, computers and anything which will help enjoy the telecast
6. Make your commercial throws as tight as the proverbial fish's ear, so no ball is missed
7. Remember this is a game of many and varied hues. As a commentator you will keep foremost in your mind that cricket contains venom and courage, drama and humour, and you will not be backward in bringing out in your commentary those aspects of the noble and ancient pastime
8. This marvellous game has many by-ways and secret things – and you as a commentator will remember that multitudes of viewers do not understand some aspects of the art, therefore you will endeavour always to add to the picture on the screen
9. Remember at all times that having practised this ancient art at the highest possible level, you may occasionally dwell on the sacred mysteries to the utter confusion of the uniformed. Therefore, you will keep it simple, never talking down to the viewer by using those bastard phrases: 'Of course', 'As you can see', or 'As my fellow commentator said'
10. Also remember your producer and director, aged and infirm, as they may be, could ask you to do things which, at the time, you feel you do not completely understand. Although your producer and director may not be properly introduced into the subtle nuances of your ancient game of cricket, they have been introduced into the puerile art of communications, so ... cencentrate, and make it work!

– *On Reflection* by Richie Benaud

FOUR GROUND *RULES* TO BE OBSERVED WHEN ENTERING THE PRESS BOX

By Frances Edmonds, wife of Test cricketer Phil Edmonds

1. No laughing
2. No applauding
3. No enjoying yourself
4. On the hour, every hour, complain loudly about a) the telephones b) the telex system c) the locals d) 'abroad' e) the telephones...

MORE ABOUT PENGUINS

For further information about books available from Penguins in India write to Penguin Books (India) Ltd, B4/246, Safdarjung Enclave, New Delhi 110 029.

In the UK: For a complete list of books available from Penguins in the United Kingdom write to Dept. EP, Penguin Books Ltd, Harmondsworth, Middlesex UB7 0DA.

In the U.S.A.: For a complete list of books available from Penguins in the United States write to Dept. DG, Penguin Books, 299 Murray Hill Parkway, East Rutherford, New Jersey 07073.

In Canada: For a complete list of books available from Penguins in Canada write to Penguin Books Canada Ltd, 2801 John Street, Markham, Ontario L3R 1B4.

In Australia: For a complete list of books available from Penguins in Australia write to the Marketing Department, Penguin Books Australia Ltd, P.O. Box 257, Ringwood, Victoria 3134.

In New Zealand: For a complete list of books available from Penguins in New Zealand write to the Marketing Department, Penguin Books (N.Z.) Ltd, Private Bag, Takapuna, Auckland 9.